Writing Travel

Series Editor, Jeanne Moskal

WRITING TRAVEL
Series Editor, Jeanne Moskal

The series publishes manuscripts related to the new field of travel studies, including works of original travel writing; editions of out-of-print travel books or previously unpublished travel memoirs; English translations of important travel books in other languages; theoretical and historical treatments of ways in which travel and travel writing engage such questions as religion, nationalism/cosmopolitanism, and empire; gender and sexuality; race, ethnicity, and immigration; and the history of the book, print culture, and translation; biographies of significant travelers or groups of travelers (including but not limited to pilgrims, missionaries, anthropologists, tourists, explorers, immigrants); critical studies of the works of significant travelers or groups of travelers; and pedagogy of travel and travel literature and its place in curricula.

Books in the Series

Eating Europe: A Meta-Nonfiction Love Story, Jon Volkmer
Vienna Voices: A Traveler Listens to the City of Dreams, Jill
    Knight Weinberger

Eating Europe

A Meta-Nonfiction Love Story

Jon Volkmer

Parlor Press
West Lafayette, Indiana
www.parlorpress.com

Parlor Press LLC, West Lafayette, Indiana 47906

S A N: 2 5 4 - 8 8 7 9

Library of Congress Cataloging-in-Publication Data

Volkmer, Jon, 1956-
  Eating Europe : a meta-nonfiction love story / Jon Volkmer.
    p. cm. -- (Writing travel)
  ISBN 1-932559-69-8 (pbk. : alk. paper) -- ISBN 1-932559-70-1
    (hardcover : alk. paper) -- ISBN 1-932559-71-X (adobe eb-
    ook)
  1. Europe--Description and travel. 2. Volkmer, Jon, 1956---
    Travel. 3. Travel costs--Europe. I. Title.
  D923.V66 2006
  914.04'5610922--dc22
                                    2006025925

"Retro Map of France" © 2005 by Nick Belton. Used by permis-
  sion.
Cover design by David Blakesley.
Printed on acid-free paper.

Parlor Press, LLC is an independent publisher of scholarly
and trade titles in print and multimedia formats. This book is
available in paper, cloth and Adobe eBook formats from Parlor
Press on the World Wide Web at http://www.parlorpress.com or
through online and brick-and mortar bookstores. For submission
information or to find out about Parlor Press publications, write
to Parlor Press, 816 Robinson St., West Lafayette, Indiana,
47906, or e-mail editor@parlorpress.com.

For Janet

Series Editor's Preface

Parlor Press's book series, "Writing Travel," seeks to publish the best works in the field of travel studies. This field has been given new urgency by debates about globalization and terrorism, by fresh dialogue between practitioners and scholars of travel writing, and by emerging insights from many disciplines (postcolonial studies, gender studies, literary studies, geography, religious studies, and anthropology) about the ways in which travel and travel writing engage such questions as religion, nationalism and cosmopolitanism, and empire; gender and sexuality; race, ethnicity, and immigration; and the history of the book, print culture, and translation. Our list will include original travel writing; editions of out-of-print travel books or previously unpublished travel memoirs; English translations of important travel books in other languages; biographies of significant travelers or groups of travelers (including but not limited to pilgrims, missionaries, anthropologists, tourists, explorers, immigrants); critical studies of the works of significant travelers or groups of travelers; and pedagogy of travel and travel literature and its place in curricula.

Eating Europe: A Meta-Nonfiction Love Story by Jon Volkmer raises the curtain on often-hidden portions of the travel experience: who pays the bills and how travel affects our relationships. Many travel writers give the impression that they are independently wealthy by omitting any mention of who pays the bills. But Volkmer's narrator—like Volkmer himself, an English professor—receives a prestigious but limited grant from his college to travel in Europe. Canny about the federal

viii ⚡ *Editor's Preface*

tax provisions for food-and-beverage business expenses, the narrator (or is it the author himself?) saves nineteen restaurant receipts to file for reimbursement from his grant. The receipts, in addition, prompt his poignant and funny meditations on topics ranging from European currency –he traveled in "the millennial year, the twilight of the guilder and the franc," when "some receipts also put the price in Euros, in small print, a harbinger"—to a translation of the nineteenth-century experience of the sublime into present-day idiom: "The nuclear power of the Alps being fed into the substation of my heart through the two-dollar extension cord of my eyes." Thus Volkmer brings to bear on the experience of travel both the administrative realities and the love of books that shape life in today's academia.

Love, too, plays its part, as the narrator traces the ramifications of one missed opportunity to affirm his travel companion's vitality. This opportunity takes place at a store—a key venue for travelers' shaping their new identities for themselves and for the folks at home—as his companion pauses to buy some small memento of the trip. Volkmer's unfolding of this missed opportunity illuminates the subtleties of both souvenir-buying and the vicissitudes of love.

This book will appeal to anyone who has ever ended a trip by sorting through those pesky receipts and wondered—simultaneously—what gets reimbursed and what to make of the fact that travel has unexpectedly opened us to evanescent snatches of love and connection.

—Jeanne Moskal

Series Editor, Writing Travel

Acknowledgments

I would like to thank Ursinus College and the Pearlstine Family Faculty Fellowship Fund for encouragement and support. Thanks also to Diane and Paul, Eric and Madeline, Margot and Rob, Daniel, Carol, Patti, Ted, Judy, Annette, Laura, Francine, Beth, Jane, David G., Richard G., Richard K., Rick D., Roger, Shawn, Jane and Scotty. Special thanks to Jeanne and to David, whose literary vision transcends category, genre and marketability. Most of all thanks to Janet, for her contributions on pages 176 to 178 and 193 to 200 and for her inspiration everywhere else.

Parts of chapters 5 to 8 and 12 appeared in the *Philadelphia Inquirer*. "An Ugly American in Paris" appeared in *The Bucks County Writer*.

Everything in this book is true, except the parts that admit to ambiguity, imagination, or deceit. Most of the names have been changed in consideration of privacy.

Contents

Series Editor's Preface   *vii*

Acknowledgments   *ix*

Introduction   *3*

Part One   *7*

1 Golden Tulip Bar: $7.89   *9*

2 L'Indochine: $60.74   *15*

3 Puri Mas: $69.43   *18*

On Cartography and the Sublime   *30*

4 AC Restaurants: $22.62   *41*

5 Restaurant le Luxhof: $37.20   *44*

6 Maison D'Issler: $22.56   *53*

7 Tropic Ice: $17.64   *57*

8 L'Auberge Alsacienne: $56.97   *64*

9 Le Grand Duc: $22.06   *71*

Part Two   *79*

On Pilgrimage and Tourism   *81*

10 Le Felibre: $36.76   *93*

11 Petit Casino: $52.31   *101*

12 Bautezar: $4.41   *117*

13 Les Moissines: $58.53   *126*

14 Les Remparts: $14.70   *142*

15 Avignon: $51.47   *157*

16 Le Clos de la Violette: $236.28   *186*

17 Domaine de Janet   *203*

18 Cassis: $114.41   *231*

19 Wancourt: $7.94   *238*

About the Author   *245*

Eating Europe

Introduction

So the college got this villa in Provence. Many bedrooms, heated pool, middle of a vineyard, two minutes from a perfect village called Rognes. The gig was for art history and French professors. I'm an English professor, but thanks to a couple of deluded newspapers, I'm also a travel writer, so I figured I had a shot, if I could come up with a good research proposal. "Travel Writing," looked a bit thin, so I tossed in an allusion to Graham Greene, added a colon, and my project became: "Old Colonials vs. New Economies: Blurring Borders in the Post-modern Post-Nation State Euro-Transitional Era."

A week later the phone rang. It was Dean Isaacs. "Congratulations," she said.

"Thank you." I said it warily. That greeting from a dean is usually followed by something like, *We'd like you to chair the campus-wide committee and write a very long report assessing how our technological infrastructure is keeping up with the demands of higher education in the twenty-first century.* But this time it really was good news. Not only had I earned a week's stay at the villa in Provence, but my proposal so intrigued the committee that I had been awarded a Pearlstine Grant in the amount of $1,000 to help defray research expenses.

"Hey, that's great," I said.

"You will need to submit receipts of your expenses, have a visible product by September 1, and give a Baden lecture in October."

"It will be an honor."

"What's a visible product?" Janet asked, when I told her the good news.

"It's whatever I write," I replied, not at all defensively.

"You didn't back yourself into a corner with a bunch of crap about postmodern this and postmodern that when you have no idea what you mean, did you?"

I gave her a look of innocent bewilderment.

"I thought so." She shook her head sadly. "And what are *research* expenses?"

"I'm a travel writer. *All* my travel expenses are research."

"Aren't they tax deductions anyway?"

"But, but . . . it's a Pearlstine."

"So, basically," she concluded, "you offered to do a bunch of extra work that you have no idea what it entails for what amounts to no money at all."

"You don't understand academe," I said.

"I understand it better than you do." She spun on her heel.

"No, you don't," I retorted saucily, almost loudly enough for her to hear.

She turned back. "And don't you *dare* set me up as some kind of a snippy foil just for the sake of narrative exposition unless you say how smart I am and mention my kicky new hair cut."

My wife Janet is really smart and has a kicky new hair cut.

Who goes to Europe for only one week? Not us. Not with a Pearlstine in my pocket. Being a student of geometry and cartography, I configured our stay as a large semi-circle with Paris, our gateway, at the center. We got a rental car at DeGaulle and drove straight north to Amsterdam. Four days later we headed east and south, inscribing an arc along national borders to the Alsace. After a couple of days studying that transnational bio-region, we saddled up our Fiat for the long day's drive south and west to join my colleagues for a week in Provence.

Meanwhile, the English professor and some time financial wizard has figured out how to use the Pearlstine without just taking money out of one pocket and putting it in another. Travel and lodging are fully deductible expenses for a professional travel writer such as myself, but restaurants and entertainment are only 50% deductible. So my insight is to submit only F& B (food and beverage—that's travel industry shorthand) and entertainment receipts as Pearlstine research, and save the rest for the tax man. One thing I've learned as a professional travel writer is to keep all of my receipts, and some of other people's, for tax purposes.

I spread out my various receipts across my desk, arranging them chronologically. Already they had the quaint air of antique scrip. It was the millennial year, the twilight of the guilder and the franc. Some receipts also put the price in Euros, in small print, a harbinger. I separated out the slips for car rental, gasoline, highway tolls, got rid of the hotel bills and all extraneous expenditures, until only an unblemished line of restaurant receipts remained. Nineteen of them. I translated them from their various currencies to a satisfying total of nine-hundred and five American dollars. This would work out nicely. Thank you, Mrs. Pearlstine.

Now about that visible product thing.

The late Mickey Mantle once said, "If I'd known I was going to live so long, I would have taken better care of myself." That applies to me and note-taking. Specifically, to me and note-taking about dining experiences in Europe. For most of my dining experiences, the receipts are all I have to spur my memory. Therefore, my guide, my inspiration, my visible product even, must be the receipts themselves. Nineteen receipts will stand in for the nine muses in this narrative free-fall across the Continent. And anyway, this is not about restaurants. They are merely the mile markers for a journey where gastronomic recovered memories will spur epiphanic insights into post-nation states in the Euro-transitional era. Or something like that.

Part One

1 Golden Tulip Bar: $7.89

The oddity of Amsterdam is that we spent four days there and have only three receipts to show for it. The scarcity might be attributable to the overwhelming cultural and historical significance of this Great European Capital. The endless splendor of the Rijksmuseum, with all those Dutch Masters; the

Van Gogh Museum; the terrible touching beauty of the Anne Frank house. These monuments are surely reason enough for awestruck tourists to lose their appetites. And for those times when one needs a shot of quick energy, there are coffee houses located on practically every street. These are not grab-and-go Starbucks stands, but cozy dens with upholstered chairs where service is languid and customers feel welcomed, even encouraged, to lounge back and speculate on the many euphonious words of the Dutch language. *Hoogerbrugge,* for instance. Odd that I never bothered to collect a receipt from any of these pleasant respites, nor from any of the delightful street vendors we discovered upon finishing our coffee breaks, where we stuffed our pie holes with falafel to the point of acute gastric discomfort.

Exhibit A is a receipt from the Golden Tulip Bar of the Hotel Krasnapolsky. Two beers, one pilsner, one wheat. The Krasnapolosky is one of the best places in town. I knew that because I stayed there on my only other visit to Amsterdam, twenty-five years ago. I was nineteen. I had relatives in the hotel business. The face of the Krasnapolsky looks properly out over Dam Square, but it has its butt in the red light district, and for two days so did I, walking at a feverish pace, sidelong glancing at the endless cornucopia of horniopia.

On this trip, Janet and I are staying a few doors down Warmoesstraat, and a few stars down the hotel food chain, at The Winston. The Winston is an edgy "art hotel" with murals in the stairwells and where, for a few extra guilders, you get a

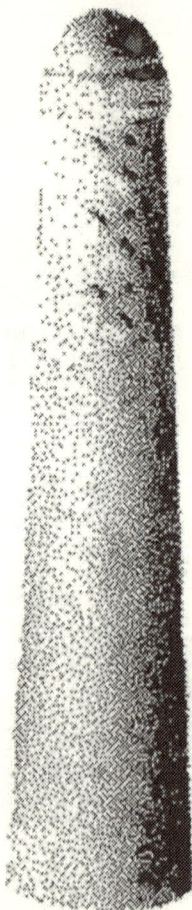

room with original art. As they say on the Winston website, if you're looking for tulips and windmills, this ain't the place for you. We were almost scared off by the home page, which features what looks like an enormous marital aid. Turns out to be an image of one of the vertical steel posts that keep drivers off the sidewalks. They're all over A'dam. You can buy postcards with the same visual gag. Our room, "The Dream," features a black and white mural of a man's head with a lot more smaller identical heads growing out of it, forming a tree-like spread, by an artist named Han Hoogerbrugge. We were expecting an Andy Warhol/Yoko Ono kind of crowd, but the hotel is full of 12-year-old British soccer players and their Dads and Mums. The edgiest thing about the place is the shower, which manages to direct a needle sharp spray straight in your eyes no matter where you stand in the cubicle.

I wanted to show Janet the Krasnapolsky, even if we couldn't afford to stay there. We are sitting at the curved bar, on round, suede-topped stools. Behind the bottles of the back bar, in beveled glass mirrors, we catch glimpses of our bar mates and debate whether the platinum blonde with the plunging neckline is the wife or the date of the sixtyish businessman beside her.

"That settles it," says Janet. "Did you see the way she just licked the whipped cream from the cappuccino spoon?"

"Trophy wife?" I speculate.

"Trophy for the night, more likely."

"Probably," I say, "but I bet she didn't meet him here. I think the Krasnapolsky is too posh to let hookers work the bar, even the best hookers."

"Or else he could have just plucked her out of a window."

We decide that he had hired her over the phone from the well-advertised call service owned and operated by a woman's collective that provides its diligent workers in the sex service industry with flexible hours, health care, child care, vacation pay, pension plan, and a way for guilty liberal tourists to be persuaded that the free market economy really does make everything for the best in this the best of all possible worlds, especially for those women who made so much less money as teachers in Kiev and doctors in Gdansk, and those poor bored girls who were nothing but somebody's grandchild in Bangkok.

No surprise that hookers are on our mind here. Besides residing temporarily in the world's most famous red light district, we have come to this bar directly from Janet's Unsettling Encounter with the Prostitute. This encounter did not involve any F&B. There is no receipt. However, since it's what sent us scurrying toward the bar as rapidly as we could go, its inclusion is relevant here.

Janet's Unsettling Encounter with the Prostitute

We are in a shop, somewhere in or near the red light district. The shop is up half a flight of stairs from street level, and borders a narrow pedestrian alley. I don't remember what kind of shop it was, probably a boutique that sold art works, ceramics perhaps, that we were thinking of buying as gifts for our art-loving friends back home. Certainly not one of those shops where walls of video boxes display every kink and fetish, where racks of dog-eared glossy magazines face walls of sex toys shrink-wrapped onto cardboard backing, where more elaborate, expensive, hard-to-figure-out implements are locked behind glass cases, and where a curtained door in the back leads to private booths where who-knows-what occurs. We have no idea what those are like. And definitely not a "Smart Shop," where legal organic and synthetic mood-altering substances are packaged and displayed with an eye to style that would make Pottery Barn jealous, and intense young men with small round glasses and pierced nostrils dispense information on dosage and effects with a precision that would make a pharmacist proud. Likewise, we have no clue what they are like.

Anyway, in our pursuit of pretty gift ceramics, Janet and I drift to different parts of the shop. As she glances through a large side window, Janet's eyes briefly meet those of a woman looking up at her from another large window on the other side of the alleyway.

In the split second that it takes for Janet to avert her eyes, she thinks, *This woman must be one of the prostitutes we've heard and read so much about, who make of themselves window displays in order to sell their services, for surely this would explain why she stands there in her underwear.* And in the same nanosecond she thinks again, *It is not right that I should avert my eyes as if she is too shameful to be looked upon. She is a human being, she is my sister, and I will salute her humanity with a friendly smile.*

But Janet finds that the woman has taken the initiative in intercultural communication by making an unmistakable international gesture. The woman's hand is extended toward Janet, knuckles outward, with all digits curled except the central one, which is vertical and bobbing slightly. My wife's first impulse is to flee. But she stops herself, thinking, *Wait one goddamn minute here.* And so Janet does not flee, but instead looks the woman in the eye and gives her the international gesture of *What in the hell did I do to you?* The woman seems to soften then, just a little. The woman's next unmistakable international gesture is to tap her own forehead hard with her index finger: *Think!*

Janet's reply, delivered from the safety of the Krasnapolsky bar, is "Well, if you don't want to be looked at, don't stand in a display window in your underwear." But Janet is one of those people who cannot stand to have anyone think ill of her for any reason, and the encounter leaves her somewhat shaken. She keeps replaying the scene. Janet wonders if perhaps the woman saw me pass by a moment earlier, and was angry with her for interfering with a potential customer.

I don't think that was it. I have read that for all the Famous Dutch Tolerance, prostitution still carries a strong social stigma. When the woman understood that Janet's smile was not condescending, and that Janet was capable of being hurt by a rude gesture, a humanizing moment ensued. That second gesture—*Think!*—was a kind of outreach, a bridge of solidarity, one woman explaining to another, "I know this is degrading. I do this for them. You don't get to smile at me like this."

And in that, I find both pathos and dignity.

2 L'Indochine: $60.74

L'Indochine
la cuisine Vietnamienne et Thailandaise

Tafel 8		Datum 31-05-2000
1	Witte huiswijn (fles)	29.50
1	Evian (50 cl)	6.50
2	Menu Saigon	104.00
	Totaal: FL.	140.00

Breslingscrow 4 1017 BA Amsterdam Tel. 020 627 57 55
Geopend van Dinsdag t/m Zondag vanaf 18.00 uur.

The thing about a city laid out in concentric circles and spokes is that tourists on foot are always passing the same places, and saying, "Oh, we were here yesterday, only we came from that direction." Driving in Amsterdam is madness. So is parking.

15

After the standard overnight flight into Paris, we drove what should have been four hours (but was six because I was too cheap to buy a map of Belgium) to Amsterdam. By the time I hit the city ring, I was missing a night's sleep, but even if I'd been fresh as a tulip, it would have been harrowing. Other world capitals have broad avenues; Amsterdam has canals with little teeny streets along the sides of them. We barely managed to follow signs to Central Station, at one point having to stop for teeming pedestrians with our front tires up on a curb and our back end in the path of an oncoming street car. We gratefully parked underground, and didn't think about that blue Fiat until we left four days later. Twenty bucks a day is a *bargain*.

After we have walked down Beulingstraat five times and have had the same conversation five times about how many great-looking Vietnamese restaurants there are, we finally figure out it's the same one, and decide to stop. It's an airy little space on a typical Amsterdam block of tall, narrow, slightly tipsy old buildings. The décor is sparse and stylish, very Zen. When we get there at about seven, the place is empty, so we're thinking, *mistake*. The waiters are too friendly, too attentive, as if having customers is a strange and wonderful occurrence for them. We order the *Menu Saigon*, a *prix fixe* meal, but we're mainly interested in those lovely translucent spring rolls.

Turns out we didn't make a mistake, we're just unfashionably early. The food is sumptuous, and by the time we're half-finished the place is chock full of happy people, with more clustered outside, waiting. I am particularly pleased with the *witte huiswijn*. After I ordered it I saw the next table had ordered an Alsacian pino blanc, and I was jealous. Holland is a beer country; who knows what they'll bring you for house wine? But what we got was not Dutch wine (is there any Dutch wine?). It was French, and it was fine. I hate making oenological blunders.

At a table by the window are four men, three of whom are Asian. One is wearing robes, and has little round glasses. He is obviously very wise. I report this to Janet, whose back is to them, adding, "It means this is a *really* good place."

"Why do you say things like that?"

"As the locust only eats the ripest grain, so the monk only sips from the purest stream."

"Stop it."

The western guy is trim, fifty-five to sixty, and wears old-fashioned glasses with black plastic on top and wire rims underneath. "CIA or missionary," I say, in that tone of unquestioned certainty that my wife finds so charming.

"Give me a break."

"They're reminiscing about the good old days recruiting Montagnards to fight the Cong. Or about building that little church in the I Trang valley."

"You said he's wearing monk's robes."

"Jesus and the Buddha are one—they have come to celebrate this Truth with holy prawns in honey sauce."

Janet has stopped listening. She is nodding her head subtly to the left, in the international gesture of eavesdropping. A couple, American, a few years our senior, at the next table. He's balding, blue blazer and striped tie. She looks like Pat Nixon. "But, then," the woman is asking, "do they just smoke it right there, or do they take it with them?" Her husband shrugs. She goes on, "But, is it already rolled, or do they have pipes? And why do they call them coffeehouses?"

Janet grins. They look like our parents. But then again, we look like our parents.

"I. R.," I say in a low voice.

"What?" whispers Janet.

"Inadequate Research." I say. "There are lots of guides on the Web."

"She's not *really* interested . . . " Janet whispers.

The woman leans forward. "I would love to get my hands on a big fat blunt and get hammered."

"I hear you," says her husband. "Remember that Dan Fogelberg concert at the Garden?" They share a special grin as their food arrives.

That really happened, almost just like that.

3 Puri Mas: $69.43

```
        PURI MAS
L.LEIDSEDWARSSTRAAT 37-41 1e
      1017 NG AMSTERDAM
   020-6277627/6391683

TAFEL    6
  2 GASTEN

  2 IJS THEE        4.99Euro    11.00
  2 RIJSTTAFEL ROYAA 56.27Euro  124.00
  1 FLES STILL       5.45Euro    12.00
-------------------------------------
            S/T  66.71Euro      147.00

BTW LAAG            3.78Euro      8.32

    TOTAL          147.00
                    66.71 Euro

DONDERDG
01-06-2000 19:55:01 P.0  1  8H NOTA   10

    For the monthly events in Amsterdam
        please visit our website
            WWW.PURIMAS.NL
```

The best Dutch food is Indonesian. I can't take credit for that line; it's in all the guidebooks. Reverse colonization, culinary. That one's mine. When it's time to do Indonesian, the choice comes down to this: To Bojo or not to Bojo. Like Pat O'Brien's in New Orleans or Bookbinders in Philadelphia, it's the place half the tourists brag about going to, and half the tourists brag about avoiding. Self-styled sophisticate and sometime travel writer that I am, I declare us non-Bojovians. No Bojo for us.

We see it, right there on Leidsewarsstraat. A gaggle of tourists waits to get in, braving the evil eyes of the door men of the empty restaurants lining both sides of the street all around it. Actually, there are two Leidsewarsstraats, Lange and Korte. Both of them come off Leidseplein, a heavily touristed square in the upmarket part of town, out near those awesome museums that we haven't had a chance to visit yet.

Leidsewarstraats are the culinary equivalent of the red light district, complete with unctuous guys out front trying to coax you in. The streets are narrow, pedestrians only, with about ten feet between awnings on either side. The restaurants all have outdoor seating. This makes a lot of sense, since it's rainy and cold 360 days a year. A'dam makes San Francisco feel like Maui. (After three and a half days of wandering around saying to myself *Who's this Adam guy on all the signs?* I finally asked Janet. So that future travelers might be spared from the laugh line "Who's Adam?" on which there is apparently no statute of limitations, the courtesy apostrophe is here provided.)

I swear the guys in the red light district are just warming up for their real jobs as door thugs on the Leidsewarsstraats. Janet and I are looking to dine, once again at the ridiculously early hour of seven, and, except for the other Americans clambering to get in Bojo, the restaurants are empty and pedestrians scarce, so the door men focus all their oily charms on us. We take refuge in Rokerjii, a coffee house in the middle of the L-street, and go back to the guidebooks, which I've forced Janet to lug around in her canvas bag. We relax for a spell and decide that a restaurant called Puri Mas seems a good non-Bojo bet, and it's right here on Lange Leidsewarsstraat.

So maybe there is something special in Rokerjii coffee, I don't know. Anyway, Janet and I walk up and down Leidsewarsstraat about ten times under the pressure hose of aggressive invitations, and can't find the place. I find it interesting that it doesn't seem to register on the door men that we are the same couple they just harassed two minutes ago, and four minutes ago, and seven minutes ago. All tourists look alike, I guess. So each time we come by that Argentine Steak House or that Pizzeria Milano, we are entreated with the same, "Best food right here!" and "Two for dinner?" and "Inside or terrace?" As if. The "terrace" is a bumpy, narrow sidewalk where white plastic chairs tilt ominously, and most tables sit in bracing proximity to the restaurant next door's garbage cans.

I don't know how Janet is taking these harangues, but, for me, the voices of the door men modulate over time into a kind of waltz-time medley, and I begin to hear the fatigue and boredom behind the entreaties. It's a job. It dawns on me that these door men have their own ethos, their own occupational identity.

The Way of the Door Man

It takes a special person to follow The Way of the Door Man. Raw, purposeful, result-oriented, he has more in common with the vacuum salesman than with the waiter or the concierge. This week he might be working for a restaurant with savory food and prompt service. Or his talents might now be in the service of what hardly qualifies as a restaurant, a disorganized mess with chefs walking out left and right so that shifts are barely covered, and it can take an hour to get your *Eisskynhoessferooss,* which isn't a real dish, but my imagined Dutchification of the German phrase *Eisen Hut,* which isn't a real dish either, but hypothetically could represent the kind of linguistic analysis required by Dutch menus, where even if you figure out the cognate, you aren't any closer to knowing what there is to eat.

"What's the name again?" asks Janet. "You're not spacing out on me, are you?"

"Of course not. It's called Puri Mas."

Eisen Hut. Iron Hat. Helmet. As a figurative name, such a menu item might turn out to be a delicate puff pastry arching gracefully over the plate, helmetlike, maybe in the shape of one of those Kaiser Wilhelm hats with the spear on top. Or perhaps the correct interpretation would be more literal:

some thick gloppy green turtle soup served in its own upend-ed shell, where you're supposed to peel the leftover meat from the inside of the tureen and consider it a great delicacy even if it is tough and chewy. And in this hypothetical restaurant you order it because that's the closest you've come to figuring out anything, because the entire Dutch menu is gobbledygook. Which itself sounds like it should be an specialty of Dutch cuisine. *Gobblyledemgook.* Goose sausage chowder.

"Are you sure it's not on the other Leidsewarsstraat?"

"I'm sure it's right here somewhere."

A good door man might entice you into such a hypothetical restaurant where the management is so bad and the turnover so high that the new Eritrean chef has never heard of *Eisskyn-hoessferoos* either and doesn't know that he's supposed to cook the soup *in the shell.* So. Those tasty bits of flesh that you wangle out of your soup? When you've slurped the soup level down far enough you see that you've been tugging on bloody stumps, wretched to look at, and the thought that you've been ingesting them makes you gag. And at that point some other customer—not you, because you are not Ugly Americans, but the opposite, one of those ultra-nice wimpy couples who put up with anything—some other customer, a French man, probably, will look at his sleek wife and say in a loud voice, "Zees ees deesgusting." And she doesn't say, "Honey, shut up," but taps her cigarette and smiles blandly, knowing there's a Gerard Depardieu scene upcoming, and she might as well look good. And sure enough he stands up, throws his napkin into the soup, and turns to follow a waiter passing with a hot *Gobblyledemgook,* harassing the man in French. And what you notice is how that Armani jacket hangs just so beneath his perfect three-day stubble, and your wife wonders where his wife got that *great dress.*

My wife is standing in front of me, looking in my eyes. "That's it. You've wandered off into the realms of the Great Hypotheticals."

"I'm *also* looking for Puri Mas."

"Well, look harder."

"I'm sure it's right around here." I set off purposefully down the street.

That's who would be complaining about the bloody stumps in the *Eisskynhoessferooss,* not you. And the copper-skinned waiter who outwardly seems impassive and uncomprehending as he whisks by actually understands every word because he's from Maritius and is thinking to himself, *that guy thinks* he's *got problems, wait until this poor American at table three digs into this chowder.* The waiter has suggested several times that the boss should post a sign up in the kitchen for new chefs:

"Goose entrails are *not* an ingredient in Gobblyleddemgook."

Pretend incomprehension is the last line of defense for this waiter; in reality he's about to fall apart. His eldest son is in an immigration holding cell and it's going to cost 5,000 guilders to get him out, and his wife is considering going into the sex industry to help pay the bills. Back into the sex industry. And it is at times like this that the waiter brushes by the door man out front, overhears his blithe repetitions, "Two for dinner?" "Best food here," and he hates him bitterly for the door man's facile ability to lure unsuspecting tourists into this pit. If salmonella ever gets put on the international endangered species list like the lovely *Wha'aa* songbird of his native island nation, this place could be a game preserve. But the door man doesn't care what the waiter thinks. Kitchen problems are the kitchen's problem. He is of the Guild of the Door Man, that special breed of men, and his job is to get them in the door and seated with plastic laminated menus in their hands.

And we are them. I understand now. The door man's friendly enthusiasm is fake, but he bears us no particular rancor. He has problems too, which aren't so bad, really, as those of the waiter scurrying around behind him. I understand so much now, and as we pass up and down Leidsewarsstraat, it becomes a kind of ballet. My epiphany allows me to gracefully parry each thrust as we sail by. "Maybe a bit later," I say, and "I'm sure it's great," and, "Thank you, not now." The door man's eyes flit to the next potential patrons without inflection, but without rejection, and I take some satisfaction in that. Intercultural understanding achieved.

"Stop." Janet stands with arms crossed.

"What?"

"I'm not walking another step until we figure this out." She digs into her bag for the guidebook. While thumbing through pages she sighs and says, "Okay, I give up. What have you been thinking about?"

"I was empathizing with the door men while realizing that there is no connection between their enthusiasm and the quality of dining experience."

"Yeah, yeah, and the waiter's kid is stuck in immigration."

"How do you *do* that?"

"Forget it. Let's just find . . ."

"Puri Mas!" I say, pointing like a scout. Sure enough, by one of those conventional miracles that we all need now and then, my eyes have chanced fifty feet down the street and landed on a metal sign hanging on the wall.

"Damn," Janet says. "We've walked right by here a dozen times." But it's said with wonder, not italics, so I know that Janet is not clinically hungry. My wife is subject to hypoglycemic dips, and when one hits, if she doesn't eat really soon she feels really bad. As in ill. Our life together is a lot easier since we both figured this out.

We figured this out yesterday.

We were walking pleasantly along through the Vondelpark, and Janet burst into outraged tears and said she *really needed to eat*. I got annoyed by her sudden vehemence, which in turn annoyed her because she had *told* me she needed to eat forty minutes ago. I remembered her saying it, but it had sounded like a casual statement, and I thought my response appropriate: that we should wander on a little farther through the park and at some point cut left in the direction of Museumplein and pick out a cute restaurant along the way. But now I admit that after her precipitous sugar plunge last year in Yellowstone I should not have been oblivious to her distress signal even if it was delivered in an offhand way by someone whose natural tendency is not to want to make a fuss over herself. It was my fault that suddenly the Vondelpark was Yellowstone all over again, only instead of driving on a narrow crowded highway through evergreen mountains and steep gorges, we were caught in the middle of a vast urban park. Kids sat in circles beside portable CD players blasting international dance music. A longhaired guy on a bench played flamenco guitar. Dogs chased Frisbees. A sweet smoky fragrance wafted through the air. Janet didn't appreciate the scene because she was having a blood sugar emergency, and I didn't notice her emergency because I was appreciating the scene. Damn. When I finally caught on, my annoyance was quickly transformed into compassion and self-recrimination. I looked around desperately for some source of protein short of jumping in the pond and rassling up a ten pound goldfish. I was reduced to a helpless feeling akin to that of husband whose wife is in labor, saying, "Come on, honey, you can do it, honey, you have to get through this," while reading in her face that she'd like nothing more, at that moment, than to grind bits of glass into his eyeballs and say, "Get through *this, honey.*" Just at the point where Janet looked close to passing out and any bistro or street vendor seemed hopelessly distant, there occurred another one of those conventional miracles that we all need a few of now and then. We came around a giant willow tree trailing its thin elegance into the fish-filled stream beside a tiny arched bridge, and saw an octagonal white building that housed the Restaurant Vertigo (no kidding). We rushed in and joyfully got club sandwiches, which were served up fast, which was amazing, and which the menu called "club sandwiches" and not something like *cloobjenpaakstaatsyndvych.* We sat out on the terrace enjoying them in the rare and glorious sunshine, and I felt deeply, reverently, grateful for many things, including but not limited to my beautiful wife, club sandwiches, the harlequin Great Dane romping clownishly among the tables, and the blonde three tables over wearing a buckskin bustier.

Too bad I forgot to get a receipt; those sandwiches deserved their own chapter.

But that was yesterday, eons ago in Amsterdam time. Which, by the way, is slower than normal time. The sun stays up until way late at night, and then pops up early the next day. Environmental and biological factors may contribute to the temporal elongation. Research is ongoing. But, as God is my witness, my wife will never have a sugar emergency again. She has graciously forgiven me for yesterday, and her sugar levels held up for the duration of my Great Hypothetical (thank God!) and we are even now walking rapidly, arm in arm, with fixed determination, toward Puri Mas.

She shakes her head again that we'd walked right by so many times, and adds some comment purporting to find a link, a connection, somehow, between our failure to find this restaurant, and our stop at Rokerjii Coffeehouse, which by amazing coincidence also happens to be practically next door. But I've got a different theory. I say, "See the crowd next door?"

"What of it?"

"See what restaurant it is?"

She reads the awning. "Bojo."

"Bojo."

"So what?"

"So that explains it. Each time we walked by here, we knew what we were looking for, and also what we were *not* looking for. We were *not* looking for Bojo, so once we saw it our eyes barely glanced that direction. Puri Mas was fixed in our minds as an alternative to Bojo, the unBojo, the anti-Bojo, and we expected it to be *spatially* in opposition as well. A clear case of proximity blindness. It was not until I *needed* the information that my mind was able to leap out of the confines of the paradigm." I take a breath, and add childishly, "My logical rational explanation supersedes your magical mystical coffee house explanation."

Janet gives me a full smile. "Your explanation indubitably confirms my explanation."

I glance at her warily. "Did you just say 'indubitably'?"

Still smiling sweetly. "No, but if you ever write about this, have me say it, okay?"

"But it doesn't sound like you. It's an affected Briticism, pretentious and inappropriate. Much more likely that I would say it."

As we arrive at the Puri Mas, Janet adds, "As long as we're dabbling in meta-nonfiction, let me remind you to get a receipt this time. I have a hunch you'll want it later."

The door opens on a steep narrow stairway that takes a left hand turn half way up. This does not seem a propitious sign, but suddenly we step out into the middle of a beautiful room. A small bar that doubles as a maitre d' station is before us. People whom I presume to be of Indonesian extraction rush to be of service. We are led around to a table near the front, where big windows overlook with Olympian serenity the hubbub of the street and the barking of the door men. What I presume to be Indonesian music emanates from what I presume to be a Japanese sound system.

We order iced tea (*ijs thee*—for real), and are presented with two bulky menus, one à la carte, and one for the rice table (*rijsttafel*) menus. The latter are big sample-everything *prix fixe* meals. And since we're in the mood to sample everything, *rijsttafel* it is. Soon the meal begins, and unfolds like another one of those conventional miracles we all need now and then—the karma for which seems particularly resonant in Amsterdam. First the low chrome braziers are laid out up the table between us, then past us, to form a T-shape facing the waiter. The short candles are lit and tinny tops replaced. Food. One waiter after another comes to us in an efficient but festive parade, bearing plates and bowls full of marvelous smells and shapes and textures. Grainy things, greenie things, and gloppy things. It goes on until there's no space left at the table on or around the T. In a practiced way the waiter describes everything in sequence, pointing to each with a flourish, but I don't remember a thing. My eyes are crossing, my hands are shaking, I am drooling. I'm having a food emer-

gency of my own, but not the official medical kind that Janet
falls victim to. This is rather its opposite, or converse, a kind
of feverish lust for instant massive consumption created mainly in the mind but abetted by a wildly willing set of glands.
We dig in, starting at the bottom of the T and working our
way toward the branches. Conversation, for the moment, is
limited to "Try this!" and "Pass that!" At my end of the T sits
a reddish dish about which I vaguely remember some warning
at the conclusion of the waiter's speech.

After an initial gorging period analogous to a scene from
the Serengeti—I mean the time right after the lionesses have
killed the zebra when the two dominant males pounce on the
carcass slashing and feasting their fill and roaring terribly at
any other lion or cub that dares come within twenty feet of
them—after that, Janet speaks.

"You know, it's not exactly what I expected."

Alert to any whiff of discontent, I growl, "What? It's
great!"

Alert to any whiff of defensiveness, Janet says, "Yes, great.
I love it. Only..." she points. "Pork, beef, veal...or is this one
lamb?"

"Lamb," I snarl. I have no idea.

"And this is chicken and that's some kind of sausage, I
think."

"But the main thing is the sauces," I say. "The hot peanut
sauce is the best, or else the green one. Is that curry?"

"Right. I like the peanut too, but. . . ."

"But what?"

"I guess I was thrown off by the name. *Rice* table. Wouldn't
you expect to have a lot of rice, different kinds of rice, or
something? This is great, but it's all meat. It's so heavy."

"Rice table," I repeat, and shrug the flies out of my mane.
"Good point. Here, you haven't tried this one yet," I lift the
gloppy reddish dish.

Her hand does not come up to take it. "Nice try."

"What?"

"I heard what he said about that one. You try it."

And so I do, and it's not so bad in a CometDranoMr. Plumber kind of way. Actually, it might have killed a lesser man, but for the moment I am the King of Beasts.

A Final Word on The Famous Dutch Tolerance

Midnight on Leidseplein. Janet is in the room. I've just come out to get some air and grab some bottled water. It's our last night in Amsterdam. Whether due to jet-lag, or that mysterious elongation of time here, we've been going to bed pretty early every night. Now I have a strong urge to run back to the hotel and say, "Janet, come out with me. We've been missing half the city." The sidewalk cafes are full, music rebounds from the clubs, people swirl across the square in a churning mass. Orange trams clank through at alarming speeds, heavy and sleek on their metal rails. Locals and tourists, piercings and tattoos and dog collars. Saris and kurtas, tights, mini-skirts, trousers and sensible shoes. People in a hurry, people lounging. The atmosphere is vibrant, electric. Edgy but open. A very good vibe.

An American voice, drunk, aggressive, shouts, "Hey, man, my turn. MY FUCKING TURN."

A sinking sensation hits my stomach, and my instinct is to walk away from trouble. The crowd has parted, peeled back from a group doing something—at first I think they're forming a human pyramid. Onlookers crowd around. I edge closer to the clearing.

"*My turn,* asshole!" the guy shouts again. "It's the Nikon, right there." The speaker is a college-age guy. He's got his arms draped over the shoulders of two uniformed police men. He wants his picture taken.

A group of five or six Americans have accosted four Dutch policemen. For a photo opportunity, apparently. Early twenties, Abercrombie clones, not meaning any harm but overly gregarious in that aggressive drunken way that college guys can be. Stoned too, no doubt. They want everyone back home to see how cool the cops are here. They're flinging arms over the cops' shoulders, posturing, taking turns being the camera man while their buddies compete to strike more outlandish poses. The crowd watches and laughs. One of the guys plucks the hat from a cop's head and puts it on his own. I look at the cops' faces. They are not enjoying this, but with grim good nature they are letting it happen. The kids are emboldened. When they start playing to the crowd, the circus atmosphere turns tense. One kid tries to get hold of a night stick, another tugs at a holster. The cops fend them off, but will not be provoked.

Suddenly it's over. The photos have all been taken. Grateful boys are pumping the cops' hands, slapping their backs, and telling them they're cool. They shout their farewells as they weave away. The crowd closes in, and the Leidseplein is once again a swirling human sea.

I find a kiosk and get a bottle of water for the room. As I walk through the crowds, I find myself picturing the young faces of those cops. Is there is another place on the planet where city police, mocked and manhandled by foreign drunks, would show this kind of restraint? If I don't write about anything else on this trip, I tell myself, I will write about this. But first I will go back to the hotel and tell Janet that I have just witnessed what it means to be a man.

On Cartography and
the Sublime

I could live in Liege. Liege clings to the hillsides above a snaking river—a little grimy and disheveled, but intriguing. Compared to its German neighbors, it resembles neither the industrial ferocity of the Ruhr nor the gingerbread cuteness of the Mosel. It lacks the drama of Luxembourg's gorges and is not haunted like the Ardennes. It is bypassed by time; it is Belgium. I would choose Liege if I were filming a le Carré novel. It has about it the brooding grayness of the Cold War. The highway along the river would show well in a car chase of bulky black Citroens, and the dark hillsides would seem to hold secrets.

As it did back in Maastricht, the road dwindles abruptly from freeway to thoroughfare when you get into town. The route flips you across one bridge into downtown, then back across to the other side as you leave the center. The effect is arresting, like being inside a zoom lens. One second we're viewing the town from the distant multi-lane roadway across the river, and the next we're in the thick of it: quick vignettes of cobblestone walks, peeling posters on lampposts, kids tossing cigarette butts, old men at outdoor cafes.

"I could live in Liege," I say to Janet.

"Could you eat in Liege?" she answers, pointedly.

"I'd love to eat in Liege," I assure her. But I am not as good as my word. By this time we're in the thick of the city center. The traffic is intense. Opportunities to jump off the thoroughfare flit by like cracks in the pavement. That's just a gas station. That's too industrial. Whoops, just missed that one. And bingo, the E-25 has regained its freeway status and Liege is a part of our past, figuratively and cartographically.

I wonder if the University of Liege has room for a Professor of English and sometime travel writer who speaks neither French nor Flemish, German nor Dutch. I could be useful to them, if for nothing more than to add some poetry to their website description of their city as the "third biggest fluvial port in Europe and the economic capital of the Waloon region." The Meuse would be my muse.

"Why do you keep saying you could live in Liege?"

"I don't know. I just like the place. It seems sophisticated and yet remote. Like Krakow."

"How can you tell? We didn't even stop there."

"I don't know." I glance across at Janet and shrug. She rolls her eyes, but sweetly. Our Fiat Punto has an electric blue interior. It's tiny but tall—room enough to juggle, but you can park it in a phone booth. Ten days hence, I'd like to check it at the airport ("What do you mean that's a car? That's my suitcase! Just twist the tag around the wiper there"), grab it off the conveyor belt in Philadelphia, and drive it home.

"So I guess we aren't going to eat in Liege," Janet says, as the last traces of the city fall away behind us.

"Sorry. We'll find some place to eat along the highway."

"I don't get it. All these cool towns with great restaurants, and you want to eat at some truck stop along the highway."

"You're thinking like an American." I remind her that this entire continent, with the exception of some parts of the British Isles, is dedicated to the proposition that great food and wine are the cornerstone of culture, and major roadways are no exception. "Remember Italy?"

"Mmmmm. Panini."

"And don't forget The Categorical Cheese Imperative."

Together we review the terms. From my European sister I adopted the custom which dictates that the first thing one must do upon setting foot or tire upon Italian soil is buy cheese. The great thing is it's always there. The first gas station you see will have better food than the entire state of Minnesota. Pump your forty liters and step inside with your credit card, and you see rows of golden crispy crusty panini stuffed with meats and cheeses. There will be three tables of cheeses—not cellophane-wrapped chunks of cheese-food but great lovely wheels with savory names, and you'll trip over bottles of local wine spilling out of wooden boxes on the floor. Whether you're coming in under Monte Bianco into Courmayeur, leaving Monte Carlo for Ventimiglia or just setting down at Fiumicino Airport, cheese will be close at hand. You buy a great hunk and you break off pieces and you eat it, right there, right then, regardless of what other obligations or intentions you may have. The Categorical Cheese Imperative is a rule to live by.

"Now I'm *really* hungry," Janet says.

My radar is picking up something. "*Really* hungry? Did I hear italics?"

"Not clinically," she assures me.

"Well, I'm sure there will be a great rest stop along here any kilometer now."

Only there isn't. We drive and drive, up and down over big hills of forests and farms, and it's beautiful, but bereft of roadside provision. Meanwhile, my cartographic imagination has been churning, and I say to Janet, "If I gave you a quiz asking which state was the closest in size and shape to the Netherlands, which one would you choose?"

"None of the above," she replies. "I would skip the quiz. It's boring."

"And I would say Maryland."

"That's nice, dear."

"Your alleged boredom is just a cover for your deep cartographic insecurity. You were afraid you'd rate illiterate."

"Bullshit." She says it pleasantly. "Any test for cartographic literacy would by definition involve a map. What you are testing for is cartographic *interest*. Mapheads will play your little game. The rest of us just don't care."

And mapheads, I am thinking, would see that the problem is that the panhandles are at opposite ends of the two states. If you flip Maryland over backwards and then turn it to the vertical, then it would more resemble the Netherlands. That would be cool. To mapheads. Out loud, I say, "I can't believe we haven't come to a rest stop yet." The weird thing is, we keep passing American style rest stops, picnic tables and a toilet building, that you never see in Europe. But where's the cool Euro-rest-stop, big square block building propped right over the top of the highway, with a hotel and at least two restaurants, accessible from parking on either side?

Janet isn't through with me. "Speaking of cool Euro-things, what are you going to write?"

"Look, there's the exit for Clairvaux."

"The grant you got?"

"I wonder if that's where St. Bernard of Clairvaux is from."

She pokes my arm. "No, really. That proposal you made had something about Euro-dollars and postcolonialism—have you thought about that?"

"One of the most beautiful prayers of all time is attributed to St. Bernard of Clairvaux. The *Memorare*. Do Protestants know that, or is it just Catholics?"

"So you don't want to talk about your project?"

"Listen to the first sentence: *Remember, Oh Blessed Virgin Mother, that never was it known that anyone who fled to thy protection, implored thy help, or sought thy intercession, was left unaided.* I would purely love to see that baby diagrammed."

"Diagramming prayers. That's the kind of thing you'd be up doing in the middle of the night. And no, Protestants don't pray to the BVM."

"They don't know what they're missing. Consider the audacity of it: opening with an imperative verb, grabbing Mary by the robe and reminding her that she is batting a thousand on all supplications, and you're not about to let her slip to .999, not on your nickel. It's like you're doing *her* a favor. But by the next line you're groveling with nice alliteration, *sinful and sorrowful,* buttering her up for another order, *despise not my petition.*

Janet is staring out at the passing countryside, uninterested in St. Bernard of Clairvaux and his prayer. After a while I say, "How are the shoes?"

She brightens. "They're great. After the second day walking around in Amsterdam I had this blister on my second toe, remember? But it's callused now, and they're really comfortable." She picks up a shoe from the floor of the Fiat. "And they look great."

"They are good. That rest stop should be coming along here any minute."

She reaches across the brake lever and rests her hand on mine. For six months prior to this trip Janet said, "I have to get comfortable shoes for the trip," and I said, "Well don't wait until two days before we leave, because they won't be broken in and you'll get blisters," and she said, "You think I don't know that? *Of course* I won't wait until two days before we leave." She didn't wait until two days before she left; she waited until one day before, and got these brown strappy sandals. But she weathered the blisters of Amsterdam, and now appreciates that I have offered a vindication of her shoe selection, and that I haven't forgotten about food.

I'm glad Janet does not accuse me of patronizing her. I do not believe that cartography and the rhetoric of medieval prayer are inherently more worthy topics of discussion than are food and shoes. By practically any measure, food and shoes are more interesting than maps and medieval rhetoric. We are defined by our fascinations, and I have the luxury to have time for some arcane fascinations. I am also fascinated by Janet. Would I be more fascinated if she loved maps and medievalism? Probably not. Common interests are all well and good, but I'm leaning toward awe of individualism. Our minds are all eclectic, no matter what we focus them on. By extension, there's as much mystery in the most prosaic of subjects as there is in the most esoteric.

"What are you thinking?"

Janet's on to me, as usual. "I could live in Liege."

"No, really."

"Really. I am thinking about the nature of attraction. Like, what was it about Liege that fascinated me. Why not Maastricht or Utrecht?"

"You don't like towns that have 'Treaty of . . .' in front of their names?"

"Was it really something inherent in the town? The look of it? Or something more intangible, some ambience? I loved the way the highway slung us into downtown, where this city, up to this point tucked up tight in its hills, suddenly lay open, vulnerable, surrendering to us its most intimate workings."

Janet's hand tightens over mine. "Are you trying to turn me on?"

"It *is* sexy. Maybe what I've meant all along is 'I lust for Liege.'"

She groans. "That's not what *I* meant."

"I know." But it does get to the heart of things, doesn't it? With a person or a place, what is it that rings the bell of our fascination? I tell Janet that I remember reading once that with men, marriage is all about timing. Men cling to the myth of unlimited sexual partnerships until it dissipates, then they marry the next woman who will have them. That's sort of how it was with Becca. I'd just come out of a five-year relationship with Sallie, that, in the end, had only for its obstacle that she wished for, and I could not abide the thought of, matrimony. I could not abide her hurt, so eventually I left Denver. I got myself accepted to grad school in Nebraska, moved to Lincoln, and got engaged to the first woman I slept with, even though I had strong doubts it could ever work.

"But that's not normal," Janet says. "That's pathetic. I like to think that the second time around it wasn't a question of your mood or that year's Stage of Male Progression, but that you found something in me that made your life better and fuller."

"Like your love of maps and the rhetoric of medieval prayers."

"Exactly."

"And food and shoes."

"Much better."

"And sex."

"Much much better." She leans over and kisses my neck.

"So where does that leave Liege?" I ask.

"She's a bawd. Forget her."

"But I *liked* Liege."

"A flirt. A weekend affair, at best. You couldn't live with Liege. Tell me about Lausanne."

I can't help smiling, if a little sadly. "I've told you about Lausanne."

"Tell me again." Janet tucks her legs lotus-style beneath her, leans back where car door meets car seat.

I tell her again about Lausanne, a story that begins on a drive from Frankfurt to my sister's place in Switzerland. She had just bought a ski condo in Nendez, and was very excited about it. *Mon refuge* she kept calling it. Her husband ran a luxury hotel, so he got free rooms in other luxury hotels, and he'd planned for us to stop overnight in Lausanne. I was twenty-three. I was looking forward to seeing the Alps for the first time. Some intimation of immortality had made me decide at an early age that I was a mountain person, and when I could go off to college, I went off to Denver. In my Colorado years I was a sometime skier and a half-hearted hiker. Mostly I ended up taking long drives by myself through the mountains, eating *huevos rancheros* at some clapboard diner, pulling off at overlooks to sit there for awhile with longing in my heart. And I always had my maps out, looking for a more obscure road, a higher pass.

Janet stops me at this point to say, "You never told me this part before. That's so sad."

"This is the full version. Where in the hell is a rest stop? I'm surprised we haven't seen someone along the side of the road holding up a gas can."

"Never mind that. Go on."

I pick up the story at the crucial point. A moment I remember vividly. We were not in the mountains yet, but we were in Switzerland. We crested the top of a hill, and dropped down the other side, criss-crossing back and forth on long switchbacks. The hillside around us was all vineyard, rows of grape leaves, bright green. Below us, the city of Lausanne stretched out, its low skyline framed in the blue of Lake Leman. And beyond the lake, almost lost in the haze, loomed the snowcapped peaks of Savoy. My response was physical. My diaphragm began pushing up against my heart—a heavy, full, feeling. If I got that feeling now, I'd be making a nervous call to the cardiologist. But at that age I could welcome the feeling and wonder at it. There may have been some conversation from the front seat; there probably was, I don't remember. I was swinging from side to side in the back seat after each hairpin, straining to see more of the view. "See" is too weak a word. I was swallowing the view, and the view was swallowing me. The pressure in my diaphragm grew stronger. I knew this was a feeling that I had never had before, and that it was precious.

I was in a daze as we drove into the city. We got out at the door of a hotel called The Palace, and someone took the car away to the garage. I was barely aware of the opulence of the lobby. They gave me a key. I got in an elevator. My room was on the top floor, and it had its own balcony looking out on precisely the same view I'd seen from the car, only closer up, more intense. The rooftops of Lausanne rolled away beneath me to the lakeshore. The deep blue of the lake was dotted with brightly colored sails—red, blue, yellow, white. The mystical mountaintops floated in the distance. The pressure in my chest doubled, and I was intensely aware of my eyes. *My poor eyes*, I remember thinking. *How can they take all this beauty? They are going to explode.* I felt that all this immense beauty and perfection, the enormity of it all, was being channeled into something equally large and powerful inside me, through the narrow conduit of my lens and retina. The nuclear power

of the Alps being fed into the substation of my heart through
the two-dollar extension cord of my eyes.

The thing is, I was not naïve about what was happening.
I was an English major. I had a name for this thing that was
happening to me. *The sublime.* It's what Wordsworth and Shel-
ley were talking about, what they came to the Alps in search
of. This was why Buddhist monks spend lifetimes in meditation: they are trying to suppress desire in order to achieve *this.*
For the first time in my life I was *completely content.* I was
completely without any desires beyond the here and now. I said
to myself, *I could die right now,* and I meant it. I don't know
what I had done to deserve such a gift, but there it was. The
fulfillment of all the longing lonely drives through the Rockies. Sitting on that little balcony I experienced transcendence.
I knew the sublime. And I knew, even then, that it would
never come again.

As I trail off into silence, I think of Janet sitting there, and
quickly add, "Not that way, I mean. Our love is transcendent
in a different way."

She shushes me. "I know. I'm not jealous. I mean, I'm
jealous of the experience, but not of Lausanne or the Alps or
God."

"Funny. I didn't think of God. I remember thinking at
the time that it was like a massive universal orgasm with the
entire environment. But not sexual, either. It was all heart and
diaphragm, breath and blood."

"Was it over that suddenly?"

"No. I remember sitting there on the balcony for, I don't
know, thirty, forty minutes, digging it. And then my sister
called and told me to get dressed up, we were going to dinner
in Geneva."

Janet shakes her head. "Women and their food demands.
Constantly dragging you down. Did you tell her, 'No problem, honey, we'll find something in a little while?'"

"No, I learned that later. I got dressed, and we went to
Geneva, and the pressure in my diaphragm slowly went away.
And I was exhausted. I remember we walked along the quay

there, by the *jet d'eau*, after dinner. I could barely drag my ass
along. I just wanted to get back to the hotel and sleep."
"So that part hasn't changed."
"Right."
We drive in silence for a while. I appreciate that Janet be-
lieves me, and that she helps keep alive in me the knowledge
of the sublime. A belief in transcendence is one of the things
we have in common.
At that moment, as if on cue, the sign appears. Rest stop,
the real kind. Massive quantities of great food, five kilome-
ters. Glory be to God.
"You could live in Lausanne?"
"I thought I could. For awhile I thought I had to. I wanted
to go live there and be transcendent 24/7."
"Doesn't that contradict the meaning of transcend?"
"The problem, as I saw it, was citizenship. And I would
solve that problem, I thought, with marriage. I was actually
considering taking out personal ads in Swiss newspapers for
a wife."
"No."
"*Oui.*"
I remember exactly when the idea hit me. The next day,
we drove on to Nendez, and in some tiny town I went into the
bank to change money. The cashier looked about sixteen—
honey blond, bashful, unaware she was beautiful. We flirted a
little. She called her village "dead and boring." And I thought,
wow, this girl doesn't realize that I am totally unworthy of
her. There must be more like her. I should take out an ad.
Normally I don't mind telling Janet stories that make me look
foolish; in fact, I'm pretty good at it. But this time, for some
reason, I hold back. I have a strange protective feeling for that
Romantic boy who touched the sublime.
"But you did go back to Lausanne?"
"Yes. With Becca. We were stuck in traffic for hours. We
fought. It was horrible."
"Same hotel?"

"No, too pricey. We stayed down by the lake, and it turned out to be the same hotel where Byron wrote 'The Prisoner of Chillon.' The irony was too perfect."

Sometimes fate hits you on the noggin, and you barely even notice. And one day twenty years later you're driving through Belgium and there it is. One should be wary of seeking transcendence, because the higher you dare to aspire, the farther down you admit you can sink. Those Romantics who stalked the sublime usually found dejection instead. When I went back to Lausanne I was about as miserable as an unhappily married Romantic can be. I couldn't conceive of divorce; nobody in my Catholic family had divorced. I was terrified that I was becoming resigned to having thrown away my chance to share my life with a soul mate. Terrified that the best I could imagine was a grim acceptance of my dungeon, like Byron in Chillon, "My very chains and I grew friends,/ So much a long communion tends/ To make us what we are." What if I had never met Janet? The thought almost makes me panic. I have to restrain myself from reaching over and squeezing her leg till she screams and smacks me, just so I can have more of her present in this moment. Damn. It's enough to make a guy swear off this transcendence business. Maybe the neoclassicists were right after all. Be safe, sane, and civil. Moderation in all things. The alternatives are too risky.

"What's wrong?" says Janet.

"Nothing," I say, wrapping my hand gently around her knee as I pull off the highway. "Just a touch of Romantic melancholy."

4 AC Restaurants: $22.62

```
AC RESTAURANTS
6700 Messancy
TVA / BE 441.544.295
Circ.6/99  Aut.23/12/99
.....................................

Jus frais 35cl              55.00
Petit Pain complet          28.00
Plat Americain             250.00
Jus frais 35cl              55.00
Ass. de fromage            110.00
Petit Pain complet          28.00
Ass. saumon fumé           245.00
Saladbar Petit              55.00
                       ............
       Total           946.00
           CAD    23.45
           CRED CARD       946.00

Clients : 2

Caisse 2  Caissier:NATHALIE B
Date: 02-06-00  Hr : 14:26 Ticket5489
Merci et bon voyage
```

"That's not ham salad." I am referring to the cellophane-covered plate that Janet has just plucked from an ice table. We have taken trays, and are standing on a cool tile floor amid a galaxy of food and beverage possibilities. Tables of cheeses, pyramids of golden crusty rolls, chilled reach-ins with rows of

41

bottles—water, juice, beer and wine standing at attention like platoons of toy soldiers.

"I *know* it's not ham salad," she says, as if I'd insulted her, and puts it back. "What are you going to have?"

I'm eyeing the hot food line over where the wall opens up to the back kitchen. Through steamy glass windows I see wide noodles next to a vat of rich brown sauce, spaghetti by a tub of red sauce, breaded cutlets overlapping like roof tiles, hot shrunken vegetables. "What are *you* going to have?"

"I don't know." She drifts back toward the cheese table.

It's mid-afternoon and we are nearly alone with all this food. I feel the tepid hand of existential food angst creeping up my spine. It doesn't matter what choices I make, but the abundance of choice is becoming a burden. I carry my tray lightly from station to station, trying not to let Janet see the symptoms. Existential food angst is highly infectious, and in its most virulent form can turn a meal into an agony of second-guessing and self-recrimination.

She intercepts me by the cold plates. "You're not getting food angst are you?"

"No, what made you think that?" I say, a trifle too brightly. Danger. I grab the plate she was holding a few moments ago. "I'm having the thing that's not ham salad."

"But that's . . . "

"I know what it is."

Her voice drops to a whisper. "You think that's smart?" She pokes it through the cellophane. "Do you think it's safe?"

"Well, now I have to take it."

"Oh no you don't," she says. "Don't you go trying to pin this one on me. You'll end up writing about how Janet made you eat steak tartare at a rest stop and you got botulism. There." She smoothes out the dimple she made. "Now you can put it back."

"I want the steak tartare." I grab a bread roll and tiny florets of butter from the next table, juice from the reach-in, and head for the cash register. Janet, under the gun, takes a smoked salmon plate and assorted cheeses, and follows. Existential food angst has been averted, but at what cost? It must be safe, I insist, first to myself, and then to Janet when we park ourselves at a table. Raw meat. Raw. Meat. They're not stingy with it either—I'm looking at a fist-sized red dollop in the middle of the plate, surrounded by capers, cornichons, slices of cucumber. It's ground finer than hamburger, almost to a paste. I discover it doesn't taste bad, especially if you have a high threshold on your gag reflex.

"It doesn't taste bad," I say.

"I know you. You don't know if you like it or not, but you'll get raw meat at a rest stop just so you can say you did it." There seems to be a hint of malicious glee in my wife's voice. A small part of her would be pleased if I got food poisoning.

"It's my travel writer's sense of adventure and risk. Like running the bulls in Pamplona."

"Like ordering fried bull testicles in Wyoming, you mean."

"Well, if you're going to limit it to things I've actually done, yes." I push the plate towards her. "Go ahead."

"So if it's bad I'll get sick too?"

"No." (*Yes, exactly.*) "I'm sure it's absolutely fine. Where are you ever going to have steak tartare? No?" I shrug and pull the plate back. "Okay." (*Take some, go on and take some.*)

Her fork sneaks across the table and tines up a blob. (*Bingo.*) "Try it with capers."

Her eyes narrow. "If I get sick, you're a dead man."

(*If we get sick.*) "Go on, it's fine. I'm sure of it. (*I hope.*)

We finish most of it, and head out to the car. Janet brings a tiny red individually-wrapped wheel of cheese that will still be sitting in the concavity between the seats when we give the car back to Budget ten days later. Ten weeks later, when the sometime travel writer is recalling with some guilt how he encouraged his wife to eat the stuff (it was fine, though), he will squint at the computer-printed receipt and contemplate the name of the dish that he had consumed: *Plat Americain.*

5 Restaurant le Luxhof: $37.20

```
RESTAURANT LE LUXHOF
67 RUE DE LA REPUBLIQUE
       GUEBWILLER
TELEPHONE: 89.76.20.89
xxxxxxxxxxxxxxxxxxxxxx
#0001          02-06-00

No compte:    808

1 D. SCHLUMBERGE 100.00
1 PATES         *45.00
1 VIANDE        *95.00
1 EAUX          *13.00
Nouv. solde:  *253.00
                  =
DIREC     0162
```

We could have saved some time if we'd known it was called Restaurant le Luxhof and not "Pizzeria," which is what the sign out front says. We didn't come all the way to the Alsace to have pizza, but there doesn't seem to be much else open. We are in Guebwiller, the town that defies pronunciation. Janet favors Gallic attempts, such as "Gyoob–wee-yay," while I keep grunting a Germanic, "Goop-feeler," which makes Janet wince. Luckily the town is charming, or we might get on each other's nerves. Just another aspect of that blended French-German culture. Hey, I'm thinking, maybe I can find something in that to write about blurring borders in the postmodern postnation state Euro-transitional era. I tell my-self to keep my eyes open. In the meantime, we're hungry. Guebwiller is strangely vacant this evening. After unpack-ing at our chateau, we wandered narrow deserted streets at twilight to find Le Luxhof spilling out onto what we guess to be the main square beside one other restaurant that also has tables outside. The other one looked more like a sports bar inside, with neon beer signs being the main decorative motif. What makes the town's emptiness so unexpected is that I had had a hell of a time finding a place to stay. In the weeks before our trip I spent hours at Alsace websites, and had sent room requests to a score of hotels in Colmar, Kayserberg, Riquewi-hr, Ribeauville, Munster, Turkheim, Eguisheim, Kintzheim, and Niederbronn les Bains. I even tried a hotel in Lorraine. I thought sure I'd get a room in Lorraine. Everybody says, "Alsace-Lorraine," but nobody goes to Lorraine. I would go there, I thought, and write about the back half of the hyphen-ated region. That would be my visible product. Make that my invisible product; Lorraine shut me out too. Getting desper-ate, I began telephoning hotels that didn't have email reserva-tion systems, and, where English was spoken, I learned they were booked too. I started asking for suggestions and some-where along the way I got the number for the Chateau de la Prairie.

This guy that answered the phone didn't speak English. "Fax," he kept saying, "Fax."

So then I called Cecile. She's a dean, but she's also a profes-sor of both French and German.

"No problem," Cecile said a few minutes later, calling me back. "And it's a really good rate."

I neglected to ask what Cecile considered a really good rate, and when I saw the place, my first thought was uh-oh, this is going to put a crimp in my plastic. After a long day's drive which might be compared on a cartography exam to a trip from Baltimore to Cincinnati via the panhandle of Maryland, we arrived in Guebwiller about 7:30 p.m.. (Hold the phone, mapheads. I'm well aware that Cincinnati was the river city stand-in for Strasbourg, and that Guebwiller would have to be some smaller town, such as, say, Xenia. Now shut up.) Our first glimpse was of large letters on a tall iron fence. Behind the fence, a wide lawn and tall trees framed a genuine chateau, mansard roof, and square gables. A narrow street led to a large iron gate, open, that gave onto a flower-lined parking area in front of the wide front steps of the Chateau de la Prairie. The date in the stone over the high doorway was 1857.

Janet and I tentatively went inside. A large staircase of dark wood led grandly up to our left. Ahead, near the rear doors that opened onto an expansive terrace and the lawns, was the hotel's front desk, which seemed to be attempting to remain unobtrusive in the enormous hallway.

A worried-looking little man came from a side hallway somewhere. "Reservation?" I said, and gave him my name.

"Oui," he said, without looking at the book, and then he was out on the front steps, grabbing our suitcases and leading us up that big old stairway, one flight, then another, then a third, then down a hallway. The tall doors we passed had shiny brass plates with names on them. We followed him around a corner, down a narrower hallway, up a narrow flight of stairs. He opened a door and—voilá—we were in a corner room very high up, with two big windows framing treetops and sky. The room was paneled in light wood, and the walls slanted up to where heavy exposed beams crossed a high ceiling. The bed was a modern take on a four-poster, a polygon of thin square pillars, unadorned, elegant. The bathroom floor and walls were tiled in light blue, and the fixtures were new and shiny. It was the bidet that worried me. You don't get new bidets in places with really good rates.

"Sign in?" I said, mimicking the action with a gesture.

"No, no." He waved me off and was gone, back down the narrow stairs.

We looked at each other for a second and then laughed. We were in the gable. The views were spectacular. One window looked out across the rooftops of the city to a vine-covered hillside. Another gave a view of the complicated topography of the chateau's roof line, dark gray slate tile amid peaks and dormers. I decided that if it was terribly expensive, we'd spend one night here, and then look for another place. Timidly I went down to the desk. The worried little man was there. *"Zimmer? Was kostet?"* Everyone in Alsace speaks German. Except him. I tried different words in different languages, embarrassed to be putting us through this over such a trifling thing as money. But, damn it, I was scared. Finally his eyes lit up. On a card from the chateau he wrote a number and smiled.

I gave him a big smile back, hoping he meant 390 francs, not dollars. Sixty bucks. He winked, said something about "telephone," and pointed to a price list in on the wall where no numbers as small as 390 were visible. From this incident I must conclude that there really is an international conspiracy among French-speaking people to do favors for each other at the expense of everyone else. *Merci*, Cecile.

So it was with high spirits that we set off in search of dinner in our unpronounceable and strangely vacant village, and ended up at Le Luxhof, which proves to be much more than a pizzeria.

It's time to get serious about F&B, starting with the Beverage. While Janet tries to figure out the menu, I study the wine list with serious attention.

"Schlumberger Gewürztraminer," I say to the waitress, making the first word sound very French and the second heavily German. She leaves without congratulating me on my obvious wise and learned appreciation of viticulture.

"You don't know what you're ordering," Janet says. "You just like the sound of the words."

"Schlumberger Gewürztraminer?"

"See? I can tell by the way you say it. You savor the sounds, so you're going to like the wine."

"I savor the sounds, and I'm *also* going to like the wine. The Alsace is the most underrated wine region on the planet."

"Why do you do that?"

"Do what?"

"Make these declarations. These pronouncements. Asserting something does not make it true."

I look her in the eyes and assert, "You are the love of my life."

"That's different."

"Would you rather I said, 'I can never be certain, since I have been on intimate terms with only a tiny fraction of the female population of the planet, but, based on this small sample, and on the feelings I have for you, and on my experiences with you, it is my considered opinion that you are the love of my life'?"

"Yes, say that. Every day."

The wine arrives. I nod in Janet's direction, so that the waitress will present her the cork, pour a sample in her glass. She sips quickly, and nods. As soon as the wine is poured and the waitress gone, Janet hisses, "I hate when you do that."

"Why?"

"Because I don't know wine. It's fraudulent."

"It's just a ritual. You look at the wine. You drink the wine. Unless it's unspeakably bad, you have them pour the wine."

"Even then," she says, "I have them pour the wine. Because what if what I find unspeakably bad is really great wine and I just don't know enough to appreciate it?"

"If you don't like it, it's bad wine, period."

"Oh yeah?" Janet says. "How much is that wine you ordered?"

"A hundred francs. Maybe fifteen bucks."

"What if it was a hundred bucks? If I thought it was unspeakably bad, would you still send it back?"

"Sure. I might cry a little."

"If it cost that much, you'd make yourself like it."

"Only if I liked the sound of its name." I hold up my glass. "And how do you fancy the Schlumberger Gewürztraminer?"

"It's speakable," she answers. "Quite speakable."

After perusing the menu awhile, I tell Janet I'm going to order the *côtelette chasseur.*

"What is it?"

"I don't know. But here's my guess. I think *chasseur* is hunter, which in German is *jaeger. Jaegerschnitzel* is a pork or veal cutlet with a thick wild mushroom sauce, usually a heavy, dark gravy."

"You're doing it again!"

"What?"

"You're choosing your meal for linguistic reasons. You don't even like wild mushrooms. Sorry, but that's kind of sick."

"I like *jaegerschniztel,*" I insist. "What are you going to have?"

The waitress appears. Janet tells me to go first, then hastily scans the menu, and says, "Tagliatelle arrabiata."

When she's gone I say, "You could get that at a pizzeria."

Janet shrugs. "It's what I feel like eating."

"And you don't want to bother the waitress by asking about other stuff, and they probably already have a big vat of it ready to serve, and you don't want to make extra work for the poor chef. Do you want to know why the Alsace is the most underrated wine region on the planet?"

"No."

"Please."

"Not unless you admit that you have no idea what the world thinks of different wine regions, and that what you're really saying is 'I like Alsatian wine' and nothing more."

"Not a chance."

"Fine." Her glance darts sideways. "Check it out."

She's referring to a group of locals who take a table near us. Five men and a woman. The guys look like they just got off work, manual labor, construction or vineyard or something. They're in dirty jeans and sleeveless t-shirts and have a couple days' stubble on their cheeks. The girl is lively, pretty, better dressed.

"Damn," I say.

"I know," says Janet, "How do they do that?"

Despite the grime, the whole damn table looks like a shoot for a Calvin Klein commercial. They're all skinny; they all have great hair, good grins, white teeth. They josh each other in big hearty sound bites accompanied by made-for-TV gestures.

"I'm not just being stubborn," I say, stubbornly returning to the topic. "In questions of valuation, assertion does equal fact, or at least influence it, since there's no way to determine factuality. Remember Margaret?"

Margaret was a friend of a friend who was taking night courses at a local college to get a business degree. Soon after she enrolled, I started getting calls from Margaret. With hardly a hello she'd say, "A crowd of people are coming over for dinner. What's wrong with that?"

"Nothing, I guess, if you invited all of them."

"I *knew* that teacher was incompetent. I'm going to let her have it. This school sucks so bad."

"Huh?" And I would have to backtrack and say collective nouns usually do take singular verbs, in the United States, anyway, and her teacher was not incompetent to suggest that a crowd *is* coming. A week later she'd be back with another grammar grappler. If I said, "Well, I might call it discretionary," about a comma her teacher disparaged, she was exultant. The school was bad, her professors ignorant, and she was a righteously outraged consumer.

Finally I couldn't take any more. "Margaret!" I said, "if it sucks that bad, transfer or quit. But if you stay, think of yourself as a stockholder, and your degree is your piece of the company. A lot of a school's value is derived from its reputation. Every negative thing you say hurts the reputation, and lowers the value of that degree, ever so slightly. Positive things make it more valuable."

"So I should protect the reputation of the college even if I know there are big problems with the place?"

"Ivy Leaguers learn that first thing. Elitism 101."

Back in Guebwiller, Janet does not see the relevance of this anecdote to me making unqualified pronouncements about the reputation of Alsatian wine.

Meanwhile, two dogs have joined us on the patio. Poodles—toy, white, untrimmed. One is skinny. The other is very fat, and when my *jaegerschnitzel* arrives I learn why. The fat guy waddles up to me with an underbite like a bulldog's. He gives a short quiet bark, almost a clearing of the throat. I toss him a spaetzl.

Little do I realize what I've started. It gets old fast, but I can't break it off. I am dealing with a member of the pampered aristocracy. And even though he's arrogant and no good to anybody and should be guillotined to make way for the rising merchant class, I am still sorry for him. So hapless. So outdated. So fat. He's having none of my pity. He looks me right in the eyes. His barks are imperative. I end up giving him half my schnitzel and nearly all of my spaetzle (it was *good*, too, damn it). It is hard to admit to oneself that one's will is being overpowered by that of a poodle. I begin to wonder if somewhere deep in my genetic memory there isn't a peasant farmer who fears the lash. Janet pointedly remarks that if I wasn't going to eat it all, then she, Janet, might enjoy a bite or two of that bold mushroom sauce. All this time the other poodle sits over by the door and looks pathetic. Janet tosses her a hunk of bread, which she daintily sniffs for five minutes before condescending to eat.

The chateau is deserted. The three big stairways and one narrow steep stairway are almost dark, and the faux Rembrandts on the walls are sinister. The brass plates gleam on the dark doors. We pass the Louis Pasteur room, the Jean Baptiste Molière room, the Emile Zola room, and climb up to ours— the Admiral Colstoun room. And who might M. Colstoun have been? Perhaps a French sea captain who came home after long years under the equatorial sun to be reunited with his young pretty wife who had waited every day in the highest room of the chateau longingly for his return? And on a night of wild weather did the thunder unhinge him so that he sliced her to bits despite her piteous cries for help? And might unsuspecting unFrenchspeaking tourists be lured by a disarmingly modest rate to occupy the Admiral Colstoun room so that on certain nights during thunderstorms the ghost himself (or his living progeny) might be appeased through the re-enactment of a grisly ritual?

"This place is kind of spooky," Janet says, just before falling uncharacteristically dead asleep—almost as if she's under a spell—so that she doesn't even awaken during the violent thunderstorm that lights up the walls of the room with brilliant silhouettes of the treetops, followed by shattering percussions.

" . . . . Janet? . . . you awake? Janet?"

6 Maison D'Issler: $22.56

```
03/06/00        000M0019
  •A• EMPL.1

ENTREE
                 45.00
ENTREE
                 40.00
VIN
                 48.00
BAR
                 15.00
        2×       12.00
BAR
                 24.00

TOTAL      172.00
```

No wonder there's no one in Guebwiller. Everyone's in Riquewihr, a place that presents pronunciation problems of its own. It's a medieval town, totally stone, except for the profusions of flowers erupting from window boxes on every wall. You park outside the city wall, walk to the nearest portal, and you're five hundred years in the past. It reminds me of Rothenburg, a hundred miles to the east, in Germany (where, by the way, the nicest hotel in town is the *Eisen Hut*). And, like Rothenburg, it gets five stars in every guidebook, and so every tourist is here.

Last night's thunderstorm has scrubbed the air. It's a warm sunny morning, and the cobbled streets are overflowing with people in sunglasses, shorts and sandals, trailing cameras. The postcards and wine glasses and scarves have tumbled out of the confines of the small shops to where they can be fingered by passersby who might then be lured toward the more expensive treasures inside—crystal, linens, ceramics.

I have temporarily lost Janet. One minute I was showing her these really cool medieval maps in this one shop, and the next she minute she was gone. This is not a problem, in itself. It's not a big place; we'll stumble across each other soon enough. But the clock on the tower signals that it's almost XII, and with my travel writer's acumen I realize that this town is about to turn into a giant game of musical chairs. There are only so many restaurant seats, and only a proportion of those are primo—that is, outdoor, in the shade, on the main street. The collective unconscious of the tourisoriate is awakening to the fact that the primo places are all gone. Soon all places will be gone, and it will be II or III before a by-then tired and snippy collective waitstaff will be attending to the by-then tired and snippy tourists. A consummation devoutly to be avoided.

Luckily, I spot her seconds later near the main square. "Janet. Quick, this way." I grab her arm and head down a side street.

"What?"

"We have to eat. Right now."

She stops. "I'm fine. No hypoglycemia." She fiddles with f-stop on her Minolta. "I was just chasing this kid . . ."

"Great," I say, "I want to hear all about it. Over lunch. Right here." I grab the last table with umbrella shade outside a restaurant with a wide arched entrance that goes deep into a dark cave-like interior.

"Now that you mention it, I am kind of hungry," Janet says, echoing the thought that is at this very moment popping into the noggins of herds of temporary Riquewihrites. The side street we are on leads to one of the portals in the city wall, and, as we watch, the tidal flow of tourists incoming from the parking lots is met by the backwash of tourists in search of an outdoor venue now that the primo places are all gone. In minutes, every seat, inside and out, at this restaurant and the one next door, is filled. There is a general clamoring for menus, and the skinny man in the apron goes into double-time.

We have wine. A carafe of *edelzwicker*, even though it is only noon on a warm day and I was up half the night warding off ghosts. We are in the Alsace, and although Janet does not want to hear why I call it the most underrated wine region on the planet, she agrees that we are obliged to indulge.

"I was following this girl—maybe ten or eleven," Janet says. "She had a cloud of blond curls, and a lacy white dress, like for a wedding, or First Communion. She wasn't with anyone, but she walked fast, with a determined look on her face. There was just something about her. I wanted to get a picture, but I couldn't stop to focus, so I kept following her. Finally I just took one from across the street. I hope it comes out."

"Could anyone else see her?"

Janet looks up suspiciously from her menu. "What are you saying?"

"There are angels in the Alsace?"

"No. There is an extraordinary little girl in a white dress."

"What are you going to have?"

Janet has escargot. I have onion cake, which sounds a lot better in French. In our separate circuits through the town, we both noticed that we heard hardly anyone speaking English.

"Are you going to assert," Janet asks, with a wry grin, "that the Alsace is the most underrated destination in France for Americans?"

"I might get there. I need more data." We pay the bill and leave our extravagant tip. I can't help it. I want the French to like us, and I can't imagine that they would disdain twenty percent as American cultural imperialism. Janet is with me foursquare on this one. She wants the French to like us even more than I do. For my generosity, I feel entitled to ask the harried, running, non-English-speaking waiter, "Tourists mostly from Germany?"

"Belgium."

I don't think he understood me. "I hear much German," I say slowly and loudly, pointing to my ears. "Tourists—many Germans?"

"No. Belgium." He scoops up the cash and darts indoors, shaking his head as goes.

As we're walking away I ask Janet, "Are you embarrassed by me or for me?"

"That depends on whether you have sense enough to be embarrassed for yourself."

"I'm embarrassed for myself."

"Then I'm just embarrassed by you."

"But that's worse."

"No. That's better. The alternative was 'both.'"

"Oh. If that picture you took turns out to have no image of any little girl at all, just an empty street, will you admit the possibility that there are angels in Alsace?"

"You're confusing angels with vampires. Anyway, if she was an angel, she was trying like hell to get away from me."

My obvious reply, that the angel was *leading* her somewhere, dies on my lips. What she said is so sad I have to push it away from me.

7 Tropic Ice: $17.64

After Riquewihr we visit Kayserberg (home of Albert Schweitzer!) and the castle called Haut-Koenigsbourg that's perched dramatically on a mountain above Ribeauville. I'm betting I can see half the Alsace from up there. What the Alsace is—cartographically speaking—is the left half of the Rhine Valley from Mulhouse to Strasbourg. It is a flat, farm-flecked flood plain with some cute cities on it—Selestat, Colmar—that rises gently and then steeply as it meets a low mountain range, the Vosges, running north and south paral-

lel to the river ("low" compared to the Alps; they kick ass on
the Poconos). This band of rising land where gently meets
steeply is green with the crosshatchings of vineyards, and
dotted with stone villages whose tile roofs are mostly red, although sometimes they're multicolored in geometric patterns.
The Alsatian wine road runs here.

The right-hand side of the Rhine, Basel to Baden-Baden,
is, of course, the same valley, with farms and villages almost
indistinguishable from these. It *should* be one big happy bio-
region, but history gets in the way. German-inflected Alsace
looks over its shoulder to sunny Champagne, while French-
ified Baden Wurtemburg leans toward the dark heart of Ba-
varia, where cuckoo clocks and cherry torts belie Faustian
bargains.

I get sweaty and out of breath trying to get to the bat-
tlements of Haut Koenigsbourg before the weather changes,
and Janet is none too happy about the pace. When we get
there, the sky has grown hazy. Thunder echoes from behind
the mountains, and it's hard for me to pick out which is Ribeauville, which Riquewihr. It's a game that Janet doesn't care
to play. We are great traveling companions, but castles are
not one of the things we do well together. They always have
those earphone audio units and I always want to get them,
even though I know they make Janet feel lonely. One drafty
stone stairwell is pretty much like the next one to her, and
she doesn't care what Charles XII of Sweden did to whom in
what year. Because Janet thinks angels run from her, I don't
get the audio unit at Haut Koenigsbourg, and we leave after
a brief visit that unfortunately involves more than its share of
drafty stone stairwells. A light rain is falling as I guide the Fiat
around the hairpin turns until foliage gives way to grapes, and
we are on our way to Colmar.

First, though, we take a detour off to Hunawihr. You can
practically spit to Riquewihr, but the ambience is closer to
Guebwiller. That is, nobody's home. The streets are barely
wide enough for the Punto, which seems to be the only car
in town.

"I wonder who waters all these flowers?" Janet says.

"I'm sure people live here," I say.

"I don't mean just here, I mean in every town, and between the towns. Everywhere."

It's a good question. We have never in our lives seen flowers like early June in the Alsace. Every window of every building in every town has window boxes brimming with them. Verbena and petunias and things we can't name. And roses! The divided highways have miles of uninterrupted red roses right down the middle, trellised on guard rails.

There doesn't seem to be a commercial center in Hunawihr, just a wide spot in the road where water comes slanting down a sluice between rows of a vineyard, and is carried by a short pipe over to a cement basin. There's a wooden awning over the basin, which also covers a couple of picnic tables. Some words are painted on the house across the road, seeming to claim it's a restaurant, but I'm skeptical. The place is utterly, eerily, empty. I park the car. It's hot again, and I go over to splash my face with water. I wonder out loud if it's potable, and Janet says, "Go ahead, try it."

I lean close to the water, coming face to face with a carp the size of my Fiat.

"You saw that fish," I accuse. Her smile tells me I'm right, but I'm happy to see the smile nonetheless.

If one is drinking a variety of wines, the palate prefers to go from sweet to dry rather than the reverse. Similarly, when one visits Europe, it is more palatable to go from big cities to small towns rather than the reverse. On a previous trip, we loved Paris and then were delighted by Koblenz. But on another, after five days sipping coffee on the Campo in Siena, we found Florence noisy and congested. Adhering to the European Metropolitan Relativity Principle, Janet and I have decided to bypass Strasbourg, capital of the Alsace. Which is ironic, since it was Strasbourg that made me choose the Alsace in the first place. Or, to be more specific, it was a moment in time that occurred in Strasbourg. A couple of years earlier. I was there overnight. I was there by myself. I was lonely and missing Janet, while at the same time lecturing myself, *Hey, sometime travel writer, it's a university town! Go out and enjoy the nightlife! Talk to the natives.* So that night I forced myself to wander the narrow streets between the timbered buildings in the old part of town. I had falafel and a Coke in a little shop with pictures of Chairman Arafat on the walls. I found a bar where music poured out into the empty street. I went inside, intent on talking to people, and plunged into a swirling mass of humanity, amid deafening dance music and weirdly pulsating lights. It was hopeless. I'd have had more chance of talking to someone on the moon. The nightclub puked me back out onto the empty cobblestones, and I wandered away, feeling very sorry for myself. I turned a corner and there, startlingly close, bathed in floodlights, in all its gothic immensity: Strasbourg cathedral. Flagrantly asymmetrical, with one ornate, sky-piercing bell tower and one sawed-off stump, the cathedral seems even more powerful for that: it can make humans feel antlike with one steeple tied behind its back. I stopped to stare. To let awe wash over me. To let me become reconciled to my own insignificance. Then I noticed a shop beside me. A lingerie shop, apparently, for there in the lighted window, laid out on black velvet, was the bare essence of clothing—a tiny, white, lacy pair of woman's panties. I stood there for a long time, looking up at the cathedral and then down at the shop window, marveling, caught between a monument to unchanging eternity and a monument to the barest flicker of time—beauty, whimsy, ecstasy. It was a deeply metaphysical moment.

But I have learned my lesson about trying to recapture moments, sublime or metaphysical, so I resisted the urge to drag Janet through the streets of Strasbourg looking for the intersection of cathedral and lingerie.

Colmar is not nearly so big, but it's big enough that I start to feel the symptoms of Metropolitan Relativity Principle. My mood sours as we pass car dealerships and strip malls on the way into town. At ambiguous intersections we debate directions and get honked at. We follow signs to somewhere near old town and finally find a place to park. I know we're close when we walk by the Hotel Rapp, one of the places that had shot me down by email. We're in one of those stone villages again, only now it's in plopped down in the middle of a bigger town. Big deal.

At least that's my attitude. Janet is delighted to see real stores, not just souvenir shops. I am to shopping as Janet is to castles, and I try to be as game in the face of beaucoup boutiques. Back in the states I call it "mall fatigue," that hopeless lethargy that hits me like a dose of Benadryl every time I set foot in Macy's or Bloomies. She is as frustrated (and trying not to show it) with my lack of interest in shopping as I am (although I try not to show it) with her castle apathy. The streets eventually open to a cobblestone church square, and we find an outdoor market, with narrow aisles between rows of canvas tents shading racks of clothes and leather goods. Janet wants to browse, but my tank is on empty, so we stop at an outdoor café called Tropic Ice. What Janet wants is a big bowl of fresh fruit but she has trouble getting that across. I order peach melba because I'm familiar with the signifier, if not the signified. Janet ends up with a vast trough of whipped cream concealing somewhere beneath its whiteness a couple scoops of ice cream swimming in wine-dark fruit sauce, possibly currant, which she promptly drops a glop of upon her white cotton top.

"Oh that's just great."

Janet comes back from the bathroom with a wet spot haloing the faint burgundy shape on her nice white top, and I sense the day dipping toward depression. I rouse myself from my lethargy, and I make it our mission to find an even nicer white top. This suits us both, so to speak: shopping is indicated, but I do much better when I have a goal to pursue rather than when trailing along behind the desultory browser. As it happens, one of the temporary shops has nothing but white clothes, racks upon racks of blouses and skirts and shorts. The problem, which doesn't occur to either of us until Janet is standing there with four garments over her arm, is where to try things on. In the back of the van to which the canvas roof of this makeshift shop is attached, as it turns out. Here the scene becomes comical, as the metal door slides open, and Janet is whisked into the dark, oven-like confines of the van by the too-tanned sixtyish proprietrix whose own gaping white top is not exactly a winning advertisement for her wares. Since the back of the van is windowless and the front seats piled with boxes, the door must be left open a bit, for light as well as air. I am posted outside, as guard and voyeur, while Janet changes.

"I *really* like this one," she says, stepping out of the van.

I like it even more. Janet has wide, regal shoulders, which are set off beautifully by thin white straps. The top is a tight cotton weave, thin but crisp as a bed sheet.

As she looks in the mirror propped against boxes her shoulders slump a little. "I love this but I'd never wear it," she says, her voice shifting to practical mode. "You can't wear a bra with it, and it's a little too transparent."

"Yeah, I guess so," I say wistfully, and she is back in the van trying on another. This one is also sexy, with hand-stitched embroidery and wider straps. She wears it back to the chateau, her stained top stuffed in her bag, and we are made happy by the purchase.

Back at the Chateau de la Prairie, we see that the place does have other guests. Indeed, the back terrace has sprouted tables festooned with white bows. A wedding is imminent. One also notices, in the light of day, that the chateau shows her age. There is no air conditioning in our garret room, and the water coming out of the hand-held shower in the claw-foot tub dwindles to a trickle when the sounds in the pipes tell us that someone in Molière or Zola is showering too. Looking out across the roof line, I see particle board in the dormers. I feel empathy for the worried-looking man at the desk downstairs. It can't be easy keeping the 143-year-old lady luxurious.

Something else. Although shielded from sight by a small grove of oaks, it is there. We pass it every time we come up the lane. McDonald's. It might not be so bad if it wasn't the only commercial establishment in the prim residential area. It might not be so bad if they had made any attempt to integrate it into the neighborhood. But it is, and they didn't. It looks as if it had been scooped up, parking lots and all, from New Jersey, and plopped down here, flattening whatever used to be on that corner—probably a tiny bistro with exquisite local foods. The McDonald's mansard roof mocks everything around it. It is an affront to the Chateau de la Prairie up the lane, trying hard, against time, to maintain its dignity. It makes me an enthusiastic founder of the American Chapter of the Jose Bove Fan Club.

Jose Bove is the French farmer-patriot who was arrested for driving his tractor into a McDonald's in his home town, causing it some damage. Along with Lech Walesa and that guy who stared down a tank in Tiananmen Square, Bove will be celebrated by history as an icon of opposition to a totalitarian regime. At his trial, thirty-thousand supporters overwhelmed the town of Millau, their signs paraded the charmingly revisionist statement "The World is Not For Sale." Do not confuse Bove's act with the simpleminded defiant destruction of, say, dumping a boatload of tea into Boston harbor to protest high tariffs, although Bove was doing that (protesting tariffs, not dumping tea). With the help of his sheep he makes Roquefort cheese, one of the food items the U.S. taxes into oblivion in retaliation for France's refusal to allow hormone-enhanced beef into their country. But he also has a global sense, and he is passionate and he is articulate, which makes him dangerous. Most of the rest of us have already been co-opted and corrupted by world corporate hegemony. Even protest gets commodified—as Andre Codrescu points out, these days, Revolution™ is a brand of flea powder.

8 L'Auberge Alsacienne: $56.97

L'Auberge Alsacienne ♦♦
HOTEL ★★★ — RESTAURANT ★★
12, Grand'rue - 68420 EGUISHEIM
Tél. 03 89 41 50 20 - Fax 03 89 23 89 32
AUBERGE ALSACIENNE

Facture

Samedi 3 Juin 2000
COMPTE No : 7

QTE	ARTICLE	PRIX
1	VITTEL 0.5L	16.00
1	SUP. MENU 10F	10.00
1	RIESLING 25CL	29.00
1	RIESLING GRUSS	95.00
2	MENU A 108F	216.00
2	CAFE	24.00

A payer : 390.00
MONTANT EN EURO : 59.46

Nro chôlberge SARL, xu capital de 15300 Euro. RCS Colmar
Siret: 428 858 302 000 18. APE: 551 A
Siège social 68420 Eguisheim 12 Grand'rue

Vous remercie de votre visite.

"How would I describe this décor?" Janet glances around the room, judiciously. "Not as busy as it seems."

"Bravo. I'll drink to that." I toast Janet and let the wine ring like a bell down my throat. The ledge that runs around the room is lined with old crockery, lanterns, butter churns, and milking buckets. Scythes and rakes hang from the walls. But the room itself is big, square, open, with plenty of room between the tables, which, like the chairs, are big boned, heavy, wooden. Large windows—I'm sitting right next to one, look out on the main street of Eguisheim. As with our room at the Chateau, there are no screens on the windows. The stone street and window boxes across the way participate in the restaurant's interior. "The most underrated riesling on the planet," I say, setting down my glass.

"Don't start."

"No, really. It's just one notch drier than the German rieslings, and that makes all the difference. You can keep your Piesporters."

"And on the basis of that one wine, you pronounce . . . "

"I've had others."

"Have you forgotten Koblenz?"

"No, I haven't," I say, a blush creeping up my cheeks, "not now that you mention it." Five years ago, when Janet's hair was long and she had never been to Europe before, we took the train from Paris to Berlin, staying overnight in Koblenz, where the Mosel meets the Rhine. There wasn't much of Koblenz left by the end of WWII, but it has a small, mostly rebuilt old town, and we found a comfortable hotel there. The recommended restaurant was small and ancient, dating back almost to medieval days, and the hostess seated us at a table where a man in glasses and stern mustache was reading a newspaper. We sat across from him, not sure how communal we were supposed to be here. Not very, it seemed. He was aloof and taciturn, deigning only to point to a specific item on the pages-long wine list, and say, peremptorily, "Get this one." We did, and then another, and another, and another. Or rather, he ordered them for us. Somewhere in there we ate something. Then another bottle of wine. At first slowly, and then rapidly, a meticulous metamorphosis unfolded before us. As our stiff German friend began to relax, his speech and gestures became at first a little, and then a lot, and then spectacularly, flamboyant. Turned out he owned a restaurant across town. By the end of the night, his boyfriend had joined us, along with the propietrix of this place, and we were drinking and laughing long after all other guests had gone. Anyway, the *German* wine he pointed to, the one we were drinking all night, was a superb riesling, which was Janet's point in bringing up Koblenz. And while I theoretically might be in a position to argue that the magical evening lent its piquancy to an otherwise typical wine, I cannot honestly do so. The wine that our friend commanded us to order had on the label the designation *halb-trocken*. Half dry. And it was genuinely divine. I don't know why we seldom see the *trockens* and *halb-trockens* in the U.S.—it seems as if the Germans are keeping all the good stuff for themselves.

Also divine was that night in Koblenz when we sloshed home and played All Star Wrestling in the shower until the whole bathroom was three inches deep so that we were afraid to show our hung-over faces in the breakfast room, which happened to be directly below our bathroom, for fear of water spots or collapsed plaster on the ceiling.

Remembering that episode brings the flush to my cheek, and enkindles a corresponding one in hers, and we hold hands across the menus we can't understand. The waiter eventually asks us if we'd like to see menus in English. Food is a big deal in the Alsace. Along with the wine, that's what Belgians come here for. Looking over the menu, I feel obliged to order the local Alsatian specialty, called *Choucroute,* ("shoo-croot" I think, but who knows? It's the Alsace) while Janet, feeling no such obligation, will try the salmon.

The restaurant is less than half full. At a big table behind Janet a large family is having a boisterous meal. It is a family of women and children, and with their noise and frequent comings and goings, I judge them to be locals. One girl in particular can't sit still. She's about eleven, and she's wearing a striped halter top. Brown shoulders sharp as knife blades twist back and forth as she clasps her hands over the high wooden seat-back and swings her supple torso from side to side.

My dish is somewhat disappointing to look at: a stubby hot dog, a hunk of thick bacon, and a bratwurst on a nest of sauerkraut. It's not that appetizing, and (nod to Woody Allen) there isn't much of it, either. This is farm food, come on. What it lacks in subtlety is supposed to be made up for in bulk. It turns out to be quite tasty, though, particularly the kraut, which is brown and tangy and crunchy.

Janet's salmon, with sauces swirled artistically over the top, is a pleasure to behold, and wonderful to eat. I concede her the win on this one, and she is prepared to be magnanimous about my kraut. After a forkful she says, "Mmmmm. You're right. Why isn't our sauerkraut at home this good? Why do we get stuck with all the sour, bleached, icky stuff?" She adds quickly, "Rhetorical question, Answer Man."

"I'm not Answer Man," I answer. "I'm Hypothesis Man."

"And you happen to have a sauerkraut theory."

"Well, now that you mention it . . . "

Janet, staring out the window behind me, lowers her voice. "Don't turn around. There's a little girl outside mugging to people in here. I wish you could see her, but I don't want you to scare her away."

"Long wavy blond hair, halter top?"

"Yes."

"How long have you known I have eyes in the back of my head?"

"She's beautiful," Janet breathes, still staring past me.

This turn of events is a great relief to me, since for the whole meal I've had to force myself to engage my lovely wife and not stare over her shoulder. Sort of like when we're in a bar together and ESPN is on behind her, only worse, because that which I can't take my eyes off is a nymphet. But if Janet is also bewitched, I am off the hook on charges of concupiscence.

The girl ends her window game and comes back inside. Janet turns her chair a little and we both covertly watch her dance and strut from the table where her people are toward the door and back again. She's just a little girl who's bored and wants to get going, and who, I suspect, likes being on stage. She is at ease in her body; the incipient awkwardness of adolescence has not so much as breathed upon her brow. And there is something sensual in that confidence. If not nearly nymphentine in the Nabokovian sense, she is not so sexless as a Maxfield Parrish sprite, either. Then what is it about this girl that makes us unable not to look at her? Here's my hypothesis: everybody's physical form gets one moment of balance in life, one time when your psyche achieves a perfect fit with your shape, when the accidents of fate and the certainties of the cosmos intersect, when your planets and stars are all in alignment. For some people, it happens fresh out of the chute. "Aw, isn't that baby *adorable?*" And for him, that's it. Nobody mentions his name and the word "adorable" in the same sentence for the next 73.6 years. Some movie stars, Meg Ryan, for instance, hang on to it for years. For most of us it's brief, and usually not recognized until afterward. Sometimes it shows up in a picture. I've got a shot of myself that I took in a mirror when I was about 28. I was playing a lot of tennis then. I have long hair. I stare at the camera, unsmiling. Damn, I look *dangerous.*

For many people, especially women, it happens at the cusp of adolescence, and the realization comes only when it is lost, often as a literal fall from grace. Janet remembers the actual moment she went from feeling like a graceful tomboy to a clumsy teenager. Gym class. Her turn to walk across the balance beam. She fell. She went back for a second try, and fell again. Laughter, humiliation, but something else. She felt some shade of her aura drain away, a part of her spectrum never to be rekindled to color. And so Janet may be forgiven if she stares at this child fiercely, agonizingly, her heart clutched for what this child has and will soon stumble out of.

There are angels in Alsace after all.

The English professor and sometime travel writer pauses here, and spends ten minutes rifling a certain section of a certain drawer where he keeps strangely personal things. Comprehensive exam results. Letters from writers. Picture with Janet in Venasque. Echinacea. Binaca. Post card of the Palace Hotel, Lausanne. And after a time he finds it. Not a print. Gave that away a long time ago to some woman he wanted to impress (who?). But a negative, a single negative clipped from the strip and saved. Even in miniature he recognizes it. The hair, the unsmiling stare, the mustache. Wait. The mustache? Even in miniature he can see he's a total dork. Shit. But there must have been *some* time when he was golden. That's necessary to the theory. Somebody should have snapped his picture on that balcony in Lausanne.

And for Janet it was most assuredly not all down hill from the balance beam. If he may be so bold as to claim an assist, the English professor and sometime travel writer remembers her account of the night he first kissed her. It was raining. She took a wrong turn on the very familiar road home. She stopped at a gas station and the woman behind the counter told her she was beautiful. And for the next few months, the glow of new love made her golden. Men were falling out of trees to proposition her. Sending over drinks in a bar, leaving their cards under her wiper blades. Her thirties were a very good decade for Janet, which makes this, the beginning of her forties, hard.

Which is why, watching Janet observe the Angel of the Auberge Alsacienne, I realize what a mistake I made this afternoon. I should have insisted on buying that white top with the thin straps from the street vendor in Colmar. If not for wearing out on the town, then only for when we're home alone, some warm summer's eve, drinking a glass of gewürz-traminer on the deck. Janet looked magnificent in that top— her kicky short haircut accentuating her graceful neck above elegant bare shoulders. In a day of doubt she was proud and sexy and alive, and dared to believe it herself, for a few seconds at least. And then doubt resurfaced, wearing the old clothes of modesty and practicality. And to my everlasting disgrace, I collaborated. I let a tiny fragment of the sublime lose its foot-ing on the slippery slope of melancholy. I betrayed the kind of courage represented by that shop window in Strasbourg, where a delicate scrap of lingerie defies the cathedral, where the moment thumbs its nose at eternity.

Like an ass, I said to her, "Yeah, maybe the other top would be better," at the moment when simple contradiction was strongly indicated. This moment will require redemption.

9 Le Grand Duc: $22.06

Not by bread alone does the sometime travel writer live, and not F&B alone can he deduct. The travel writer is obligated by his professional oath to experience and report faithfully on the entertainment scene in the locales where he finds himself.

Driving back from our authentic Alsatian dinner in Eguisheim, we see from miles away the night sky above Guebwiller ripped open by a roving spotlight. We refrain from making any bad taste jokes about defenses against the unwholesome intentions of a certain large and sometimes unruly Teutonic neighbor across the Rhine, but damned if we know what it is. Our highway leads us nearer and nearer to the source, and finally our curiosity is satisfied by a large, floodlit sign on the roof of what appears to be a large warehouse in an semi-industrial part of town.

"But we hate discos," Janet points out.

"We used to hate what used to be called discos," I say. "Who knows what this is? We have to check it out."

Janet is dubious.

"So far nothing has happened on this trip. What am I going to write about, restaurant receipts? I have an obligation to experience and report faithfully on the entertainment scene in the locales where I find myself." By this time we're almost back to the chateau, but Janet is not unwilling, so I turn around in the McDonald's parking lot, and head down what appears to be an industrial road.

"This is a gift from fate," I continue. "We happen to be driving by at eleven o'clock on a Saturday night. Prime time. We will submerge ourselves in the local disco obsession."

"Must be a repressed obsession," says Janet, as we pull into a vast and completely empty gravel parking lot.

We sit a few seconds, trying to decide what to do. But what the hell, we're there. If nothing else, there's the mystery of why all that wattage isn't attracting barflies.

Inside the windowless double doors is a foyer, a hallway really, with a ticket window on one side and a bunch of posters—advertisements for the place—on the other. A woman behind the bars asks for 150 francs. My riesling-seasoned brain is trying to figure out if that's a lot of money, and what we might be getting for it. A couple of guys, door men I guess, drift out from inside, about the time that I get a load of the pictures on some of those posters.

"One-fifty franc," says a door man, as if I might be making trouble.

"Is this a strip joint?" I ask, pointing to the poster.

He doesn't understand. "Strip?" I shout, as if even more volume will render me intelligible. "Strip? Strip?"

More remonstrations in French.

"Do women take off their clothes here? Strip?" I dance around, miming what must look like someone being attacked by large mosquitoes. The door man strokes his chin gravely.

Janet has her head down. "Just whatever," she says through the fingers covering her face. "Let's just whatever."

I turn to her, still in talking-to-foreigners voice. "You don't want to go to a strip club, right?"

"What*ever*," she says, through gritted teeth.

I wouldn't do that to her. I try again with the boys.

"No club," he says. "Disco. One hundred fifty franc."

I punch the feather boas on the poster and point to the inner door. "Strip?"

"No strip. No." For a second I think he's about to chestbump me.

"Okay," I say, holding up my palms in the international gesture of *hey, cool it, man.* I push some bills into the ticket cage. "Okay. No strip. All I wanted to know."

Along with my change I get four yellow cards. Drink chits, I realize. Which makes the 150 francs more tolerable. We plunge blindly into a dark, cavernous space pulsating with the beat of Donna Summer. As my eyes adjust, I see that the ceiling is black, the walls mostly mirrors flecked with gold. The room is disconcertingly multi-level—we stumble, trying to discern where we have to go up or down a half-step. The lowest level is the dance floor, which has light strips embedded in it, like a miniature runway where all the planes are supposed to crash into each other. Just above the dance floor looms the DJ station, combination control room and high altar. A line of tall stools follows the weaving length of glossy bar. Along the walls and off into nooks and crannies, built-in benches, covered with black shag carpeting.

Holy Bee Gees, Batman. We have stepped into The Museum of High Disco, circa *Saturday Night Fever.* And like many museums at 11 p.m. on a Saturday night, the place is utterly empty. We take seats at the middle of the bar, and the bartender dutifully appears, a youngish woman in a spandex top. As we redeem two of our yellow cards for beers, I notice Janet still has a hand covering her face. "What?" I shout over the music.

"For you, but mostly by you," she shouts grimly.

"What? Embarrassed? I was trying to . . . "

"It sounded like you *wanted* a strip club."

"No, I was . . . "

"Like you were *demanding* a strip club, like you were going to be mighty pissed off if stripping is *not* what happens here."

"Oh. Sorry. I was just trying to . . . "

"I know." Janet rolls her eyes a little. "It's okay."

We sip our beers for awhile. It's hard to talk over the disco beat thumping up through our diaphragms. Eventually I try to start a conversation with the bartender. When she wanders by I shout, "Speak English?"

She smiles apologetically, and shouts, "Français?"

I shake my head. "Deutsch?"

She purses her lips, then brightens. "Italiano?"

I throw up my hands. "Español?"

"Si! Si! Español!"

"Bueno!"

"Si! Bueno."

We are both happy as hell about that, until we discover that neither of us can remember much Spanish, and we can't hear each other over the noise, and we don't have anything to say to each other anyway.

"Vive Usted en Guebwiller?" I shout.

"Si. Yo vivo en Guebwiller!"

We stare at each other.

Janet smirks. "How's the research coming?"

I turn to her. "How do you say 'crowd' in Spanish?"

"Going to ask her why there's nobody here?"

Since I'm already shouting, I might as well revert to the international language I know best. "EMPTY!" I yell, even louder than before, and waving my arms around. "WHY BIG EMPTY?" Janet gets involved too, motivated less by curiosity than by a desire to curtail my hollering and flapping. Pretty soon the bartender catches on. She says something excitedly, again and again, but we can't make it out. She flies over to one of the door men lounging at the end of the bar, consults for a moment, and comes back.

"One o'clock," she says proudly.

"One o'clock?"

"Si. One o'clock. One o'clock." Her gesture takes in the whole place. "One o'clock. Mondo mondo peoples!" My watch says 11:17. Janet and I look at each other and start laughing.

"One o'clock!" says the bartender.

"It's a long drive to Provence tomorrow," I say.

"Thank you, thank you, thank you," says Janet. "I was so afraid you were going to want to stick it out."

"One o'clock?"

Gentle reader, we didn't make it. We didn't even use the other drink chits.

A NOTE FROM THE AUTHOR

Hi, it's me, Jon Volkmer. I'm going to drop the pretense of the first person "narrator" and speak to you, my readers, directly. I want to come clean with you here, as we are about to leave the Alsace for the South of France.

The fact is, I am not about to leave Alsace for the South of France. I have to suspend my recreation of that mythic journey because next week I have to teach *Gilgamesh*. Also Job, Plato, Homer, Aristotle, Ovid, Virgil, Dante, Galileo, Raphael, Machiavelli, Descartes, and Montaigne. To freshmen. The renowned Common Intellectual Experience class. I pushed for Cervantes to make the list, but I lost. The world needs more itinerant unreliable narrators, I say.

Speaking of Cervantes, did you know that the second half of *Don Quixote* did not get written until the first half had been widely read? In fact, Cervantes had to take up the pen again, and quickly, because imitators were trying to pass off their own further adventures of the Man from La Mancha. I am aware that the same thing could happen here. European restaurant receipts can be had for the price of a meal. In order to confound would-be copycat narrators, reliable or otherwise, I present you here with some of the highlights of the true and authentic second half of *Eating Europe*.

- The Palace of Popes, Avignon, full of wacky installation art
- More wine tips from Janet's least favorite amateur oenologist
- Dinner at a really expensive place
- Road trip to the Riviera—*oooh la la!*
- Redemption

Stay tuned for the fascinating narrative of Receipts 10 through 19.

In the meantime, I invite you, my readers, to join me in an experiment in interactive authorship. Remember when kids used to launch a hundred helium balloons with their address attached, and see how far the balloons got, and who wrote back? My plan is to make one hundred copies of this manuscript in an attractive, low-tech format, and send them to everyone I know, and a few people whom I don't. If you have gotten one and have read this far, thank you. If you think it's a good read, or if you like the idea of active reader response, *pass the thing on to someone* else. And here's the bit of paper attached to my balloon: *EatEurope@flashmail.com*. I welcome your comments.

The notion of a reliable narrator is problematic, since history is fabrication. The lens influences the shape of the image at least as much as the object under scrutiny. The voyage of Part I of this book will influence the writing of Part II.

What we have here is newly minted genre: *Interactive Meta-Nonfiction.*

When I get around to writing the true and authentic second half of the book, the responses to Part I will be influence the writing of Part II. Your comments might just make it into the narrative!

Thank you for spending some time with me, Jon Volkmer. I hope we got to know each other a little better, and I do apologize for interrupting your enjoyment of the thrilling narration *Eating Europe*. Let's rejoin our hungry couple as they head for the south of France to eat, drink, and share more thoughts on cartography, oenology, and the human condition. I promise I will finish it, if only for manuscript readers—we few, we happy few, we noble band of brothers. And sisters.

In the meantime I'll see if Howie at the *Inquirer* wants a travel piece on the Alsace. And to demonstrate to my employer that I am a productive scholar, I will go back on the conference circuit. I will submit my proposal, and, if it is accepted, I will eventually take the podium in that Marriot meeting room, and five other college professors will hear me read my paper entitled, "Old Colonials vs. New Economies: Blurring Borders in the Post-Modern Post-Nation State Euro-Transitional Era."

Remember, it's *EatEurope@flashmail.com*. I look forward to your responses.

Part Two

On Pilgrimage and Tourism

Pilgrimage and Tourism, the sacred and the profane of travel. One is an enlightened quest for personal growth or restoration via the difficult attainment of a cartographical goal. The other is self-centered unseeing escapism, using a land and its culture and cuisine with the same reverence one treats a video tape of *Home Alone II*. I have been thinking a lot about pilgrimage, since a return to Provence is, for Janet and me, a return to a kind of holy place. To this end, I have been reading *The Art of Pilgrimage: The Seeker's Guide to Making Travel Sacred*. It is a very silly book that makes me want to put on a loud Hawaiian shirt and hit the road chanting the sacred mantra, "Can't they even get HBO in this country?"

Actually, the trouble with the book is that it's not silly enough. Not silly anywhere. This guy, Phil Cousineau, thinks that by stringing together an endless lot of ponderous quotes by Zen masters, beat poets, Arab mystics, country western singers and Folk Sayings of Indigenous Peoples of the World, he can tell us how to make our travel as sacred as his is. Here's Phil telling us how to pack:

> For my long journeys, I take a woven *kilim* bag I bought in the Grand Bazaar of Istanbul. Because it has only two end pockets and one interior space, I'm forced to severely limit what I can carry. My satchel holds my writing journal, cameras, sketch pad, pencils and watercolors, letter-writing paper, *blank* postcards (I make my own drawings on them for

a personal touch), mini-binoculars, guidebooks, and language dictionaries.

For *my* long journeys, I take an electric blue Fiat *Punto,*
rented from Budget Rent-a-Car at Charles de Gaulle Airport.
Because it has a loads of interior space, I can fill it up with any
kind of crap I want. Littering the floor of my Fiat are apricot
pits and cherry stones, bread crumbs, plastic water bottles in
various stages of emptiness, a ragged envelope for travel receipts, shoes that no longer give Janet blisters, postcards of
flower boxes in Alsace (in order to show friends back home
what the place actually looks like), and a tiny red individually-
wrapped wheel of Belgian cheese.

The apricots and cherries are from Dole, not the international conglomerate but the town that occupies the cartographical and geographical point one-third of the way from
the Alsace to Provence, and where a few shops are open in
an otherwise deserted downtown on a Sunday morning. Our
fingers sticky with fruit and gooey cheese, our laps full of
breadcrumbs, we sail southwards, skirting the Alps, heading
for the sun.

Our mood is light but fragile. We do not speak of the fragility, because we both know its origin. At day's end we will
be joining a house full of my colleagues and their spouses,
and our vacation, heretofore a duo and a dialogue, will become a commune and a cacophony. Janet knows the house in
Provence provides the rationale for the trip, and she genuinely
likes my colleagues. But still. After the intimacy of Amsterdam and the Alsace, I believe that for Janet there is a feeling
that the vacation is, in a sense, over. That what remains is, in
a sense, work. What I should do is invite her to talk about her
fears, and reassure her that I will not let her feel abandoned
among the nutty professors. Instead, of course, I talk about
the scenery.

"We could," I say, "go *over* a part of the Alps, instead of
swinging around them."

"I vote for the scenic route."

"The scenic route is to skirt Lyon, head down to Grenoble, go over some mountains and hit the expressway in Sisteron. Remember Sisteron?"

"Sisteron?"

"We drove through there the last time," I say. "On the way to the Route of Napoleon."

"Don't remember it."

"How about Saint Vallier de Thiey?"

"I remember how much you like to say it." Janet smiles.

"We used to think it defied pronunciation. But that was before we ran into Guebwiller."

"*Goob-ve-yay*," Janet corrects.

"*San Val-yay de Teh*," I say.

Janet sighs. "Venasque."

Our last trip to Provence. Just a two-day swing, a stopover on the way from Paris to Tuscany, but still. For us the name Venasque has become a synonym for romantic escape. The town—or rather, our experience of the town—was so perfect that I claimed I would never write about it, so as not to let anyone else in on our secret. I couldn't resist, though, and the piece appeared under the twee headline "Romancing the Stone Cities of Provence." That was the travel editor's doing, hatched at a time when that movie had just come out. Anyway, the point is that whatever we do during the upcoming week in Provence will almost certainly pale in comparison to our initial visit.

What else do Janet and Jon talk about as they drive the empty French freeways in their Fiat from Budget? We wonder if there is any connection between the twin absences of police and road kill. A week in Europe and we have not seen one car pulled over for speeding. And we have not seen one dead animal smashed and flattened on the roadway. How is Europe so civilized that it can avoid these twin carnages? France even builds overpasses across the freeways just for animals, and then puts up pictorial billboards featuring silhouettes of deer and boar to let you know that's what they're for.

"When I was young," Janet says, "I thought that 'deer crossing' signs were for the deer. That's why they used pictures, because deer can't read. Every time we came to one of those signs, I got excited, because I thought I'd see a deer, because this was where they were supposed to cross the road."

"Did you ever see one there?" I ask.

"No."

"It's still a sweet idea."

From the hilly country around Lyon a number of highways pour down a vast flume into genuinely alpine Grenoble. As the highway drops away and the big-shouldered mountains come into view, my pulse quickens. Grenoble was the first specific place name I ever heard of in the Alps, thanks to the 1968 Olympics. The associations are speed, danger, and sexy reckless courage—as personified by one Jean-Claude Killy. The vast swoop of wires from huge valley stanchions to mountain-top perches is dizzying to me. I wonder aloud what it is about mountains that gets me going.

"You found the sublime there," says Janet.

"Yes, but I started looking for it way before that. This love of mountains, it feels as if it's hard-wired."

"Like some kind of genetic memory from your Sherpa ancestors?" Janet laughs. "Come on. Your family took vacations to Colorado when you were a kid. Basta."

"So you would argue for environment, not essence. Nurture rather than Nature. I think that makes you a behaviorist."

Janet starts to say something, pauses, and then says, "You do that a lot."

"What?"

"Make generalizations. Put things in categories. You always want to say what kind of an –ist someone is."

"But that's how we make sense of things. We put them with like and unlike things. A or not-A."

"Do you think the world was made by computers? Everything isn't reducible to binary code."

"No, but . . . "

"Let's see if you can just tell me about *one* childhood vacation without making generalizations about it. Just try."

"Of course I can, but . . . "

"Why are you getting irritated?"

"I'm not *irritated.*"

"Then why are you driving so fast?"

I let up on the gas and take a deep breath. "Okay," I say. "I can do this. A short vacation to the Ozarks. Silver Dollar City. It was new then, a kind of a low-tech Disney faux Old West town . . . "

"Hmm?"

"Okay, damn it. No categories. I remember raised wooden sidewalks that creaked when you walked on them. A saloon door that pushed open in the middle and swung both ways on hinges. We drank sarsaparilla. It seemed exotic, but it was just . . . it seemed exotic. Chris and I got tin sheriff badges with our names stamped on them."

"Good. Keep going."

"A longer vacation was to Colorado. A full day's drive following the Platte river. Interstate 80 wasn't finished yet, so most of the time we were on two-lane highways. The awful smell of alfalfa processing plants. I remember the first time I saw a snow-capped mountain range shimmering on the horizon. My uncle's house, Cheyenne, Wyoming. I got butterflies in my stomach. We stayed overnight in Estes Park, Colorado, and the next day drove Trail Ridge Road through Rocky Mountain National Park, and *that* was the epitome of thrill and terror. In Grand Lake we stayed in a knotty pine cabin named Pal-Ca-Ni-Ta. Wow. I can't believe I remember Pal-Ca-Ni-Ta."

"Excellent. Go on."

"And what I'm just realizing is how the higher the elevation of the destination, the longer and better the vacation was. Ozarks, low mountains, short vacation. Rockies, higher mountains, more thrilling, and longer . . . "

"Jon!"

"I know, honey, but I just figured this out. A kind of cartographical-spiritual equation. The higher, the more distant, adds up to a kind of . . . "

"See." Janet crosses her arms. "You can't do it."

"I can," I say. "I did. I gave you facts, but then I . . . "

"No, you didn't. You immediately had to . . . "

"No," I insist. "I did what you wanted, and *then* I . . . "

We go back and forth like that for a while, neither one of us willing to concede anything or to admit that we are growing annoyed with each other. Finally we lapse into silence and stare at the mountains until we stop for gas at the north edge of Grenoble.

Janet buys bottles of water while I scan the map. "*Col de la Croix Haute,*" I say, when she comes back to the car. "That settles it. We must live to say we have crossed over the Pass of the High Cross."

She matches my fresh-start tone: "Pass of the High Cross it is."

The south end of Grenoble is all torn up with highway construction, and we end up on a road that snakes its way up the mountain above, below, and around a freeway where cars are go whizzing by. And I can't find how to get on it. So we're stuck on the slow road with the bicycles and the tractors pulling hay wagons. After a few miles the freeway ends and dumps all of its traffic onto our road so that we can all proceed up the endless hill together in bumper-to-bumper fashion, the bicycles, the tractors pulling hay wagons, and the impatient Parisians taking a short cut to Cannes. The BMWs and Benzes try to lord it over the rest of us with their accelerative prowess. Any time there's the tiniest whiff of an opening they roar out to pass, oncoming traffic be damned. And since it is Sunday, the oncoming traffic is thick with impatient Parisians trying to take a short cut back from Cannes.

"This," Janet asks gently, "is your idea of fun?"

"Adventure," says I, mentally calculating how much time and aggravation I would have saved had I simply taken the wide and wonderful *Autoroute de Soleil* at Lyon. "The important thing is to go where we haven't gone before. It's like Wordsworth says, you can go back to Tintern Abbey and remember how fun it was as a kid, and maybe write a poem about it, but you can't recapture the original adrenaline. It's bound to be second rate."

"So Provence is going to be second rate?" Janet says.

"Walked into that one, didn't I?"

"Not really," Janet says. "You're presuming that your attitude applies to everyone."

"Mine *and* Wordsworth's."

"For my family," Janet says, staring off into the distance, "it was the shore. And it was the same shore. We'd rent a house in Ocean City every year, and I couldn't wait to go. I loved the familiarity of it. I still do. I love planting my chair in the sand and opening a big novel and knowing I don't have to do anything else that day if I don't want to."

"Repetition, the rhythm of the moon. While I'm always looking for new peak experiences."

She gives me a look.

"I know, I'm doing it again. But I find it so interesting how we play out male and female sexual archetypes. Don't you?"

"Not as much as you do."

"Anyway," I continue. "The good news is that you can go back to Provence and have wonderful experiences, just like you had the first time."

"Hope so," she says. "It's just that . . . well, you know. Being there with your colleagues will make it a little more stressful. Nothing I can't handle."

The Pass of the High Cross isn't so high as all that—1176 meters, less than 4000 feet. More of a New Hampshire than a Colorado kind of pass, and the Alps here resemble the White Mountains. Now we're headed downhill, and the dance of death goes from waltz to jitterbug. A certain cooperation and trust builds up among the dozen cars snailing along behind the old man in the old green Peugeot creeping down the mountain oblivious to all those behind him. Aggression and timidity vie with good sense as one by one the cars take their turns finding places to pass, and the rest of us judge the attempt. Was that attempt too bold and risky? Did the Citroen miss an opportunity that others of us think we would have taken? A delicate dance indeed. Of course, at frequent intervals comes an impatient Parisian or nutty local who blows by everyone with an apparent death wish that leaves the rest of us steaming. And in this direction it's not limited to Beamers and Benzes. Gravity is an egalitarian force of physics: even the Ladas and 2CV's can pass with the same insanity.

I adopt a sensible moderate-aggressive posture, and when my turn comes, finally, to be the first in line behind the old Peugeot, I pick my spot, feeling the pressure of the eyes of a dozen drivers behind me. It's a great feeling once you get around the old Peugeot, to have the open road before you, to leave the others stuck behind in the slow lane. To be rolling down hill full tilt, ahead of the pack.

"You'd Better Get it Right."

Narratus Interruptus

Janet wrote that. I mean the part about getting it right. I wrote the pseudo-Latin heading to give notice that it's been three years since Janet warned me that I'd better get it right, and I stopped writing. And just when the road was opening up, and seemingly all down hill for awhile. The electric blue Fiat successfully negotiated the Pass of the High Cross, but the narrative that described it missed a curve somewhere, went off the road, and tumbled headlong into a deep ravine.

Three years have passed since that journey down the mountain. Three years since my bold promise, at the end of Part I, to manufacture copies of the story-so-far, distribute them to friends, and let the responses influence the writing of Part II, as Jon and Janet carry on through Provence and the ten remaining receipts of *Eating Europe*. A lot can happen in three years. In three years a shiny new century can become as ugly as muddy shoe.

In three years the jolly anarchist image of Jose Bove's tractor crunching a McDonald's can be smashed under the tread
of an A1 Abrams tank churning through a sandstorm. A line
of Auden keeps popping to mind, the one where all the living
nations wait, each sequestered in its hate.

I am back in France. I am living with my American expat
friends, George and Erica, just outside of Paris in the tiny village of Chapet. My country is at war with Iraq on the battle-
field, and with practically everyone else—especially France—
in the field of public opinion. Janet is back in Pennsylvania,
suffering the consequences of her political awakening. Like
millions of other Americans, she discovered that humane values and progressive ideals do not enact themselves into public
policy merely because they are right or true. She has become
an Internet warrior, to the befuddlement of Seth and Tristan,
who have found that the new Janet does not suffer knee-jerk
nationalism gladly.

In a time of war and separation, it seems ironic that so
much beauty surrounds me. Here, where the furthest fring-
es of Normandy intersect the lengthening tendrils of Paris
suburbs, it is spring. Lilacs fill the air with perfume. Fields
of rapeseed blaze yellow over the rolling farmland. Finches
and sparrows cavort at the feeder outside the window. Morn-
ings, fresh and raw, give up their low-lying fogs to sunny days
flecked with passing showers. If I forget my umbrella on my
morning walks to the chateau of Bazincourt, the spring sky—
just that scrap of cloud hiding behind the hill—will pounce
like a cat, soaking me. The chateau is a squat frowzy building
with two half-turrets and assorted chimneys. Adjacent to it,
sharing the walled grounds, is a modern building, square and
plain. Together they comprise the Bazincourt Clinic, a reha-
bilitation center for physical accident or infirmity. I am not a
patient, but when I see through the windows men learning to
walk again, I cannot help but identify.

I'm not sleeping well. Most nights it seems as if I don't
sleep at all. I turn on my side, my back, my stomach. I crunch,

fluff, and punch the pillows. Vague half-dreams pursue me, and sometimes Janet is there beckoning, and I move toward her, until I startle awake. Sleep taunts me most just before dawn. I could close the steel shutters and prolong the night, but I don't. Like Dante's sinners, I am drawn to what I dread, and the first birds tell me to open my eyes and see the glimmers of light along the windowsill.

If I am going to figure this place as hell, I must admit it has many comforts. George loves working for an international software conglomerate. He drives to Paris each morning, returning at eight in the evening, seeming oddly refreshed. Erica is a brilliant but troubled woman with reclusive tendencies, and she spends much of the day in her room. My morning walk to Bazincourt takes an hour. My evening walk, much shorter, takes me down the narrow curving street to *Le Relais des Saveurs*, where the owner, Daniel, has made me his friend, and the regulars at the bar shake my hand when I arrive and depart.

My two rooms on the second floor have large windows that overlook a green flat valley that hides a crook of the Seine. Both rooms are filled with floor-to-ceiling bookcases, and the library is subtle and complex. Books of poetry, novels, and history books predominate, although two whole shelves are devoted to guidebooks and maps.

Living in this library, swooping in and out of a dozen books a day as my whims carry me, I sometimes feel detached from my body. I imagine my spirit communing with these books the way that the shades of the noble pagan poets converse in *Inferno*. Janet hates it when I go off on pretentious literary tangents of dubious relevance. She would say that one Dante reference per chapter is quite sufficient. But she's not here. Limbo, where the wise pagans converse, is the best address in hell, but it is still hell. And while they converse, they suffer from Absence. *Without hope, they live on in desire.*

But I do have hope, so the appropriate analog is not hell but Purgatory. Absence *with* hope; punishment with purpose. Expiation. Like Dante, I must keep moving. My journey, my purgatory, runs through Provence. Not now, literally. The journey can only be made in the Fiat Punto, and in my memory. If I can fulfill the promise of the end of Part I, if I can make the perilous journey by the Route of the Ten Last Receipts, if I can find Janet there, then I can find her, I hope, in real life.

Perilous? When I wrote the first few pages of the trip to Provence, I gave them to Janet. She saw the direction it was headed. She remembered the difficulties we had there. She put that five-word warning on the page. Funny thing happened then. I lost my nerve. I didn't know if I could "get it right." I became a full time English Professor and no time travel writer. I abandoned Jon and Janet. In retrospect, it seems a double failure of mine: I could not face up to the difficult realities of the narrative, and I could not face up to our difficulties in real life. The personal stress was leveraged by geopolitical distress. There was a catastrophe on a blue September day, and, after the mourning, a backlash catastrophe as America became the land of the freaked and the home of the bellicose.

Janet is not here with me, but I am determined to evoke her spirit. And I must be sure to get it right. So back to Provence I will go, to the lavender and the broom, the sunny doorways and pink wine.

Do I have a Virgil to guide me? I made the mistake, three years ago, of beginning this chapter talking about a bad book. Life is too short to read bad books, much less to waste time mocking them. *Adieu*, Philip Cousineau, *bon jour* Patrick Leigh Fermor. I have just finished his memoir, *A Time of Gifts*, the greatest book of travel writing of all time. Leigh Fermor, bounced out of a fine British public school at eighteen, decides to walk from England to Constantinople, and does so. This is 1933, and the Nazis have just taken power in Germany, casting some dark shadows on the journey. In my home country, the spirit of nationalism and the intolerance have made me sick with fear for our future. It makes me makes me glad to be in exile now, and more sad for Janet, especially since the fear propaganda has gotten to Seth and Tristan, turning them into advocates of pre-emptive war.

A Time of Gifts was published in 1977, more than forty years after the journey depicted there. I am emboldened by that. Compared to a forty year gap, three must be both miniscule and manageable. Somewhere on this continent, considerably to the south of me, in Hellenic climes, Leigh Fermor lives, a very old man now. From this distance I will let him be my unobtrusive Virgil, the shade who guides my footsteps through the Purgatory of Provence.

Nineteen restaurants in fourteen days. That's what I promised, and that's what I'm going to deliver. In the name of honesty, the three year gap had to be acknowledged and its origins owned up to. But for the sake of storytelling, this meta-narrator is now putting on the cloak of invisibility. The resurrected receipts will be the guide, and the narrative will run them like a rack of pool balls. No more pretentious literary tangents, tendentious political detours, or self-indulgent asides on the author's current woes and whereabouts. It's all about Janet and me, and the (im)possibilities of truth between two people.

All I can do is try to Get It Right.

10 Le Felibre: $36.76

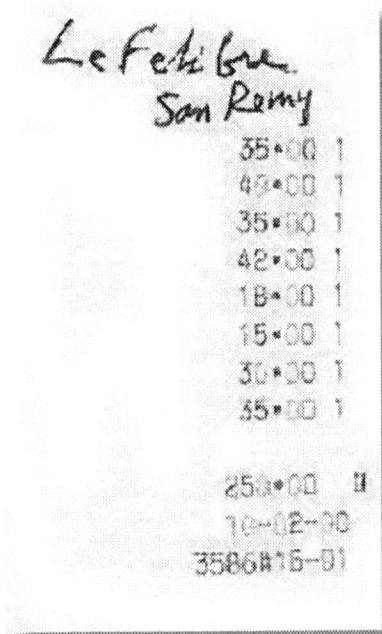

```
Le Felibre
San Remy
        35*00  1
        45*00  1
        35*00  1
        42*00  1
        18*00  1
        15*00  1
        30*00  1
        35*00  1

       250*00   8
      10-02-00
     3586#16-01
```

There is a city where bulls are loosed to run madly down stone streets, where courageous locals and drunken tourists dash before them, ducking into doorways at the last second, or getting gored, or even getting trampled to death. Heroic and foolhardy—it is the stuff of novels, backdrop for wayward ladies falling hopelessly in love with gorgeous toreadors while rivals for their affection engage in drunken fisticuffs.

The importance of being Ernest having vastly diminished in recent years, we come to a sorry pass where even a Lost Generation seems quaint. The novel has devolved to travel narrative, fiery romance to middle-aged monogamy, epic binges to wine tastings. Is it any wonder, then, that our narrative takes us next not to Pamplona in the Basque but to San Remy in Provence where the intrepid visitor can witness and even participate in the awesome spectacle of The Running of the Sheep?

"The sheep come right into the middle of town?" Janet asks.

The young man across the table shrugs. "I guess so. I haven't seen it myself." His name is Jeff. His hair is held back in a neat blond pony tail, and he has a big black Nikon slung around his neck. Brandon, the other young man, is neatly groomed and perpetually pensive-looking. Watercolor is his métier, and after lunch he wants to visit the Roman ruins at Glanum, to paint the arch that, Dana tells us, was once a stopping point for young British aristocrats making the Grand Tour. Dana is a Victorianist, so she knows such things. She's at the next table, along with Natalie, an Americanist with a lately-developed passion for photography, and two more students.

It is a gorgeous day in San Remy—sunny, warm breezy. I'm happy we're with Dana and Nat, smart funny women with whom Janet is at ease. A day to sit outdoors, under the jumble of umbrellas of the cafés lining the old street. There are too many of us, so we are relegated to tables just inside the cave-like restaurant Le Felibre. The lone waitress—a blond woman in early Sophia Loren housedress—seems both harried and indolent at the same time. We wait patiently like good Americans to order our crepes while she hustles by us to become a silhouette in the sunshine. Her dress has a wide neckline that sometimes slides across her shoulders, revealing a round tattoo—some eastern religious symbol—on the front of her shoulder. Janet asks Jeff about his photography and Brandon about his painting and both of them about the flat in Aix that the school has rented for them.

When the waitress finally saunters around to us, we all order crepes. When I order the "Crepe Saracen" Janet gives me that funny look.

"You're doing it again," she says, when the waitress leaves. She turns to the two boys. "Jon orders from menus based on which words he likes. If there's anything strange or exotic sounding, or fun-to-say, that's his choice."

"That's only partly true."

"What is the Saracen crepe?" she challenges.

"Uh, I'm guessing something North African. Dates maybe."

"See?" She turns to Brandon. "Isn't that a strange way to order food?"

It turns out that Saracen crepes are made with whole wheat rather than white flour. "Are they called Saracen," I ask the waitress, staring at her tattoo, "because the Saracens had darker skin than the natives?"

"I do not know," she says, tugging the neck of her dress. "There are towers on the coast. Saracen towers."

"So the Saracens colonized here?"

"I think it was to watch out for them."

"Oh. So not built by them, but in defense against them."

Backing away, "I think so."

Janet covers her face with her hands. "He does this," she says resignedly.

"What?" I say.

"Does anyone want this water?" Dana asks from the other table. "I forgot you have to say *sans gazeus.*" She gives me a droll look, waiting for some remark. Dana is very particular about what she ingests, and I, the omnivore, tease her about it. Office neighbors in the department for a dozen years now, we fall into the same kinds of patterns and habits as married people do. Today, I just grin at the offending water, and Dana knows I have recognized the opening and am letting it pass.

As we're waiting for the waitress to bring the bill, Jeff is talking to Janet about the vacations his family took every year to Disneyland. Janet asks if there was ever any period when he thought his parents were insane—when he was fourteen, say, or sixteen.

"No," Jeff says. "Things were always pretty cool with my folks."

I say, "What about you, Brandon? Insane parents, right?"

He shrugs. "Not really."

"Oh come on," Janet says. "You never went through a time when you didn't want to be around them?"

"Maybe I was weird," Jeff says. "But we hung out a lot at my house. I looked forward to Disneyland and stuff."

"Oh," Janet says. "Well, you're lucky."

When the bill arrives the boys politely reach for their wallets, but I wave them away. "I've got a research grant."

Jeff snickers. "Crepes are research?"

"I'm a travel writer," I say modestly. "Everything is research."

"Cool."

"That's how we scholars work. This lunch could be the basis for an essay on the relation between the Saracen towers and the crepe of the same name."

Nat puts her head into our group. "Don't listen to him. He's not a good influence on young minds."

"Can I be a travel writer when I grow up?" Jeff asks.

"It's far too dangerous," I say.

On the sidewalk in front of Le Felibre we have one of those eight-sided two-car discussions about who wants to go where and who needs to take whom to what location and who needs to be at some assignation somewhere by some time. Janet wanders down the sidewalk, past the racks of postcards, towards the galleries and craft shops. A few minutes later I catch up to her to say that we're taking Brandon to Glanum. "They've excavated most of the Roman city. Isn't that cool?"

She pauses a moment, and says, "Yes. That's cool."

"What?"

"It's fine," she says. "It's just that . . . you know, when we were looking for a place to park, we saw all these little streets with cool shops. We said we would wander around after lunch."

"You're right," I say. "Well, Brandon has to walk back to Nat's car to get his stuff, and he needs to buy some water. I'll tell him to meet us here in fifteen minutes."

"Fifteen minutes?"

"Twenty. I'll tell him to meet us here in twenty minutes."

"Fine."

We walk mostly in silence down the small stone streets of San Remy. I realize that twenty minutes is hardly the compromise that my tone suggested, and I'm grateful that Janet doesn't call me on it. The shops appear prosperous. Galleries with original art at outrageous prices. Specialty food stores with chevre and olive oil at outrageous prices. I can feel Janet's barometer dipping.

"What am I going to do?" she says finally.

"What?"

"The boys. Look at this stuff. What can I possibly get for the boys?"

"I'm sure we'll find something."

"Yeah, maybe," she says doubtfully, and walks down the street.

"It's the globalization problem again," I say, following her. "San Remy t-shirts and Ursinus College t-shirts, made in the same Honduran sweat shop. Wine. The last local product. That's what we'll get them."

Janet sighs. "I know I should be able to joke about it, but I can't. We said we wouldn't go to Europe again without them. I have to get them *something*. And it has to be nice, not just some crap."

"I know," I say, taking her arm. "We've got another week. We'll find something."

"I don't know what." She keeps walking.

Janet seems to have grown sad since about the middle of lunch, and I am just figuring out why. It has to do with Jeff and Brandon. Polite, engaged, funny young men. College students. Artists, better yet. This is what she would want for Seth and Tristan. This would be heaven for her. The good news is they have the talent. Unlike in so many ways, they are alike in this. I remember back when they were ten and twelve they would sit for hours at the table, side by side, paper in front of them, frowning with concentration. Then they'd leap up, yelling, "Hey mom, look at this." And the battle-bots and guns and graffiti were remarkably adept, brilliant really. "That's wonderful," she would say, "that's really good. Now why don't you draw a real person, or Nina. Draw Nina." The Dalmatian would bark, hearing her name, but by that time the boys had dropped the pencils and were running outside or downstairs. At sixteen and fourteen, even while their bodies are vaulting into their six-foot adult frames, Seth and Tris have withdrawn into the mysterious netherworld of adolescence, abandoning the woman who made them her life's work. Seth the socialite, always gone. Twenty minutes in front of the mirror getting just the right gelled spikes, and he's out the door. Tristan, buried in the basement, killing things on the internet, uncommunicative and withdrawn. And when they are rude or when the report cards are disappointing, she feels that she is to blame, that she has failed them.

And back at the restaurant, while admiring the maturity of these boys, she tried to confirm the solace that many, including me, have urged upon her, namely, that Seth and Tris are going through a phase. That boys on their life orbits go around the dark side of the moon and come back as well adjusted young men. Jeff and Brandon, with their casual protestations that they never thought their parents insane, showed it didn't have to be that way.

I buy postcards of doorways and windows with flowers on them, in them, around them. While I stare at these depictions of the impossible beauty of Provence, out of the corner of my eye I see a pretty woman down the sidewalk, and only after doing a double take do I realize it's Janet. She is in front of a store with heaps of wicker baskets outside. A strange little pain of sadness hits me that I did not recognize her at once. It's as if I'm having trouble focusing, or as if some orbit is pulling her away from me.

Pilgrimage and Tourism are orbits. They each comprise an outbound leg and a return. Tourism is associated with the outbound—escape from the everyday, from the known, into a new world. Pilgrimage is more about the return—how your life will be different as a result of this travel. Tourism is the lightness of the present. Pilgrimage has the weight of history, past and future. It occurs to me that what happened to Janet and me in Provence may be framed in these terms. The more the burdens of pilgrimage weighed on her, the more I tried to insist on the joys of tourism. I would have been better off if I'd remembered The Bullwinkle Effect.

Set the Way Back Machine for first grade. For reasons I still don't understand, I was terrified by Sister Marie Carol. It's not that I was unused to nuns; the convent was a block from home, and the sisters were frequent guests at our table. We even had one in the family—a cousin named Sister Albertine. And yet, all through first grade I would fake sickness every morning. To call it "fake" is inaccurate; my stomach really did hurt at the prospect of facing that fearsome creature. The fear of school resulted in a curious weekend psycho-spiritual odyssey. Each Friday I was overjoyed in the afternoon, carefree in the night time, loving life. Saturday was a provisionally happy day, with half-decent cartoons in the morning and pure freedom or some family outing during the day—but also a growing uneasiness that Monday lurked. Sunday morning meant Mass at St. Mary's, and then the high point of the weekend: a special breakfast, hot cocoa and cinnamon toast, accompanied by the king of cartoons, "The Bullwinkle and Rocky Show." I loved Moose and Squirrel, Peabody and Sherman, Fractured Fairy Tales. Even Dudley Doright. Witty remarks, historical awareness, political savvy, puns, and a wry self-awareness. No wonder it appealed to me. But no joy is ever completely untainted. The intellect of that show was also a warning shot across my bow, the first intimation of the school week. Sunset effect, last hurrah. After Bullwinkle, at 11 a.m. came a show called "Discovery." Educational programming. Here's how the pyramids were built. Here's how the mongoose eats the scorpion. Exactly ten minutes into it I got a killer headache. Every single week, same headache. It lasted through the afternoon and into the evening where it begot queasy, guilty feelings about homework. My point here is to map an orbit where the outbound journey is light and joyful, but the inbound is a real drag. I should have realized that our journey across Europe was in danger of succumbing to The Bullwinkle Effect. When I felt her flying off into a different orbit, I should have sprinted down that street in San Remy. I should have grabbed Janet and wrapped her in a wild passionate embrace that sent wicker baskets flying everywhere.

Here in Chapet, in the suspended orbit of exile, I am at work in the dining room, where it is curtained and dim. The kitchen windows have no curtains. The doorway to that room is a portal of light, and haphazard kitchen things are refulgent with the yellowy morning. The green striped wallpaper. The table and its clutter, hyper-real—newspaper, cigarettes, ashtray, purse. Janet sits at the table, glowing more real than reality, like Mary at Lourdes. It seems she has been listening to me blather about Rocky Pilgrimage and Bullwinkle J. Tourist, and she's trying to suppress a grin. She's looking off to the side in a cute Princess Di kind of way. Her fuzzy green sweater has slipped fetchingly down over one shoulder, revealing the strap of a black tank top. "Wicker baskets flying everywhere?" She shakes her head sadly, turns her head to look at me and whispers, "You're not looking in the right *place.*"

"What do you mean?" I ask. "What place?"

But then there's an electronic hum, her image twinkles for a moment in that transporter room kind of way, and she's gone. I get up and walk slowly into the kitchen, staring at the empty chair. Warmth radiates through the windows. I stand very still, the way people do when they're about to get beamed up, and I concentrate real hard, but nothing happens. The only way I can follow her is to return to the dim dining room, flip up the screen, and set the Way Back Machine to A.D. 2000, Provence.

11 Petit Casino: $52.31

PETIT CASINO
MAURICETTE ET FRANCK
30 BD DE LA TOULOUSE
13840 PUYRICARD
TEL:04 42 92 17 06

GEWURZTRAMIN   44.15F
RIESLING   30.25F
GEWURZTRAMIN   44.15F
COTEAUX AIX   17.25F
RIESLING   30.25F
COTEAUX AIX   17.25F
EAU CASINO   2.70F
EAU CASINO   2.70F
RCE NAPO 420   7.95F
RCE NAPO 420   7.95F
CHAIR TOMATE   6.75F
CONCENTRE TO   4.35F
LAIT FRAIS   7.90F
SODASUN X4   12.40F
TAPENADE   14.75F
F FRUITS/LEGUMES 5.50%   11.90F
PATE NTDG   5.95F
PATE NTDG   5.95F
PATE NTDG   5.95F
F FRUITS/LEGUMES 5.50%   11.90F
F FROMAGE COUPE 5.50 X   25.90F
F FRUITS/LEGUMES 5.50%   1.50F
F FROMAGE COUPE 5.50 X   18.45F
F FROMAGE COUPE 5.50 X   17.10F

≈ T O T A L (24)   355.35F≈

≈ T O T A L EURO   54.17≈
(1 EURO = 6.55957 Francs)

CARTE BANCAIRE   (CB)   355.35
MONTANT EURO   54.17

001 / 1 / 07/06/2000/18:16:09
Numero de Ticket : 137215
VOUS REMERCIENT DE VOTRE VISITE

But the Way Back Machine isn't working right now. No matter what adjustments I try, it just blinks at me. It's temperamental that way—a real pain in the ass, frankly. But there's nothing to be done about it now, so I close its lid and grab my little spiral notebook and go for a walk. That's what I do here in Chapet. I take walks and I drink wine and I curse the malfunctioning Way Back Machine, and after a long and joyful day of walks and wine and mental disturbances, I lay me down to not sleep. Then I toss and turn and have strange dreams. And then the morning birds sing, and the whole episode starts over again. My very own suburban Parisian *Groundhog Day.*

I now find myself sitting at a small table at a brasserie called *La Marcotte,* in the town of Les Mureaux, across the valley from Chapet. It's also an off-track betting facility of some kind. On a large screen at one end of the room horses are milling about a paddock. A half-dozen TVs are hung in various locations, above the bar, above the door. The place is crowded. Most of the men hold racing forms, and make bets on small paper chits.

Nearly everyone here is of a darker shade than I, although they are by no means uniform. They vary from the sand-colors of the Levant to the blue-black of equatorial Africa. One sturdy man, looking perplexed, stands motionless in the middle of the room. With his bushy mustache and full face, he bears a striking resemblance to a certain recently deposed dictator. And maybe this is he, newly arrived from Baghdad, trying his luck at a new game. He had quite a run at the old one. Several of the men wear the robes and scarves of Africa, long flowing things that remind me of the cassocks that some priests still wore when I was a child, only these are of bright patterned cloth, royal purple, burnt orange.

To get here I walked across the green fields below Chapet. I crossed a scraggly margin of trees, broken fences, old mattresses and assorted debris, and found myself in a vast low-cost housing complex where vertical and horizontal blocks of apartments sit in equipoise. It was four in the afternoon, and the place was swarming with children. Many of the women were veiled. A poster at several bus stops said "Stop La Guerre" above a picture, in profile, of a gasoline nozzle pointed like a gun barrel at the forehead of a small girl. But no one looked at me askance, there nor here in *La Marcotte.* A man who looked

Middle Eastern stepped back grandly to make a place for me at the bar. The bartender was dark, handsome, clean shaven, and he wore a tie. For some reason I guessed Egyptian. When he looked at me I panicked and for some reason barked, *"Ein Bier, bitte."*

"Which beer?" he said in English.

So much for trying to pass myself off as a continental. I pointed to one of the taps. I paid for my beer and took it to a little table next to a window that looks out on the parking lot, and pulled out this notebook to record my walking tour up to the present moment. And where I must stop writing right *now.* Why? Because, as I just realized, I am freaking people the hell out. I feel the tension in the quick stares, the half smiles, the covert glances. The place is crowded, except for the three empty tables closest to me. That's me, as in the middle-aged crew neck-sweatered white guy looking at people and jotting down notes with insolence of one who doesn't care if anyone sees him jotting down notes. Idiot. And yet, some perversity in me prolongs the discomfort by continuing to describe it. Okay, gentlemen, I'm done. I have my little black book full of names that I'm selling to French Immigration and the Islamic Fundamentalist Union. Kidding. Absolutely nothing to be concerned about. So stop, already. Click pen with thumb, reach under sweater, return to pocket. Someone's going to stab you in the parking lot. Really. Stop. You're making them very nervous. And writing very small does not help. No, it doesn't.

Meanwhile, three years earlier, Jon and Janet, having recently sampled restaurants in several parts of Europe, are attempting to adjust to life in a rented villa called *La Bastide* surrounded by a vineyard called *Beaulieu.* The villa is a three-story stone house with a red tile roof. It's supposed to look old, but it's practically brand new. The spaces inside are huge, and the amenities top notch. Leather couches. African art on the walls upstairs, abstract canvases below. Outside, three stone arches give partial cover to a large porch that overlooks the pool. A wide stone stairway curves up to the main entrance on the second floor, but everyone usually just walks under the arches to the ground floor. The roof of the porch, above the arches, becomes a lovely terrace from which it would be unwise to attempt to jump into the pool. Seven bedrooms on three floors. It would be hard to imagine a more tasteful or luxurious retreat. The only problem is that we have to share it with other people.

I am standing at the window of our bedroom. "Look," I say, "the vines are right outside our window."

"Lovely," says Janet.

"No, really. Look, you can practically touch them."

Janet tosses postcards of San Remy on the bureau and comes to stand beside me at the window. "It is beautiful." She eases herself onto the bed, and it creaks loudly. I smile. Janet rolls her eyes. It is the loudest bed we have ever encountered, containing a veritable symphony of sounds. The unspoken point is that there will be no sex here, not in this bed, not with all these people around.

"So what's up this afternoon?" Janet asks from the creaky bed.

"Drink wine and hang out by the pool?"

"Okay."

"It's only our second day. You know, we're not supposed to treat this place as a hotel. The whole idea behind it was 'community building.'"

"I said okay. Save the public service announcements."

"But the way you said it . . . "

"Listen," Janet says, "When something isn't okay, I promise you'll be the first to know, okay?"

I nod. "Okay."

Janet nods. "Okay, who's in charge of dinner?"

"I don't know," I say. "Maybe you and I could make dinner for everyone."

Janet looks at me and says dubiously, "All right. . . ."

"Not okay?"

"Well . . . " Janet tilts her head back and forth. "It's not the *making dinner* I mind. It just seems a bit *presumptuous*, I guess. What if people were planning to go out to eat?"

"We'll take a head count." I sit down on the bed next to her. It creaks loudly. "Well, you know, after last night . . . "

Janet puts the back of her hand to her forehead, and speaks in a movie star voice. "It was ghastly, my dear."

"It is amazing that we survived."

Janet heaves a big sigh. "I shall never know how I summoned the strength to endure."

Yesterday, our first day, we took off and visited Rognes and Lambesc, the local villages. Lovely. Picturesque. When we returned, around seven, everybody else in the house was seated around a big table, a dozen or so people, nearly finished with the pasta and capers dish that someone had prepared.

Cecile said, "Come and sit down!" and others chimed in. But I felt awkward, intrusive, and thought Janet did too. So I said, "No thanks, we just ate," at the same moment that Janet said, "Great, I'm starved." Everyone pretended we hadn't just done that, and soon we were grafted onto the corner of the table, pushing bits of pasta onto the freshly washed plates of diners who said they were done. Later, when we were going to bed, Janet was kind of pissed off that my lie could make her look like a liar. I argued that mine was so much more obviously a lie—in fact, it *was* a lie—that everyone at the table was thinking that *she* is the well-adjusted spouse, and I'm the one that's given to panicked moments of social ineptitude. She wasn't buying my explanation, and it got to the point where she was ready to jump out of creakybed, throw on a robe, and run around the house polling everyone that was still up. Janet can be really stubborn.

Today, the movie star shtick is Janet's way of showing that she doesn't take it all that seriously, after all.

"Come on," I say, getting up off the noisy bed. "Let's go get the food now, so we don't have to run around later."

"All right." She gets up. "But it seems very Catholic to me."

"Have you seen the car keys?"

In the eastern part of the United States of America, if one drives around for very long at all, one will almost certainly pass a grocery store. This turns out not to be the case in Provence. While we're crisscrossing the vineyards on narrow back roads, looking for food, I ask her about the Catholic comment.

"Oh, you know," she says. "The whole penance thing. Making dinner as a kind of public atonement."

"Not at all," I say. "It's just a nice gesture by the new members of the community. To show them we want to do our fair share."

"You mean, and not stroll in right in the middle of dinner and expect to be fed?"

"Weren't we just at this roundabout?"

Janet looks around and shrugs. "Different one, I think."

"Purycard. Do you think that's a town or a brand of soap? We'll try it that direction." After the turn I add, "Anyway, if anyone is making public atonement, it's you."

"Me?"

"You bet. They all know you were lying, and I went ahead and had dinner again to cover for your insatiable appetite."

"They're not going to think that . . . " Janet says warningly.

"Whoa . . . was that our turn?"

" . . . because you, Jon, are going to get up on the table before dinner and announce that you were the liar, and that you are very sorry to have made your lovely wife, who has great shoes, appear in any but the best light."

"You want self-flagellation with that?"

She wrinkles her nose. "No blood."

"Thanks."

Purycard is the name of a town, not a soap, and the store is called *Petit Casino*. We are leery of a place that makes grocery shopping sound like a gamble, but it's a nice little place with lots of fresh fruits and vegetables. We get pasta, sauce, bread, and assorted cheeses and pates, wine.

It does not escape my notice that this receipt, being from a store, belies the restaurant motif of this work. So sue me.

While getting lost on the way back to the villa, I say, "How about this: tomorrow, we'll take off early and check out Les Baux. Just you and me."

"What? Abandon the community?"

"My plan is that we alternate days. One day with the villa people, the next day by ourselves. One day on, one day off. How about it?"

"We don't have to be strict about it," Janet says. "We can be flexible. But yes, that would be nice." She touches my arm as she says it.

"Cecile was in Les Baux last week, and says it's beautiful."

"That's enough for me, Map Man. Only, it's not too far, is it? I don't want to spend the whole day in the car."

"Nothing's too far here, my cartographically-challenged dear one. Provence ain't that big."

Janet and I make dinner, with Cecile helping us find things in the new kitchen and refreshing the salad from last night so that we will have another course. This is the same Professor Cecile who booked our Chateau in Guebwiller, and who now functions as a kind of de facto house mother, because somebody has to coordinate, with all these faculty coming and going, which must be like trying to herd cats. She's been at Ursinus for about thirty years, although she looks much too young for that. And in the kitchen, as ever, she is generous, vigorous, upbeat. We lay a table for ten, and everyone tucks in.

"What *is* this?" Nelson Barge, the historian, holds his clear plastic glass away from him, as if it held turds.

"Yes," Dana adds. "It's so strong."

Someone else says it's sour and someone else says it's skunked and someone else says it smells like cat urine. I stand up and shout to everyone, "It's gewürztraminer!"

"*Gesundheit!*"

"Ha Ha. Now listen . . . " Since most of my colleagues do not share my passion for oenology, I go on to explain that this wonderful word applies both to the grape and to the wine from this grape, that a very dry version is typical of Alsatian wine, a particularly delightful species of which they happen to hold before them at this moment.

"That may be true," says Nelson, "but it still smells like cat pee."

"I like it," says the painter, Finn. "No, I mean it. This is a *good* wine. I don't know if I rank it up there, you know, with a good chardonnay, but I can drink this. Maybe the rest of you had something in your glasses, I don't know, like maybe they weren't *clean*, because as far as I'm concerned, this is a drinkable. It reminds me of the time I was in Napa, *no,* the Willamette Valley, that's right, I was at a seminar in Portland, and I drove out. I mean, I think it was after the seminar, and I needed to hang around because my cousin lives there, but she wasn't flying in until the . . . "

Cecile steps in to agree that it's a nice gewürztraminer, but offers that everyone is probably used to the Provence rosé, so the Alsatian seems bitter. She says there's plenty of rosé in the plastic jug in the kitchen, if anyone prefers that. I consider throwing myself in front of the stampede to the kitchen, but a steadying hand on the arm keeps me in my place. I whisper, in a pouty voice, "But they're pouring my wine in the sink."

Janet tries, not successfully, to look sympathetic.

"And they're drinking that *pink* stuff from plastic jugs."

She tries, with equal unsuccess, not to grin.

" . . . so the Willamette Valley, *that's* where I had the gewürztraminers, not Napa . . . "

Cecile proposes that Nelson, Paige and I talk about research projects. Cecile has a sense of duty, and is not one to let the stated justifications for this experiment in community-building slide under the table. But I suspect it might also be a maneuver to parry Finn, who is blessed with more than his share of the blarney. Cecile continues to drink the Alsatian wine, showing more sympathy to my feelings than someone who shall go nameless who joined the rosé parade as fast as her cute shoes would carry her. While I'm refilling Cecile's glass,

I whisper something about a plot to derail Finn. She laughs a noncommittal laugh, but her eyes sparkle. Finn is one great painter. He does these incredible hyper-realistic portraits that look more like the people than the people look like themselves in real life. But he also has logorrhea, an affliction to which we in the professoriate are particularly susceptible. He's been around about as long as Cecile, and, like her, he has a Dorian Gray quality. Finn has fine, jet black hair that hangs down to his shoulders. He punctuates his commentary with lively hands that are always pushing his hair back over his ears.

Nelson is happy to tell us about his historical research. It concerns the Cathars, also known as the Albigensians, a sect that lived not far from here, in Languedoc. A tall man with thinning white hair, Nelson has a habit of speaking with interlaced fingers resting across his sternum, which adds a visual impression of earnestness to his somewhat dry delivery. He talks about the Cathars through the end of dinner and while the plates are being cleared. A lot of different things have been written attempting to explain the nature of the alleged Albigensian heresy, but most historians seem to think it was Manichaeism. Of course, the theological disputes were pumped up with accusations of sodomy and black masses and the like. So the Pope and the king of France and other good medieval Christians—this is the early 1200s—decided that it must be suppressed. One might see it as the Crusade mania turning inward on itself, and it did so with a brutality as least as fierce as anything unleashed upon Muslims.

I get another glass of gewürztraminer, and one for Cecile, since she is beside me. Janet, the defector, can get her own pink wine. The talk goes on.

In one town seven thousand people were massacred at once. Many of them inside the church. It went on for decades until the Cathars and those accused of being Cathars were all pretty much fully exterminated. Nelson's monotone has wry flecks of irony that creep in at the edges when he relates something particularly heinous. He goes into some detail about the various methods by which the depopulation of Languedoc was brought about, although he insists on pointing out that if one wants to get comparative about it, many of the really imaginative atrocities do not come into vogue until the next century, when torture becomes something of an art form. Now if we would like him to tell us about what happened to the Templars . . .

I am trying to catch Janet's eye, but she is attempting origami with her cloth napkin. It looks like she checked out of the lecture somewhere mid-pasta.

Cecile says we would all love for Nelson to tell us about what happened to the Templars, but we should be hearing from Paige and Jon also. If we were all back home and this were some kind of school-social dinner, people would have been rattling their keys and coughing and pleading children duties by now. But we are deep in the countryside of Provence, and there's nowhere to go. And there is wine. There is always wine. It turns out, by the way, that my disdain for the local wine is completely misplaced, and I am duly ashamed of myself. Rosé in the summertime is one of the most charming of the many charms of Provence, and possibly the best thing about life at *La Bastide*. As Janet and I will quickly discover, every day someone goes into Rognes with our two five-liter plastic containers. At the local cooperative, large upright metal tanks have hoses that look very much like antique gasoline spouts. For a few francs, they fill the plastic jugs with the wine of your choice—white, red, or rosé. No one back home ever thinks of rosé wine, but in Provence it is the wine of choice, and it becomes ours as well. It is light and delicious and cheap and in endless supply. A quick stop for cheese and an armful of baguettes, and we are set for the day.

The bottle gone, I fill my glass from the spout of the plastic urn and return to the dining area so that Paige can tell us about comparative health systems and wellness systems in the United States and France. She is smart and enthusiastic about comparative health systems and wellness systems, and there are many polite questions. It all has a slight air of artificiality to it, though, and Janet asks me about it when I join her on the corner of the terrace overlooking the pool. It takes me awhile to find her. After Paige finished, Cecile had declared a twenty minute potty break before we heard from Jon. I used the bathroom, and wandered around until I found Janet. She was sitting on the wide stone railing with her back against the side of the house, deep in shadow.

"It's chilly out here," I say. "Shall I get you a sweater?"

"I'm fine."

"I saw you spacing out in there. You're not going to pass the history exam unless you take better notes."

"What's going on with Paige?" Janet asks flatly.

"She's great, isn't she?"

"Yes. She is great," Janet says patiently. "But everyone is acting just a little weird. What's the back story?"

"I can explain." I sit down on the rocky edge next to her. "Paige is from E-S-S. Back at school, the negative voices on this overseas experiment came from the hard sciences. They claimed that it was a junket for the humanities, because *their* summer research requires big labs and expensive machines. You can't just pack up the old spectrometer and take it to France, I guess."

"What's this have to do with . . . "

"Well, E-S-S is in the sciences, and . . . "

"E-S-S?"

"Sorry. Exercise and Sports Science. Anyway, since the E-S-S department is classified as one of the sciences, and since Paige is here, doing legitimate research, it undermines the objections of the chemists and biologists. So everybody is very anxious to be nice to her. Not that she isn't very nice, it's just that . . . "

Janet raises a hand. "I got it. Thank you. Office politics."

I glance inside. The second-floor living room is empty. "I guess we should go down. I'm supposed to talk about my legitimate research now."

"Do you mind if I just stay here? I think I know enough about your research."

"Yeah, sure," I say, "but it's cold up out here."

"I'll be fine. You go on. They're waiting."

While I was talking to Janet, people moved to the living room sofas and chairs. There are no spots left, so I pull in a dining room chair. I describe my project in clumsy and banal tones, thinking that no one really cares. But then, out of nowhere, Pleckman starts peppering me with questions.

"Yes, I understand," Pleckman is saying, "but what I'm asking here, what I'm not sure about, is where the *research* component comes in."

"Well, *as I said*," I say, my smile growing tighter, "since I am a *travel writer*, everything I see is, in a sense, research, and . . ."

"And I am a philosopher," says Pleckman, "so everything I think is, in a sense, research. But that's not going to get me a grant, is it?" General laughter.

Pleckman is in the deep cushiony chair next to me. He looks like a philosopher—lean and bald, with fierce, penetrating eyes. His specialty is Spinoza, and his position is that everything written about Spinoza up until now has been dead wrong. Like Finn, Pleckman is a regular in the faculty lunch room, and likes to arrive early. This presents later-arriving diners with a classic choice—Finn's verbal whirlpool or the chance of a biting Pleckman interrogation. Like Odysseus, I usually point my prow towards Scylla.

He continues, "I may well get a research grant for what I think, *ultimately*, but provisionally, there has to be a subject matter of some kind, an object for contemplation—Spinoza's *Ethics*, say, or, at least a context or framework for speculations upon ethics. I understand that you're a travel writer. All I'm asking, I guess, is what you're travel-writing *about*?"

"I don't know yet."

"You don't know yet?"

Cecile jumps to my aid. As one of the organizers of the Provence program, she has a stake in the justice of this enterprise. "You had this idea in your proposal, it was very good. Something about old colonials and new economies in the postmodern world . . . "

A general groan goes up at the word "postmodern."

"It's about borders," I assert. "Blurring borders. Janet and I just came from Alsace, where you have the French and German, and there's the EU—next year they'll have the same currency—and my research, if you want to call it that, is about cultures in transition, about people, how they live with blurring borders, and how the preconceived notions that I bring to the area blur in the actual practice of observing them and blur again in trying to record them." That made no sense. Too much wine. I'm blurring my own borders.

"I can see how that might apply to the Alsace," says Pleckman, "even if they can't make decent wine." He pauses for the chuckles. "But then what do you do in Provence? This is the most homogenous culture I've ever . . . "

"Not if you look back across history," says Cecile.

"Are you looking back across history?" asks Pleckman.

"Yes. I mean, no." Laughter. "Not like Nelson, I mean. I take in history as I look at things. It has an impact on my observations."

"You read guidebooks."

"Yeah."

"He reads guidebooks." Pleckman waits for his laugh. But he has overplayed his hand; sympathies are shifting. His tone becomes mollifying. "So if what you're doing is journalism, say it's journalism. I have nothing against journalism. I was just trying to find out . . . "

"It's not journalism," I say, emboldened to recklessness. "It's postmodern meta-narrative inquiry. And if you want to know what that is, listen up and I'll tell you. Journalism adheres to established standards of reporting. A so-called objectivity. What I'm calling postmodernism is really just an extension of the modernist paradigm, exploding the myth of objectivity. It's not about Provence, it's about *me experiencing Provence*, and that includes things I *don't* experience in Provence, because they're already inside me. I'm talking nonlinear chronology. The viewer contained in the view. Fucking Cezanne."

"Fucking Cezanne painted right near here," says Cecile, deadpan. "You could research his perspectives of *Saint-Victoire.*"

"Van Gogh was in Arles," someone pipes up, even less helpfully.

"Wait a minute," says Pleckman. "So you're saying, for example, that you could write this conversation, as it happened, to the best of your memory."

"Sush as it ish."

People laugh as if I slurred intentionally. I smile knowingly.

"Or you could change it, say, to make yourself look better."

"Could do that."

"Or you could make it up altogether! Maybe I'm still at Stanford, maybe I don't get hired until next year, and maybe you're writing this later, and nonlinearly back-loading me into the story just to give yourself an excuse to sound off about what you think of as 'philosophy'."

"Maybe I am. Or will. So what?"

Pleckman snorts. "If you're writing a novel, just say so."

"I'm writing *truth.*" Childish and shrill, I stand up in order to look even more ridiculous. "It's not journalism and it's not a novel. If the word 'postmodern' puts a bug up your butt, call it 'meta-nonfiction.' That's what it prefers to be called."

"I call it pomo-pathetic," Pleckman says. "*Bug up my butt?* You can take the boy off the farm, but you can't . . . " He stops and smiles at me. "Are you at least taking good notes?"

"No, and here's why. Every articulation puts the agent one step further removed from experience—notes are an interpretation that later gets re-interpreted into text. I collect primary research instead. Indisputable things like wine labels, and . . . " I reach in my pocket and come up with a strip of paper with pale blue printing, "grocery receipts." I wave it in front of his face. "There is more truth here than any notes I could make about what happens tonight." I'm starting to feel on top of my game again, and I'm remembering what I like about Pleckman. You can argue with him all through lunch in the faculty room. Extended, exacting arguments, bloody arguments, with no quarter given. And then, walking back to the office, he'll ask how your son is doing in track, and you realize it's not personal, it's philosophy. It's funny how, when philosophers come right down to it, so many of them will contend that the highest human activity possible is engaging in philosophical debate.

And many of the greatest poems are about the greatness of poetry.

And many of the greatest rock songs are about being a rock star.

I guess it's not so surprising. Self-regard is the animating force of the universe. Descartes almost got it right. I think about myself, therefore I am all about myself.

Janet is already in bed and at first I think she is sleeping. When she mumbles that she's awake, I'm anxious to tell her how I'd gotten the Pleckman treatment and everyone was laughing at me, but in the end I kind of said some things that made sense, and scored some points of my own.

"That's nice."

I pause and stare at her. "What's going on?"

"What do you mean?"

"You," I say. "You were fine at dinner, and then when I came up and found you on the terrace, you seemed bummed out. And then, I can hardly believe I'm saying this, you actually behaved as if you genuinely didn't care to hear me talk at great length about myself and my work."

It's too dark to see if she smiled, but she does turn on her back, fluff up the pillows, and sit up a bit, to the accompaniment of the noisy bed springs. "I'm sorry, hon. It's just that, gee, all that talk about how all those people were tortured and massacred, it kind of brought me down."

"You mean Nelson's stuff? The Cathars?"

"Oh," she says, with phony brightness. "Was there *more* torture and massacre that I missed?"

"No, it's just that . . . I thought you weren't listening after awhile. You looked checked-out."

"No, Jon, I was listening. I heard all the earnest discussions about burning at the stake and tying people's legs to horses, and sawing them in two with their head down to keep them conscious as long as possible. And if you want to know, yes, I will tell you. It makes me sick. Why is everyone always so ready to go to war? It's like, if you've got a hundred thousand men massed at the borders, and you have to feed and house them anyway, they might as well invade, right? You might as well get some use out of them. And if the inspectors say they need more time and everyone in the world but Tony Blair agrees, why, screw 'em. We're ready to roll . . ."

Wait. That's not the Janet of Provence. Obviously, that's newer, that's now, that's the Janet who gets goaded to fury by Fox News. The Janet who writes to senators and signs email petitions. The Janet who put a bumper sticker on our car that she got from the Quaker meeting: "God Bless Everyone. No Exceptions." The Janet who can be brittle, caustic, and get angry with me for not being angry enough at what's going on in the world. Anachronism is an admitted risk of the non-linear meta-narrational inquiry method. I do believe she was strongly affected that night in Provence by all the talk of Albigensian cruelties. But when I try to picture her, she's standing by the kitchen counter in Pennsylvania, pointing angrily at the television as she speaks, and I have to question whether my view of Janet as angry sorrowful woman has been backloaded into the past.

12 Bautezar: $4.41

```
BAR   RESTAURANT
      BAUTEZAR
       Grand Rue
13520 LES BAUX DE PROVENCE
   TEL: 04.90.54.32.09.
      MERCI A BIENTOT

05/06/00          000000
#0049                 01

2x 25.00
GLACE 2 BOULES     50.00
2x 15.00
THE                30.00
S/TOT              80.00
TVA 20.60%         13.11
H.T. 19.60%        66.89

ESPECES         80. OO
                 e12.20
```

"Do you know," I ask Janet, "or can you guess, the substance that was first discovered and mined here, and gives this castle its name?"

"Strangely enough, I don't."

"Here's a hint. It's pronounced 'Lay Bow,' right? But it's spelled Les B-a-u-x." I point to it on the receipt for the iced tea we are drinking. How might you pronounce it?"

"Lay Bow."

"But if you were a stupid American you might say . . . " I notice Janet's gaze wander out over the balcony, towards the steep gorge below. Tapping the receipt, I say, "Box . . . which

117

sounds like? What mineral?" She ignores me. "Bauxite! This is the place that bauxite is named for!"

I am in a good mood, and trying to drag Janet along with me. Janet was already up when I rolled out of bed. She was sitting out by the pool, in early morning sunshine, chatting with Paige about health systems and wellness systems. I took my coffee on the upper balcony where I imagined Pleckman on a chaise lounge, Spinoza open on his lap. I asked how *his* research tied to Provence. I imagined him cheerfully saying that it didn't; that his proposal was pure hogwash, and that he was here to do the same things he'd be doing back home. "Plus wine, cheese, et cetera. Complete junket. As alleged."

"Would you have said that last night?"

He laughed. "Hell no. But I wasn't here last night, just like I'm not here now. See, this is where the meta-nonfiction thing loses all credibility. You're just using me."

"But when I admit to fabrication, the narrative reclaims its veracity. As now."

Pleckman bowed to acknowledge my metaphysical superiority.

And then I'd wandered downstairs, found Janet, and swooped her off in the car without saying a word to anyone, just as I'd promised. The highway approached Les Baux across the flat sandy fields, vineyards, and olive groves. The ruins of the castle stood out above the valley, growing out of the chalky rock formation, almost indistinguishable, except that one part of the ridge seems to have square windows. We drove up where the highway slices through the rock, and found a parking place. Les Baux occupies a plateau, perfect for defensive purposes. The castle, or what's left of it, dates as far back as the ninth century. It occupies the highest part, commanding the valley. On the back side of the plateau, overhanging a cypress gorge, the village resembles a haphazard pile of children's blocks, bright painted shutters relieving the gray-white stone. The sun was shining, and the climb from the parking lot to the entrance was surprisingly hot and tiring. The first thing we needed was a cool drink, so we found this place with its excellent iced tea. Actually, the *first* thing I did was buy a guidebook. I'm giving Janet fun facts on Les Baux over tea.

"Saracen towers! The castle has Saracen towers." I take her hand across the table. "This is the perfect place for both of us. I like castles, and this one is cool, even if it is mostly ruins. And there's this incredible village, with all these shops."

Janet takes her hand from mine. Her fingers slide absently up her glass, collecting condensation. "So," she says. "You go look at your castle. I go look at my village. Fine. What time shall we meet?"

"You know what I meant. We've got all day. You go castle hopping with me, and I'll wander the village with you."

We pay an entrance fee at the castle and are offered little audio machines and ear phones to hear the history of each part of the castle.

In hindsight—and this is me stepping ahead three years, to my lonely corner of Chapet—in hindsight, it is easy to single out this moment, and say, *There. You should have known better.* And I should have. Also, in hindsight I might say, *Hey, Dipstick, you know how, when couples fight about leaving the cap off the toothpaste, it's not really ever about toothpaste?*

Yes, older sadder exile me?

Well, when your wife gets angry about Albigensian persecutions . . .

It's not really about the Albigensians?

You got it.

I honestly thought it was, at the time.

I know, moron. That's why you're—why I'm—stuck in Chapet right now, alone and missing her.

Isn't there any way we can just put this part behind us, and Janet and I—Janet and you—can just be together and be happy?

"Jon?"

"What?"

"Do you want the audio or not?"

"Huh?"

"The *audio* thing. They have it in English. Do you want it?"

"Yeah. Two please." I hand money to the impassive woman at the desk, and she hands me two units and headphones. Giving one to Janet, I say, "It was like that flash you get, something kicks in and you remember a part of the dream you had last night, and you go, 'oh yeah!' and then as soon as you try to bring it into focus it's gone, totally."

"Well, try not to do it when someone is asking you something."

We stay together during the first part of the tour, up through the chapel of St. Vincent. We nod and smile at each other, and press buttons on our machines, get confused, and press other buttons. Then we wander away from each other. There's a large open area. At one end, the corrugated floor indicates the roof of a huge stone cistern, and there's this wide area where all the rainwater is caught and channeled into it. Apparently, after some siege or other when everyone died of thirst, it seemed a good idea to build it. Up on a flat area near the edge sits a trebuchet—a giant graceful praying mantis kind of engine that looks like it could hurl a rock half way to Monte Carlo. Trebuchet. I look around for Janet so she can tease me that I like the word "trebuchet" more than I like the siege engine itself. But what if trebuchet were used against the Albigensians? And what is the plural of trebuchet? They probably were used, so I hurry away from there. At times I spot her a long ways across the open rock ruins, and then I don't see her for a long time. I listen dutifully to the centuries of history, most of it bad and bloody, surrounding Les Baux. In the back of my mind is Pleckman's taunt that my historical research amounts to reading guidebooks.

At the farther end, I am in that part of the fortress you see while approaching across the valley. Staircases are carved into the stone of the wall, long steep staircases, and, with that European disregard for safety and litigation, anyone is allowed to climb them. So I do, acutely aware that my footfalls are echoing down through history. How many people have climbed this staircase, in flight, in turmoil, in glee—running to a secret assignation, hurrying to defend a rampart, moving with resignation toward certain death? Some of the stairs are so worn that they form deep concavities. I climb and climb. It gets scary near the top, high and narrow. There are a couple of rooms, and an overlook where I can wave, and people driving up the valley, if they have binoculars, can see me wave. Turning back to the inward side, I overlook the ruined ramparts and walls, trying to find Janet. As I turn to go down the stairs I spot her. In profile, in the distance, *above* me. She is perched on the very top of the fortress, sitting with her feet in front of her, arms loosely around her knees. You can't get there from here—she must have gone up an even steeper staircase somewhere else along these walls. Seeing her there nauseates me with fear. She's sitting too near the edge. I yell to her, but it's too far. I turn back to my stairs, and have to move cautiously because I am dizzy with fear and apprehension. Other tourists are coming up the stairs, and passing each other is delicate. Finally I make it down, and I'm looking up to where she was but I can't see her. I can't even tell where it was I saw her in this giant maze of stone. I stalk up and down along the walls, looking for her, not seeing her, then suddenly she is next to me.

"Hey," she says, without inflection.

"I saw you way up on top. You were sitting right on the edge. You scared the hell out of me."

She shrugs.

"Are you crazy? Don't do that anymore! Where's your headset?"

"I took it back a long time ago. Are you ready, or is there more castle you have to listen to?"

"I'm ready."

We don't say much on the long walk back to turn in my audio unit. I ask her what she saw, what she liked, and she gives short answers. My manner is unctuous. "Now you've done my castle thing," I say as we approach the village. "I'm ready to check out the shops. Are you hungry?"

"No. Thirsty."

"Let's go back and have another iced tea. That place had great iced tea."

Janet is amenable. So we go back there, and the place is practically filled now, and everyone is having these tall, beautiful ice cream concoctions in tulip-shaped shiny steel serving dishes. We get the menus, which have pictures of them all. We point out our choices and we soon have iced tea and luscious ice cream.

BAUTEZAR II: $11.76

```
       BAR  RESTAURANT
           BAUTEZAR
            Grand Rue
    13520 LES BAUX DE PROVENCE
        TEL: 04.90.54.32.09.
           MERCI A BIENTOT


       05/06/00          000000
       #0048                  01

       2x 15.00
       THE                 30.00
       S/TOT.              30.00
       TVA 20.60%           4.9
       H.T. 19.60%         25.08

       ESPECES             30.00
                           e4.57
```

"I really love that castle," I say, spooning in the ice cream.

"I thought you would."

"Did you like it?"

"It was fine."

"Is everything all right?"

Janet looks down at her ice cream and then up at me. She seems to be making a decision. She takes a deep breath. "Okay, I admit, it was kind of hard for me. When you put on those headphones, it's like you've walked back into history and left me here."

"I was trying to keep contact. I waved to you."

"And it felt like you were waving to me from a train window."

"I don't think you're being fair."

She sighs. "Maybe not. Maybe I'm not making the transition to communal living as smoothly as I'd like. All I know is I'm feeling sad and a little lonely and I need you to just be with me a little more."

"I'm with you. I'm with you every second almost."

"I don't mean just physically being together. I can't describe it. I just know how it feels to me."

"Tell me how I can be more there for you."

"You don't have to be there *for* me. You have to be there *with* me. I know it sounds like I'm splitting hairs, but there's a difference."

"Okay. I'll try to be more *with* you. I think I know what you mean. When I saw you sitting up on the very top of that rock, it really scared me. It looked like you were going to fall or fly away or something. I felt helpless."

"I'm not sure that's the same thing," she says. "Anyway, thanks." She shakes her head as if to clear it, and looks around. "Let's just go check out the village. I saw a place that had essential oils. Maybe I can find something for Nance."

Janet and I wander through the narrow stone streets and bright shops of Les Baux village, being kind and solicitous towards each other. Perhaps we are trying too hard, because there's a slight air of artificiality about it. Janet buys a yellow and blue Provençal tablecloth for her sister. Many shops feature the local olive oil, much touted—elaborate bottles nestled in exquisite boxes. The Italian side of Janet cannot quite make the concession to French olive oil. She loves the soaps and oils and lotions and shampoos. She gets lavender-scented lotion for her mother and honey soap for her other sister. Nothing here looks suitable for the boys, however, and that distresses her, although she doesn't make a big deal of it.

In the interest of maintaining the suspension of your disbelief, I am not supposed to tell you that I have spent days crafting the Iced Tea Dialogues. But you already know that I am reconstructing it three years later in Chapet, and so this confession of inexactitude should actually serve to *enhance* verisimilitude. I remember the feeling of isolation caused by the audio headsets, and I vividly remember the feeling of terror when I spotted Janet sitting casually on the edge of a precipice, but I am having trouble recapturing the way we tried to speak of our vague and dispiriting sense of distance from one another. Certainly the distinction between being there *for* someone and being *with* someone has come up in our conversation in similar circumstances; I'm just not sure if it came up in this one, in this way.

When I get depressed about how far I am from both the real Janet and her literary doppelganger, which is every day, I stop to read *The International Herald-Tribune*. And then I get more depressed because it's all about the war, and there's all this ridiculous talk of "punishing" France for opposing the war. It seems to me that one of the less ignoble reasons for the war is so that Iraqis can criticize their own government—or those of other countries, presumably—without fear of reprisal. Now I read that the Department of Defense is especially keen on punishing France. I haven't been away that long, but already I'm feeling the expatriate's bewilderment over permutations back home. A kind of horrible continental drift is pulling the United States farther from France, and Janet farther from me. I am embarrassed to show my face at Daniel's pub, and yet I do, every day. And the locals shake my hand and call out *"Bonsoir!"* in friendly voices, every day.

Trying to build bridges, I wrote a "Postcard from France" and sent it to the travel editors at the *Philadelphia Inquirer*. They wrote back and said my piece wasn't travel writing. Send it to the editorial page instead.

"What then *IS* travel writing?" I demanded of them, rhetorically.

Letters

Don't give in to stereotypes of the French

When I bought toothpaste at a CVS store, I mentioned I was leaving for France later that day. The lady behind the counter guffawed. "He's going to France!" she announced to everyone in the store. "They're going to hate him over there."

I have been in France for more than a week now, and I plan to stay a month. After dozens of encounters with French people, I can report that not a single one has been anything but friendly and polite — and I speak no French.

At the open-air market I bumped a woman and mumbled, "Sorry."

"American?" she asked.

When I said yes, she beamed and said she loves Lansing, Mich., and hopes to go back soon. "Only, you know," she shrugged sadly, "events...".

The bistro in the village was closed for the break between lunch and dinner. The proprietor heard me, came outside, and took me out for Chinese food in the next town. In his car. And he paid for lunch.

My new friend said, "I heard from a travel agent in Paris that all the Americans have cancelled for this summer. They think French people will spit on them or something. It is not true. Politics is politics, but friendship is friendship. Americans should understand that."

It pains me to think that French people who visit the United States might not receive this same kind of hospitality. France is our friend. Let's not give in to small-minded stereotypes and caricatures.

Jon Volkmer
Telford

ivolkmer@...—

Where to Write

The Philadelphia Inquirer
Box 41705
Philadelphia, PA 19101
Fax: 215-854-4483
E-mail: Inquirer.Letters@phillynews.com

Letters should be no more than 200 word and they must include a home address and phone number (day and evening). The Inquirer reserves the right to edit submissions and, because of the volume of mail, it cannot acknowledge each letter. All submissions be property of The Inquirer and n republished in any form or m more information, call 215-85

Read today's pages online at:
inquirer.philly.com/opinion

of a modern
come a "remai
fense of freed
Western values.

I am not clear
ern Muslim natio
ern values,"
convinced tl
"freedom," i.
out of this "li
facts yet to ji
so far.

I take issue
of war's cost it.
states that "Iraqi c
up roughly equalin
Saddam Hussein'
Bowden definitely
many Ir
wdr. No
The n
to any o
got to
th

by the entire Middle East
deeds there, as anywhere
volumes.

Starting with the criticall,
12-year-old Baghdad h~
arms ~~

13 Les Moissines: $58.53

About half the people residing at the villa at any given time have rental cars. It wouldn't make sense for everyone to have them. In practice, however, what it leads to is a kind of mobile aristocracy who have to deal with the unwheeled rabble. Car people have two choices. They can get up early and take off without telling anyone, as Janet and I did yesterday, or they can hang around for a second cup of coffee, mention where they are going, and ask if anyone wants to come along. This morning Janet sits patiently by the pool, second cup in hand, waiting for me to enact the *noblesse oblige* arrangements for today's adventure. But it must not *seem* to be trickle down transportation, so everyone stands around endlessly as we try to decide where to go, who hasn't seen what yet, who's going with whom, who has to be back at what time for what purpose, etc.

It ends up that we have two cars headed for the nearby hill town of Ansouis this morning. Natalie's husband Peter has just arrived for an insanely short visit. In a couple of days he'll head back to his helpless clients, but we are happy to see him. And we're all headed to Ansouis. Nat and Peter drive Dana. Janet and I take Finn.

While we're standing by the car, waiting for Finn to gather up his painting supplies, I say to Janet, "You look great."

Her look is distrustful. "Thanks."

"I mean it. That's the top you bought in Colmar, right? It's great."

She looks down. "You like it?"

"Goes great with those pants." The pants are cornflower blue, with small white flowers. They are baggy and loose, but made of a cotton so thin that it whispers sexiness without a hint of transparency. I say something to that effect as Finn slouches toward the car, pushing his hair back.

"Why didn't your wife come?" Janet asks as we're driving toward Ansouis.

"My wife . . . " He takes a breath. "My wife," he repeats, "not come." It reminds me of a symphony tuning up. And the baton comes down: "Well, it comes down to cats. Cats, can you believe it? I know, why can't we get someone to watch the cats? We should have someone to watch the cats, other people get someone to watch the cats, you know, house sitters, they watch cats while they're sitting houses, it's part of the deal, you know. Sometimes they call it cat-sitting, or dog-sitting, you know what I mean. But Merlin, that's one of the cats, the other is Matisse—I know, how does that work together? They should both be painters or they should both be magicians but what are you gonna do? I can't think of another magician, come to think of it, well Simon Magnus, but then what do you call the cat, Simon or Magnus, both sound pretty stupid if you ask me. But anyway it's the other one, Merlin, that has the problem. Yeah, it's like an infection or something, anyway it's fucking gross, man, the bandage has to be changed twice a day and that's not something you can ask a kid, I mean if it's a veterinary student or something, okay, but just a regular cat sitter, like one of our students, man, that would be too much to ask, you know. As it is I have to go out and get the medicine and come home and then all the way back to school again, and I tell you . . . "

Janet taps my knee and smiles. She is enjoying this.

" . . . I tell you if I could go back and start again, march down the aisle and all that, this time I would *insist* that she learn to drive, because this . . . "

"Finn," I say. "Your wife doesn't drive? Does she have a license?"

"Never had one. Every year she says she's going to take lessons, because, I mean, of course she could never stand to have *me* teach her, I don't blame her there, you should never take lessons from your spouse, especially driving lessons, and . . . "

"That must be inconvenient."

"Inconvenient?" His laughter explodes at the understatement.

Janet and I join in, and somehow the mood is lighter, and Finn rambles on while I hold Janet's hand between gear shifts.

Ansouis is different from the other hill towns in that the hill it crowns is rather small, and isolated from other hills. It rises out of the valley of the Durance on the carpeted plain that unrolls south of the Luberon range.

We meet the other car in the parking lot, and the six of us climb the wide path that makes a gentle conical circle up into the old town. The women are together, a little ahead of the men. Peter is a tall guy, computer consultant, science fiction buff. Like me, he is interested in the mechanics of things, the way things work. When he and Natalie come over to our house, we can spend a lot of time in good-natured debate about the best shape of the stack of logs in the fireplace for maximum caloric efficiency. It's good he wasn't with me when I came across that trebuchet yesterday. We might still be there. Today we mostly listen to Finn, who describes the fortification strategies of the hill towns and how they changed over the centuries with the increasing perfection of canon range and velocity. It's like the live version of The History Channel. Peter and I exchange happy grins while Finn carries on with great enthusiasm.

Natalie is in a manic phase, bouncing back and forth across the path with her big Nikon and black bag full of lenses, snapping flowers along stones and flowers in window boxes and flowers with the broad valley behind them. Watching her, I feel a sense of her urgency to capture some of this, to hold onto it, to bring it home. Snap snap snap snap snap. Change film. Snap snap snap. I could never be a photographer. All those rolls of film, all those frames, all those adjustments, those contact sheets—all that to try to find one or two good moments where everything hangs together. And the rest all gets thrown away.

While Natalie makes photos, Janet and Dana move together slowly, tall women, deep in conversation, and I have no doubt what they are talking about. Dana has boys the same ages as Seth and Tristan. Dana is a quiet, thoughtful woman, kind of the anti-Finn, in that she speaks seldom and chooses her words very carefully. I find it calming to see Janet talking with Dana. Stanley meets Livingstone in the trackless jungle of adolescent boy lives.

Our groups converge in the main square of Ansouis, which is tiny. Although our path climbed steadily from the car, this square gives no hint of altitude. Rather the opposite, in fact; it feels like a refuge, hemmed in on all sides by stone and ivy—city wall, church, castle, and village buildings. The church is small, ancient, and beautiful. It is cool inside, dim and empty, with that smell of sanctified stone and incense. Someone has put white bows on the pews, as if to welcome us. Natalie is in a zone, some kind of photographer trance. I marvel at her hand movements—each one crisp as she juggles lens caps, film canisters, cameras. She seems intent upon capturing every ripple in the stone robe of every saint. Her movements do not impinge on the sense of peace I feel here. Janet settles on the pew beside me, and I know she shares the contentment of the moment.

Across the courtyard, the only business in town is a gallery, and the artist is in. She is a gracious but businesslike woman in her late fifties or sixties who continues her work in the back room while we paw through the piles of framed paintings and prints leaning up against the walls. Finn has wandered off in his own direction, so we are left to our own tastes, and Janet loves the works and the woman who makes them. All the paintings are abstract water colors and acrylics, usually featuring vertical dark ovals, overlapping shapes in dark hues, dripped and flecked with red. Janet and I are long past the poster age, and have moved beyond the Reproductions-of-Impressionists stage. We have been talking about the scary move into Original Art stage, but timidity and finances have kept us from making the plunge. And we still don't achieve the O.A. standard, but the print that we buy from her is, if I understand correctly, a limited edition of some kind. Janet is pleased. Art from France. To bring home and put on our very own walls.

A year or so later we will be sitting in the living room with friends, talking about art and France. We will point to the work on our very own wall above the fireplace whose inflections match the brick so well, and one of our friends will say it's beautiful, and admire that we choose to make such a bold statement of gynolegiance in our living room, and I will be like, *What?*, and Janet will be like, *Well, duh!*, and I will say, *Do the boys know?* and Janet will say, *Of course not, they're kids. But what did YOU think it was a picture of, all this time?* And I will shrug sheepishly and say I thought it was an abstract, and Janet and our friends will have a good laugh at my inability to see what is right before my eyes.

But for now, the yoni rendering is paid for and rolled up in a cardboard tube for safekeeping. The others are gathered at a small sign affixed to the yellowish stone wall of the court-yard.

"Castle tour at two-thirty," Peter announces as we arrive, "I am all over that shit."

"No thanks," I say, "yesterday we . . . "

Peter whips out a brochure. "The Chateau d'Ansouis," he reads, overcalling my objections, "was built as a hilltop forti-fication sometime before the year 961. It has evolved over the centuries to its . . . "

"The castle at Les Beaux took us . . . "

"Wait," Peter says, waving a hand aloft, "you're going to love this part. 'Evolved to its current form of fabulous state house, but retains some of the walls and watchtowers . . . '"

"What time, again?" Janet asks.

"Two-thirty," Peter says.

"So we've got a couple of hours."

"Roger that."

"Then let's do it," she says. "Sounds great."

Peter slaps the brochure across his hand. "All *right!*"

Janet nods. "I just had to make sure we weren't going to do that thing again."

"What thing?" I ask.

"That thing we do where we drive somewhere or tour something and then suddenly it's three o'clock and we're starving . . . "

"Oh," I say. "You mean that hour when every single res-taurant is closed."

"Yes, that."

"Aix, yesterday," Peter says. "Nothing but falafel."

"Les Baux, yesterday," says Janet. "Tea and ice cream."

"But we *loved* the ice cream in Les Baux," I say.

"You loved it," Janet says. "And it was fine with me too, after I saw that they weren't serving lunch any more."

Peter shrugs. "Beats falafel."

"I would have killed for falafel," says Janet.

I take her arm. "Why didn't you say so?"

Janet pats my hand. "There was no falafel," she says. "That's the point. There was only ice cream."

"The point," Peter interjects, "is that it's going to happen again today if we don't find a place to eat soon."

The rest of our merry band, who had contracted closely around us upon our arrival, had drifted off in different directions as the conversation progressed. But it seems their thoughts were running along the same lines, for they have reconverged across the square where a sign points to something called *Les Moissines,* and are waving to us.

The restaurant has an intimate outdoor courtyard, its outer wall covered thickly with vines, and there is a small window—we call it the keyhole—that frames a generous view of the plains and farms below. I am sitting with my back to the vines, and emanating from them is a sound like an electric motor. But it is not an electric motor, it is a million bees that we do not see but we hear.

Peter, sitting to my left, looks up from the brochure. "It says here that the current mayor is from the same family that has held the mayor's office since 1170."

"Aren't you guys nervous?" Dana asks.

She means about the bees, and she's addressing our side of the table, where our backs are eighteen inches from ivy.

Peter and Janet say no. "It's strange," I say. "I can't imagine another situation where I'd be okay with parking my butt so close to so many bees, especially with food coming. Think about it: back home, a half dozen bees can take out a whole picnic."

"Maybe this buzzing is at a different frequency," Peter speculates, "one that we understand in our animal brain is not aggressive."

Natalie and Janet attempt to imitate the buzz, and this reminds Finn of the space ship sound effects in a famous early science fiction movie, which he proceeds to describe in detail. "And I swear, the space ship, it looked just like this." He picks up a plastic Perrier bottle, and moves it sideways through the air above his plate, managing to capture the particular wobble of early sci-fi effects, and in the meantime he's buzzing loudly. "RRRRR. RRRRRRRRRRRRRR RRRRRRRRRRRRR," he buzzes. "And when the thing lands, it looks just like this." He drops the bottle and it bounces on his place mat. "Swear to God, man. RRRRRRRRR." He drops it again. "Just like that. And you know what they used to make the noise?" He looks around and finishes triumphantly. "A Norelco electric razor. I am not making this up."

Finn keeps buzzing and dropping the bottle over and over again, saying, "I kid you not" and "just like this," and our laughter goes up a notch when we catch sight of our waiter, a sharp-featured handsome guy in his twenties. He is posing, pen poised above the tiny tablet he holds in front of him. Observing Finn, he raises an eyebrow theatrically to the rest of us. He doesn't speak English, and there is little French among the six of us, but he is indulgent of our fumbling questions, a willing straight man to our ongoing hilarity, the French waiter in a fifties film.

Dana is as careful and precise with her food as she is with her language. She spots the word for corn, *mais*, and in various ways tries to ask the waiter if she is reading this right, "Chicken salad with corn?" And the waiter is cheeky, flirty, giving her back his few bits of English. *Jess, Corn. Jess, weeth cheeken. Why not?* Then Dana wants to know if it is made with mayonnaise, and the pretty boy mugs and rolls his eyes for the rest of us.

Dana may have provided the warm-up act, but Finn is the main feature, of course. Swooping his hair back, he careens from subject to subject with mad enthusiasm. Finn knows an awful lot about a huge number of arcane things. In fact, before day's end I will begin to believe that he is a certifiable genius, if they can claim to certify such things anymore. If they can't, then my nomination is as good as anyone's.

It seems that each time the waiter comes back to our table he catches a Prime Finn Moment, so that the boy gets another chance to play along with eye-rolling, head shaking, or shoulder shrugging. He does it all with great verve—a real ham, this kid—and we banter across languages through the whole meal. The other tables sit empty, looking almost like props. It's as if the restaurant and the waiter materialized out of rock and flower for our benefit alone. The day had started rainy, but the sun comes out while we sit there, and the deep blue sky is punctuated by giant brilliantly white clouds shaped like castles and trebuchet. Through the keyhole, the clouds look even more dramatic, ghost frigates in full sail, casting slow-roaming shadows over the green plain. At different times one of us will go to the hole in the wall, and shout back, "Oooh, you should see it *now*."

After lunch, we are ready to head back to the castle. I pay the bill, of course, the Legend of Deep Pockets having been established at San Remy. I wander around outside, waiting for Janet. When she comes out she is flushed and smiling. "The bathroom is beautiful," she says. "It's like a stone cave done up by Pottery Barn."

"Cool," I say. But her face betrays more than nice fixtures. "And what else?"

"Well, when I came out of the bathroom, our waiter was standing there. It seemed like he'd been waiting. And he looked at me and said, 'You are very charming.'" She imitates his accent, laughing.

"And then what?"

"Nothing. He just sort of stood there, looking shy."

"That guy? *Shy?*"

"Well, what do you expect? Laurent doesn't speak English."

"Laurent!"

"He said his name was Laurent."

"What else did he say?"

"Nothing. That was it." She laughs, and starts toward the castle. "Come on, everybody else is already up there."

"You slew the waiter!" I chant. And who can blame him— Janet *is* charming, and she looks especially great today. "And what did you say?"

"I didn't say anything! I couldn't even remember '*merci*.' I just smiled and stood there for a second, and walked on. I'm sure he thinks I'm a dork."

"I doubt that's what he thinks." I take her arm as we head toward the castle, proud and happy. "Did you have any clue this was coming?"

"Some significant eye contact during the meal. But I thought I was just imagining it. Or else that he does that to all the women."

I stop, and turn to her. "Janet, listen. If you want to pass on the castle tour, we can just hang out. I don't have to see another . . . "

"No, it'll be fine."

"Really?"

"Really," she says. "You just go on the tour. And can you take this?" She hands me the cardboard tube with the art-work. "It would be tricky on the motorcycle."

"Motorcycle?"

"We're just going down to Laurent's place. Back in a couple of hours. And if we're not, well, I'm sure he can find the villa . . . " She shrugs nonchalantly, and can't suppress her laughter any longer. "I had you!"

"Naw."

"I did! Admit it." She takes my arm and marches me toward the castle.

"Well, maybe a little."

At the door, Peter hands us two tickets. I turn to Janet. "You want to do this?"

"Sure," she says, snatching a ticket from my hand.

I want her to be with me. I want her like this, happy and pretty and teasing. I am afraid the castle will bring her down. So far, this day has been a gem. Wonderful weather, gorgeous town, almost no other tourists. The darling church with white bows on the pews, the strong woman painter, the flirtatious waiter—all of these have conspired to alter Janet's course, at least temporarily, away from the slough of despond.

On Melancholy

Janet is subject to melancholy. I prefer that word to "depression," as the latter indicates abnormality. "Depression" implies that the "normal" state is in some way elevated, relative to that which is lowered or depressed. Americans, with our unbounded sense of entitlement, have come to believe that the elevated state is universal and deserved. That any deviation must be a pathology, to be treated by the most expedient means. In dealing with others, such thinking has made us a litigious nation: if anything bad happens to me, it must be someone's fault, and someone should pay. In the inner life, melancholy used to be called a neurosis, and the treatment was talk, lots of talk. Since friends or relatives could not be expected to refrain from harmful interference, a professional class arose with scrupulous training in the fine art of not responding. This system proved too inefficient in the age of HMOs. Let the brilliance of biochemistry shine on the dark recesses of the soul and discover them not depressed, but merely imbalanced.

Melancholy, also, may be seen as an imbalance—an excess of black bile, in medieval parlance—but one that cannot be corrected by injection. Anecdote: Back when my first marriage was breaking up, I told my doctor I was strung out from stress, couldn't sleep, and asked him for sleeping pills. He said my symptoms indicated that I was depressed, and wrote me a scrip for Prozac. I took it for the required three weeks, and then it started to kick in, creating in me an odd sensation. I still felt the melancholy, but it was separate from me, as if on the other side of a big muffled wall. I pictured the melancholy as a big clumsy robot—*something* was clanking around over there. The noise was irritating, but it couldn't get to me. But in some odd way I felt sorry for it. So after a couple of weeks I quit, on Christmas day. I can see how the insulation is necessary for some folks, I said to myself, just not for me. I was fine until New Year's Eve. That's when the robot tore through the wall and ripped me into shreds. Only it wasn't a robot. The metaphor no longer applied. It was just me, miserable lonely me, standing there in front of a window in abject hopelessness, crying and crying. I could not stop crying. That window happened to be in Paris, Rue Theophile Gautier, my sister's apartment. My sister took care of me as best she could. And here I am again, melancholic on Le Grande Rue de Chapet, relying on the kindness of friends.

France, my refuge and my strength.

But my point is that the doctor should have given me the fucking sleeping pills I asked him for. My marriage was breaking up. Becca and I were together eight years. I could no longer sustain a life with her, but that did not mean I did not have a powerful love for her and a deep sympathy for her pain. The balance of my humors *should* have been off. *Not* to be affected would have been pathological. But regaining the balance is a slow process, and in the meantime, I submit, there's nothing wrong with treating the symptoms. Can you imagine an Old West scene where the hero takes a bullet and is lying there grimacing and Doc won't give him a belt of whiskey because it might contribute to alcoholism? When I came to him strung out and insomniac over my broken marriage, my doctor should have said, "Yeah, it's a painful ordeal. It will take a long time to get over it, and it's not surprising you can't sleep. Here's some tranks."

The ancients understood. For Buddhists, melancholy *is* life. Suppression of all desire is the answer. But then you run into the basic Buddhist paradox: the intention to suppress desire is itself a desire. Then you have to embrace paradox, which is why you need meditation, because paradox is not easily embraced. I spent five weeks in Japan trying to be Zen. Every once in a awhile I thought I had it. I thought some deeper understanding of the Right Path was taking shape for me. I would try to express it, saying something idiotic, like "You know, man, you really do have to suppress your desires," and just that fast, with a tiny plink like breaking glass, it would all come crashing silently down, and I would be left with nothing but the clichés of Buddhism in little fragments heaped around my feet. Again. That Zen acceptance thing is so close to being easy that it's damn near impossible. Paradox redux.

Buddhists and Christians agree that relief cannot be found in worldly riches or success. The original Slough of Despond shows up in the cartography of that early work of travel writing, *Pilgrim's Progress* (that fun guy, Bunyan, also put Vanity on the map, noted for its Fair, along with the lesser known but still delightful Town of Carnal Policy). Bunyan tells us that at one time the King made a sustained attempt to reclaim the Slough of Despond. The wetlands swallowed up twenty thousand cartloads of the best materials, and remained swampy as ever.

Janet and I will freely admit that we are more fortunate than most of the souls who have ever inhabited this vale of tears—wealthier in monetary terms, and in finding our human spiritual camaraderie as well. And yet, when one's legs are bemired in the slough, it is hard to take solace in all the clean pants back home in the closet.

Instead of thinking of the swamp as something we can avoid, we must negotiate it as best we can, and remember that without melancholy there can be no transcendence. Without the lonely drives in the mountains of Colorado, no sublime moment in Lausanne. In fact, there may be something in melancholy to embrace, as we are taught by the master, Aristotle. The *Poetics* explains the mechanics of why we are drawn to the vicarious experience of tragedy on the stage, and not just to comedy. Tragedy ends in death, comedy in marriage. Look at Shakespeare. All those closing tableaux, the entire cast on stage, with some lately-restored benign figure of authority pronouncing the blessing upon the betrothed couple, their contretemps and misunderstandings resolved. That's comedy. But why is it that the ages bestow the highest wreathes upon the plays where the hero's corpse is what it all comes to? Why is dismal tragedy valued above life-affirming comedy?

Because tragedy is the plot of each of our lives. The hero dies in the end. Marriage is but a stay, a bubble, a blossom against the inevitable. But death takes all. Is it true then, Horatio, that we all come to this, a fire hose of formaldehyde pumped up the ass for some bizarre mummification ritual? E'en so, my lord.

But in the meantime, Aristotle tells us, we can strengthen ourselves against this cosmic certainty by the vicarious experience of the morbid emotions in manageable doses, on stage or screen or in print. Pity and fear. The former that it is unmerited, the latter that it could happen to us, coming together like a chemical reaction, producing that psycho-spiritual effect that the master calls *catharsis.*

But why do I linger so long over the workings of melancholy? Perhaps because it is the humor that rules Chapet, where my recollecting is done now, three years hence. And where unexpected emails from strangers have knocked me smack into the Slough of Despond. Letters to the Editor now feature that wonderful quick reply function.

We must return to enchanting Ansouis. Look, Janet is still there, beautiful in the sunshine of a stone courtyard, surrounded by flowers, having been recently complimented by a handsome young waiter. *You are very charming.* She does not decide to stay among the sunshine and flowers, but follows me into the castle, where I am praying that it is not all drafty stone corridors and dungeons that will drag her mood downward.

If prayers were never answered, the practice would have died out. For this castle, which looks so cold and fortified from the outside, is, on the inside, the mayor's home, filled to the bursting with furniture and carpets and tapestries and statuary and paintings. There are a dozen of us taking the tour, and so the tour guide in black, who looks disconcertingly like a nun out of habit with bright red lipstick, whispers first in French, and then in English in each room. And meanwhile there is Finn, throwing up his arms and whispering ecstatically at everything in sight. "My God!" he says, pointing to a bust, "that's a Houdon! You know, Houdon, he's the guy who did those statues of Washington and Jefferson! In fact, when Washington got tired of having to spend all his time sitting for portraits, Houdon was the guy who did a plaster cast of Washington's face, so then the portrait guys could just paint from that!" Finn is nearly delirious, and a profane prayer explodes from him at every new sight. "My God!" he keeps saying. "Do you see the work in that tapestry?" His enthusiasm is contagious, and we are all smiling and so is the tour guide, when she comes to understand that Finn really does know about this stuff and is not just some noisy American tourist.

Only a part of the chateau is on the tour. Now and then the guide points to a door we are not allowed to open, and this pleases Janet. She whispers over her shoulder to me, "I would hate it to be traipsing through this guy's whole house. Imagine if someone did that to us?"

"And here," I say, *sotto voce*, "is where Nina scraped all the paint off next to the front door sometime in the last decade of the twentieth century. And over here . . . "

"Shush."

"My God!" says Finn, clapping his hands to his head, "can you believe that?"

The tour ends appropriately, with a room that is part of the tour but also a regular part of the house. It is the massive, modern, ancient, picturesque, practical kitchen, featuring the finest culinary equipment from the medieval to the present day. Something about the combination of art and utility captivates Janet. She edges to the front. She asks questions of the tour guide. And finally someone asks about the mayor. Is he in town? Is he here now?

He is. And he has a very important duty today, and when we step outside, we will see what she means. Thank you for joining us on the Chateau Tour.

We hurry outside and find we are now on a wide garden above the central courtyard. We look over the parapet and see that a crowd has gathered. Well-dressed people mill about, talking and laughing and slowly drifting into the church. Cars arrive, and women in flowing white emerge, along with a gorgeous flower girl in a wide brimmed hat to match the bride and bridesmaids. Gallants in tuxedos await them, and they all wave up to us gaily at our perch along the parapet and we wave back gaily and the man emerges from the church with a large red sash across his breast to welcome them, and this must be the mayor and this must be his important duty and Finn is clasping his hands to his head saying, "My God! Can you believe this?" and Natalie is snapping off rolls of film and Janet and I are holding hands, giving squeezes of delight back and forth. Tears of sweet cathartic comedy swell my eyes and a sweet cathartic burning tightens my throat as the marriage preliminaries unfold in the courtyard before us. If joy is fleeting and tragedy final, how much sweeter the occasional comic triumph, especially when it blossoms unexpected on a warm and perfect day, scattering the minions of melancholy before it, and culminating, in fine Elizabethan fashion, with the joy and pomp of marriage witnessed from a sunshiny balcony?

14 Les Remparts: $14.70

Les Remparts

BAR - HÔTEL - RESTAURANT
Cuisine Provençale - Terrasse Panoramique
84210 VENASQUE
Tél. 04 90 66 02 79 - Fax 04 90 66 61 67

We have been speaking of pilgrimage and tourism. Transcendence and melancholy. Exile and expiation. My first marriage took place in a cold stone cathedral. My first wife needed an emergency root canal on our honeymoon night. My first marriage lasted eight years officially, four years functionally, and in my inmost heart, I would rather not say. My second marriage took place in a sunny garden by a pond, with dragonflies everywhere. My second wife was whisked off to St. Croix for a surprise honeymoon where she wore tiny island dresses every day and we made mad love every night. How long my second marriage will last, I do not know. In my heart, it is forever. Or, to be more precise, until death do us part.

And yet I am apart from her, and not dead. While Baghdad burns, I am in Chapet, trying to resurrect from restaurant receipts a true account of certain days in Provence, and find my boat beaten by headwinds into the rocky shoals of disquisitions on melancholy. Erica and George have taken off to Heidelberg, leaving my sole contacts with countrymen (and women) to come in email replies to my letter in the *Inquirer*.

> Liberal Naiveté! "Politics is politics, but friendship is friendship" utter nonsense! Friends support each other, just like family. The deciding factor that you missed is the Almighty American Dollar that the French and the rest of the world want. Stop the Yankee Dollars and you'll see how fast they'll change sides. I don't know where your head is but it's time to get a moral perspective!
>
> D.J.M.

Wait! There's more where this came from. Emails from enlightened American newspaper readers!

> Has it occurred to you that this friendly (perhaps pandering!) reception you received in France was BECAUSE we finally stood up to their nonsense and that— stubborn as they tend to be—they are taking notice and (perhaps) trying to respond? Quite frankly, I see this as a good thing. A dose of reality that they are letting penetrate their (oftentimes) hard heads! France is weak power on the world scene—and they resent the U.S. for its strength. This is not complicated. This is what we are seeing to some degree from Canada, as well. We don't tend to put it in their faces—but a good look at what they (France) were doing politically in this war situation—at the expense of a lot of lives, both Iraqi and American, and what they've done

in recent history, well—it's ridiculous. I traveled in France some years ago—out of college when I was completely enamored with the very idea of their great culture—and all the romance that goes along with French culture (art, music, architecture, etc.), but I was horrified by the people's blind arrogance and pseudo-sophisitication. I thought they were obnoxious. I denied it for a long time—even to myself. I actually couldn't believe how bad it was. I thought the country people would be less so when we traveled in the wine country—staying in out-of-the way places, but no such luck. The French have been obnoxious—both politically and personally—for years. Chirac is slippery—and the people put the government in place. Our taking a stand against French hypocrisy is long, long overdue.

Best regards!
Katie W

And my favorite:

Take a bath!

Sally

I feel dirtied by reading my email. So thank you, Sally, I will. My cleansing rite will be to describe the hallowed ground of Venasque. The word itself is like a whispered secret or a sip of young wine, opening on a quiet note leading to a small epiphany —ah!—with a finish so light and quick you aren't sure it was there at all. To explain Venasque will require a further detour back in time, eight years back instead of only three. Bear with me.

Janet and I took a trip to Europe before we were married. It began like the trip these pages relate, at a car rental counter in Charles de Gaulle Airport. Only instead of an electric blue Fiat Punto, that time it was a burgundy Renault Clio. It was April, chilly. Neither of us had ever been to southern France. Through a guide book, we had reserved a room at the Inn of the Blue Shutters in a town called Venasque that we had never heard of. It was nearby to Gordes and Rousillon, towns equally unknown to us, but apparently more famous on the Provence tourist trail. We left the *Autoroute du Soleil* at Orange, where the road through town curved around our first castle so tightly we could almost touch it. We drove on to Carpentras, whose gridlike center suggested its Roman origins. We found what we thought must be the right road, though it seemed impossibly narrow, and cruised down a lovely valley of vineyards, looking for Venasque.

"Yes, and you found it and it was beautiful?" asks Natalie. "What happened next?"

Since Natalie and Peter also want to hear the story, I might as well let the narrative do double duty as we drive toward Venasque from the other direction five years later in the Fiat Punto. According to our every-other-day plan, this was supposed to be a day when Janet and I went somewhere alone. But our last private getaway, to Les Baux, hadn't gone all that well, and then yesterday's trip to Ansouis had been so nearly sublime that we decided to break the pattern. And we had jabbered so much about Venasque, Gordes, and Rousillon. Venasque, Gordes, and Rousillon. Perfection. What was I supposed to do when Natalie came into the kitchen this morning and said, "Oh, you're going to Venasque, Gordes, and Rousillon! Can we go?"

Well, one thing I could have done would be to explain that we were sorry, but this visit had intimate personal meaning for us. Actually, I did say that. Yeah, I remember now. I said that to Natalie. But then what happened was, Natalie went over to Peter on the couch, talked with him, and then came back and said that, well, not to be copy-cats, but they had been planning to go to those towns too, since we'd talked about them so much. Peter only has another day, and she had wanted to visit Rousillon—that's the one that's all ochre and rose colored, right?—she wanted to hit that place on a day with good light, which it looked like today was going to be. So they would just take their own car, and maybe they'd see us in one of those towns or maybe we could have lunch together, or if not, that was fine with them.

And I said, "Okay, lunch maybe."

And Janet said, "No, this is ridiculous. We should all just go together."

"Really?" I said.

"Really?" Natalie said.

Peter, from the couch, contributed, "Hey, whatever, dudes."

"They understand," I said quickly to Janet. "Venasque is our song. It's okay. We can just drive separately, and maybe . . ."

"No," said Janet. "It's not going to be the same. That was special, seeing it for the first time. Now it will be fun with you two seeing it for the first time."

And so, in the car, on the way, Natalie keeps prompting us to tell the story of our magical first trip to Venasque. "What happened next?"

"It was getting towards dusk," I say, "and we weren't sure we were on the right road. And just when we thought we may be lost, we looked up, and saw, way up above us on this mountainside . . . "

"Blue shutters!" Natalie exclaims.

"Remember, honey?" I look across at Janet. "We both saw it at the same time and said it just like that."

"Yes," says Janet, "we did."

Natalie says, "I can't wait to see the blue shutters above the valley."

"Um, we're not going to see them," I say.

"We're not? Why not?"

Peter says, "Because we're coming from a different direction?" Peter's no slouch in the cartography department. "In fact, we'll be reversing the order you guys did, right?"

"Roger that," I say. "Rousillon, Gordes, *then* Venasque."

"Rousillon," Natalie says rapturously.

Venasque, the first time *was* special. After we spotted the blue shutters, we crossed through the valley of vineyards and I guided the burgundy Clio up the steeps of a long switchback. Like Les Baux, Venasque perches on a slanted plateau—a smaller, narrower one. At the lower end of the town, a small stone church. After that, the town had, it seemed, just four roads, in the shape of a cross. At the intersection was a fountain—*Place de la Fountain*—with barely enough room for the car to squeeze by. At both ends of the two short streets that formed the arms of the cross, the hillside dropped away. At the end of one of those streets was the Inn of the Blue Shutters. April, too early for crowds. It was hard to believe there ever were crowds here. A single tiny parking lot, down by the church, had places for six or eight cars. I remember how my heart dropped when I figured out that the sign warned people to lock their cars. It seemed impossible theft could occur here. The town seemed sacred, reverent, perfect. We felt like we should whisper while we discovered its few streets.

A single restaurant looked out on the main square, *Restaurant de la Fountain.* The proprietor of our inn asked us if we wanted reservations. Yes, we said, and Janet asked if it was really so busy that we needed them. The proprietor, an artsy-looking woman in a bandana, was amused. It was the other way, she responded. If there is nobody to come to eat, they will not bother to open. We only saw one other family of tourists, both at the inn and at the restaurant. They were Dutch. A well-scrubbed couple and a darling boy of four or five. Every time we saw them we exchanged furtive grins, sharing the greedy knowledge that, for this night anyway, we had this jewel all to ourselves.

Chapet, where I sit now, recalling all this, sits on a hillside. As I have mentioned, my view looks out over a green valley, albeit with much more habitation than the valley below Venasque. The jumble of horizontal and vertical rectangles— the low-cost housing of Les Mureaux—squats in the near distance, along with one of those water towers in the shape of a golf tee. Like Venasque, Chapet is a one-street town, and it too has just one restaurant. Although the hill is much lower, there is here, too, a small steep switch-back where the road enters town, and the first building in town, an old stone villa, has shutters of bright Provençal blue. The coincidence is both painful and comforting. What I haven't yet mentioned about Venasque, and did not mention in any descriptions to Natalie or Peter, is that the reverent isolation of the town somehow spurred us to fits of glorious, wild, carnival sex. Riotous sex, dangerous sex. Wonderful exhausting sex. I am not the kind of writer who can describe such things with cheery detachment. I will just say that we did something that day that in our private lexicon ever since, and seldom repeated, has been called "a Venasque." Now, when I walk back from Les Mureaux, the blue shutters of Chapet that I can see from afar across the fields seem to mock me. During the war, locals tell me, this Chapet house with the blue shutters was chosen as the headquarters of the Gestapo.

And so, with Natalie and Peter in the back seat of the Punto, we arrive at Rousillon. With its narrow steep streets, window boxes teeming with flowers, and all those gorgeous shades of rust and red, it lives up to its posters, calendars, and postcards. Janet and I are good hosts, showing Nat and Peter the places we remember. Nothing has changed. A sculptor is still in the same studio we remember working in the same sensuously curving stone. One piece, in black, a couple embracing, attracts our attention. We return to see it twice. We have crepes at an outdoor restaurant. We climb to the overlook above town where we can see across the valley to Gordes on the far ridge. We laugh and joke a lot. Good fun. Janet seems fine, but I am wondering if she feels the same small ache in her heart that I feel. You can only see Rousillon for the first time once. Natalie and Peter seem genuinely enchanted by the place, and that makes Janet and me happy, but it also serves to emphasize that we are visiting the archeological site of a more enchanted Janet and Jon.

Gordes is the most magnificent of the three towns. Monochrome gray rather than multi-colored, it perches precariously on its outcropping of the Luberon range. Somewhere I read that Gordes is the most visited of all the villages of Provence, and it's easy to understand why, but also easy to see the results. The souvenir shops jump gaudily to the foreground with postcard stands and t-shirt racks spilling out into the main square, competing madly with each other, less discreet than those of Rousillon. We wander around and lose track of each other in Gordes. Janet is, I think, still looking for something to buy for the boys. I follow a steep street downward that eventually becomes a stairway, and dead ends at a gate with a nice view of the valley. I sit on a bench, trying to pick out Rousillon across the way, and remembering when Janet and I were here, in Gordes, the first time. It was the morning after Venasque, we were sore and exhausted, and by turns shy, shocked, and very pleased with ourselves. Our proprietor took one look at us, pointed up the valley and said we must see God. At least that's what we thought she said. "Go to God," she said, in her heavy French accent. "You must visit God." And it did seem like we were going to God, as the Luberon ridge was shrouded in fog, and we crossed over the ridge to find Gordes seeming to hover in gray space. The town was cold and mysterious. The yawning vendors were just putting out their wares and the first tour buses of the day had yet to arrive. But we could tell by the size of the parking lots that even this early in the season the buses came in force. We didn't linger long, and went on to Rousillon, where the sun came out and the colors were warm and the enchantment continued.

A funny thing happens in Gordes this time around. All of the sudden, a freak wind hits the town, and hits it hard. I am just coming out of a little store where I have been contemplating, once again, buying some of that expensive local olive oil. I am almost knocked back into the store. Umbrellas collapse at the restaurants, and waiters rush to close others. The roar of wind is punctuated by gunshot-loud bangs as white chairs get folded by the wind and hit the pavement hard. Racks topple, postcards scatter. Paper cups and souvenir bags shoot across the plaza. The dark sky churns and the wind blows cold. I'm expecting the cloudburst any minute, but no rain comes. Ten minutes of this, shocking in its ferocity, and then, in the space of a minute, the wind dies, leaving a cold grayness in its wake, and I'm wishing I'd brought a sweater.

People emerge, looking a little shell-shocked, and slowly the square fills again with people. I look around for Janet, for Natalie and Peter. I cross and re-cross the plaza, and go down a couple of the main streets, and still, no one. I am annoyed. Finally I see Janet through a store window. I go in and say, a bit impatiently, "Where have you been?"

"Here," she snaps, "trying on clothes. Where should I be?"

"Did you see that wind?"

"No, what wind was that?"

"Nice. Where were you?"

"I was here. As I said. Trying . . . on . . . clothes." She un-crumples something blue and returns it to a hanger. "I was going to ask you if you like this, but never mind. Apparently we don't have time." She marches out of the store.

I trail her saying, "I didn't know where the hell you were, that's all. Go back and put on the dress."

"I said never mind," she spits over her shoulder. "You're in some kind of goddamn hurry all of the sudden, so let's go. Where are Peter and Natalie?"

"I thought they were with you."

"Well they're not, are they? I don't suppose *you* found anything for the boys."

"I was looking at olive oil."

"Great. The boys love olive oil."

"Just cool it, okay."

"You cool it."

As we stand there glaring at each other Peter wanders up, rubbing his eyes. "Did you see that wind?"

"What wind?" we say in chorus.

"I was over by the parking lot, and it blew all this sand up. God damn, it's still in my eyes. It really hurts. I've got to find somewhere to rinse my eyes or something." Peter rubs at his eyes and says, "Ouch, goddamn."

"Where's Natalie?" I ask him.

"I don't know, I can't even see. Do any of these shops sell Visine?"

He goes to look, and Janet and I growl at each other for awhile, and then focus our collective irritation on Natalie, because we've all been standing around here for a long time and she should at least check in with us instead of getting lost in her little photography raptures. When she finally wanders into the square, she looks as if she can barely hold up her camera.

"Hi guys," she says wanly. "I kind of got lost."

As Peter joins us, Natalie says, "I don't feel so well."

We slump towards the car, and the melancholy stabs me like a knife. The feeling is accompanied by a simmering anger at Janet, which is mainly because I feel her simmering anger at me, and it seems so wholly unjustified. We pile into the car without a word. The steep road twists down the back side of ridge into the narrow hidden valley that holds the stately Abbey de Sénanque, and everyone is telling me how to drive. Peter wants to stop at the abbey and so we do. It's almost five and so the abbey is closing, which disappoints me and Peter. The women are relieved. There's a large bookstore with a lot of books in English on medieval cartography and theology. I read dust jackets, trying to decide which one to buy, uncertain about the prospect of lugging a thick hardback around. One that I'll probably never read. One that I'm just buying out of some pretentious impulse. Finally I give up and wander out to the parking lot, feeling sad and empty, and meet the three of them waiting by the car. Janet is furious and demands to know what I've been doing and why I kept everyone so long and Natalie isn't feeling well—did I even consider that?

"Why didn't someone just come get me?"

"They wouldn't let us back in." Janet says it through gritted teeth.

The car is silent on the ride from the abbey to Venasque, and as we get closer Peter looks at the map and says he thinks it would be faster just to go on towards Carpentras and around that way to head back home.

"Maybe we should just bypass Venasque," I say.

"Maybe we should," says Janet.

"No," says Natalie. "You guys have to go to Venasque. I'm okay." She sounds as if she can barely get the words out.

As predicted, we do not enter across the flat valley by the way of the blue shutters. Coming from the other way, we squeeze into the tiny town from above, and find it as blessedly deserted as it was when Janet and I visited it years earlier. The Place de la Fountain has room for one car, maybe, and I stop there.

"You can't park here," Janet starts.

I am about to respond but Natalie interrupts.

"Look," she says, with an invalid's weak excitement. "Blue shutters."

The arched entranceway arrests me, sends me reeling into the past, and I give Janet a small smile, which she returns.

"Do they have a restaurant?" Peter asks, adding, "Natalie has a really bad headache."

"No," I say. "At least they didn't before."

"What's that?" Janet asks, pointing to a small sign saying "bar + restaurant" next to a steep path. We hike up there and find Les Remparts, and hear a click of pool balls as we enter. We pass through a dining room of empty tables, and into a bar that looks American. On the right side is the bar with its stools, beer taps, and jumble of bottles. The back side of the room has a flashing juke box, and the left wall, all glass, opens onto yet another balcony with yet another breathtaking view over yet another green and forested valley. It's chilly outside, so we stay in and endure the too-loud bobby sox music, the crack of pool balls, and laughter of the players. We all order coffee, and the waitress, an inattentive girl in a short skirt, is in no hurry to bring it. She idles on a bar stool, facing out, watching the pool game. We sit there, almost too enervated to make bitchy comments to each other. Peter, still complaining about his eyes, goes off in search of a lavatory.

The grip of melancholy rises inside me. I have been trying to fight it but it feels inexorable, like muscular arms are climbing hand over hand up my spine, one vertebrae at a time. Soon they will reach my head, and then one arm will put me in a headlock while the other fist punches me in the brain. I sit sideways in my chair with my back against the wall and indulge in crude fantasies about the waitress, spitefully enjoying her indifference. Neither Janet's purse nor Natalie's camera bags yield up any pills, and Natalie is looking worse all the time, and somehow I don't care. Venasque has been ripped from me, and I am angry. And the anger includes Janet for unspecified reasons too blurry to track down. The way she yelled at me in the parking lot of the abbey will do.

When the coffee finally comes, tiny cups, hardly worth waiting for, Janet haltingly explains to the waitress that Natalie is sick and asks if there is any place in town we might find medicine.

"One minute," says the girl, and returns promptly with a tall glass of water into which she drops two fizzing tablets. Some French Alka-Seltzer thing. "This will make you feel better."

"I don't know what it was," Natalie says, "after that wind hit, I felt suddenly, I don't know . . . "

"Mistral," says the waitress.

"Mistral!" I repeat, sitting up.

"Mistral," she agrees, matter of factly.

"It's the evil wind," I say. "It has some kind of mystical dark power. It messes with your psyche."

"So the mistral made me sick?" Natalie asks.

"Of course," says the waitress, shrugging her shoulders like it's a no-brainer. "This will make you better. Drink it all."

I am so grateful to her. In thirty seconds she's transformed from object of perverse anger to angel of mercy. "Janet," I say, "didn't you feel it?"

"Yes," she says in her regular, unspiteful voice. "Ever since we left Gordes, I've felt like slitting my wrists. Or else yours."

"And I've been pretty fucking annoyed with both of you," adds Peter.

The muscular hand reaching for my top vertebrae hesitates and withdraws. Hand over hand the thing retreats down my back.

"I read about it too," says Natalie. "It's why tourists don't come here too early in spring. More chance of mistral. Hey, I'm feeling a little better."

"We were all affected," I say. "We all got some kind of psychic poisoning. Just like it says in the book. I can't believe it never occurred to me."

"Well," says Janet, "the mistral didn't keep you twenty minutes in that abbey while we sat around in the parking lot. But I know what you mean. It feels like a weight has been lifted."

We leave Les Remparts in a much lighter mood than when we arrived. We walk by the fountain, linger in a couple of galleries, and converge on the small church. It is tiny and dark, but since the air outside has grown cold, the chill of the church feels more embracing than bracing. It is smaller, even, than the church at Ansouis, and there are no white bows, no incipient marriages, to brighten it up. Exhausted physically and psychically, I sit down. It feels good to rest. Peter leans over to whisper that the part of the baptistery here dates from the fifth century. The fifth century! I walk to where Janet stands, at a corner of the church, looking at a dark metal plaque with a dozen names inscribed. The local contribution to the charnel house of World War I. Tears streak Janet's face.

"All these boys came from this little town," she whispers. "Seth's age."

"Yes," I say.

"Do all the churches have memorials like this?"

"I think they do, yes."

"Why haven't I *noticed* before this? How could I be so blind?"

I take her hand and squeeze it. The strength of her self-recrimination is startling. To be with Janet is to learn never to underestimate the depths of her empathetic capacities, especially where suffering is concerned. I am still learning.

Now she sits down, takes a tissue from her purse, and dries her eyes. We sit there for a while, not saying anything, while the church, this church, performs that office that churches are built for, bringing comfort and strength to the weary-hearted.

As we walk back up the hill to the fountain and our car, the four of us are quiet but not unhappy. Natalie and Peter hold hands. Natalie is feeling much better. Janet and I hold hands. Venasque has been restored to us. Or rather, a new Venasque has been given to us without obliterating the earlier one. As we get in the car, I glance back at the sign for Les Remparts, and get a sudden powerful sense of déjà vu. I suddenly remember that we *did* go there the first time we were here. It was late in that orgiastic night, and we had prolonged our ecstasies with a trip out on the town, Janet wearing a short skirt and red lipstick. And, and . . . there was a sexy waitress that night too . . . it all comes back. I don't know if it was the same girl, but she became part of our fantasy after we drank our campari-sodas and could stand no longer not to be making love so we hurried back to place of the blue shutters.

Did that déjà vu occur then, getting into the car with Natalie and Peter, or now, as I sit here in Chapet, remembering? Either way, it is a sensual memory that makes me miss Janet all the more. I feel like Schliemann, setting out to discover Troy and finding nine Troys, one layered on top of another in the profound vastness of time. Which were Priam's towers, which cups did Hector and Paris toast, and Odysseus discard as unworthy loot? And what marriages and what slaughters attend the ashes of the unsung Troys? I struggle to uncover Venasque I and Venasque II, so distinct in some ways, layered like lasagna in others, and discover on top of them another layer here, my neo-Venasque, my archeological laboratory, my blue shuttered Chapet.

15 Avignon: $51.47

The problem is not that we are all going to Avignon. The problem is that I did not tell Janet that we are all going to Avignon.

"It's not like we can bow out," I say. "They're counting on us to drive people. It's been planned all week. Everyone goes to Avignon today."

"I know," Janet answers, rinsing her coffee cup and setting it in the drainer. "And that's fine. It's just that we'd made the every-other-day plan, and nobody told me . . . "

"It's not fair that Cecile has to schlep the students around every day."

"I *get* it, all right?"

As we move through the general hub-bub of the living room, I put my arm around Janet's shoulders as a coach might with a little leaguer. People are criss-crossing the room in all directions, gathering cameras and maps, talking about directions. "Come on," I whisper, giving a squeeze. "The Palace of the Popes! Don't you want to see that?"

"Sure," she says, in a tone of resignation.

"Are we talking about Popes or Anti-Popes in Avignon?"

"I don't know," she says.

"They must be Popes, right? Otherwise they would call it the Palace of the Anti-Popes."

"Actually, it's both." Nelson is beside us. "Gregory XI returns to Rome in 1377, but then you have the Great Schism, and after that you have Anti-Popes in Avignon."

"The Great Schism!" I squeeze her shoulders again.

"You'll hear all about it when we get there," Nelson says.

"When we get there?" I say.

"I've been asked," Nelson says, trying to sound beleaguered, "to give a talk on the history of the Avignon Papacy."

"Great!"

"I'll get my purse." Janet shrugs away from me and heads for the bedroom. I try to find out who needs a ride. Without Cecile to direct traffic, the process is chaotic. Finally, we end up with Dana and Finn in the Fiat, which is fine with me. Ever since Ansouis, I love hanging around with Finn. Provence has created—or allowed to blossom—an altogether different Finn than the one we see back at school. The practiced cynicism is gone, replaced by a boyish rhapsodic wonderment at everything that he sees, coupled with knowledge that is beyond encyclopedic. His expertise is not limited to art. He is well versed in history, architecture, cinema, popular culture, and, yes, cartography. He seems to know the make and model of every plane, train, and automobile ever made, and also does well with botany and geology. I learn and forget more on an hour's drive to Avignon than in eight years of graduate school. And with what enthusiasm. How many times do we hear Finn shout, "My God!" clasp his hands to his head and say something like, "That's Orgon! That must be the Notre Dame de Bueregard Chapel right there. You know there's a great museum here—antique cars, right? Knights of Templar were big here in . . . " All Janet and Dana and I can do is smile and shake our heads and hang on for the ride.

We park in the grass outside the city wall, walk through a portal, and find ourselves in a residential neighborhood, a good ways from the imposing citadel on the hill. After a long walk culminating in a lot of steps, we arrive at the vast courtyard in front of the Palace of the Popes. About half the group is already there, including Nelson, who is rocking back on his heels with his fingers interlaced in front of him, waiting to begin his lecture. Janet and I wander across the broad plaza to one of the restaurants that has outdoor tables. We sit down and order coffee.

We watch our straggling crowd gather and mill about. From where we are sitting it appears as distant, silent pantomime. After a few minutes, everyone stops moving and faces Nelson. Natalie points an accusing telephoto lens at us.

"Nelson speaks," I say.

"Go on," Janet says, "you want to hear about the history. I'll catch up."

"I'm fine," I say. "I haven't finished my coffee. I'll get a guide book."

"You don't have to demonstrate your loyalty. I'm not a delicate flower."

"I'm perfectly happy sitting here." But, in fact, as usual, she has sniffed me out. I do want to hear what Nelson has to say, and I am sitting here as a demonstration of loyalty. So when Janet talks idly about how ugly and forbidding the place looks with its hodge-podge of ramparts and towers, I am driven by some perverse bent to defend its stark façade on aesthetic grounds.

"Oh come on," she says. "You're just being stubborn."

If I weren't being stubborn, I would agree with her opinion. Very little about the place suggests holiness, or reverence, or even a palace. It looks like the biggest, most bad-ass medieval fortress we have ever seen. Tortures R Us. Makes Les Baux look like the Alhambra.

But as I look from the dark stones to my wife's dark hair and Mediterranean skin, it occurs to me that her reaction may go deeper than I first supposed. Janet's father was a second-generation Italian Catholic. But something happened—God knows what. At eighteen he angrily denounced the Church, declared himself a Baptist, and by the strength of his personality and conviction took the entire clan with him. The rituals and mysteries of Rome were replaced by a plain and strict Bible regimen. A couple of years ago Janet came across her old devotional notebooks from when she was twelve or thirteen, and was at first surprised and then angered by what she found there: page after page of her own handwriting asking God to show her how unworthy she was, reminding herself what a miserable wretch of a sinner she was, what a worm, a gnat, a maggot. While she has never forgiven the Baptists, she has been, I think, fairly successful in overcoming the anti-Papist strain with which she was injected at an early age.

"Well, it's not like I *admire* Catholicism," she says, when I tell her what I'm thinking. "There's that birth control thing, the stupid celibacy rule . . ." She stares at the palace and takes a deep breath. "But you're right. I find this place creepy and oppressive, and when I think it was built by *Popes*, it's like . . . " She shudders and shakes her head.

"Would you say," I ask her, "that this place epitomizes the human abrogation of The Almighty's sole franchise on being a vengeful and jealous God?"

"No. That's something you would say."

"I think it was Petrarch who called this place the filth of the universe."

"That's closer to what I would say."

We pay for the coffee and head across the square to join the others. Janet is quiet, a little tense. If people girded their loins these days, that's what Janet would be doing right now. When we get our tickets and head inside, we discover that the place is filled with installation art. Avignon is one of nine cities named to represent the cultural diversity of the European Union at the dawn of the third millennium. The others, since you ask, are Bergen, Bologna, Brussels, Krakow, Helsinki, Prague, Reykjavik, and Santiago de Compostela. The French national exhibit, installed here at the Papal Palace, is entitled "*La Beaute*" and it promises a retrospective of the concept of beauty in the twentieth century. No portraits or busts or homey artifacts such as filled the Chateau at Ansouis, no sir. All the original art that used to be here was burned or looted in the revolution (thank you, Nelson). What we get are wires and stones arranged like a big S on the floor. Continuous looping film of man being doused with water and disappearing, then burning and disappearing, to thunderous sound effects. Repeated slide projector images of a young girl. And in the main courtyard, a giant grotesque topiary by Jeff Koons. A cartoon or animal head of some kind.

Finn, for once, is speechless. He has nothing against contemporary art, he mumbles, but he would have liked to see these rooms without the distractions.

Janet is quiet as we wander past the exhibits, and her demeanor makes me uneasy, and increasingly chatty. It's as if I need to off-set her cool with my heat, as if I have find all of the works fascinating. After awhile, Janet asks me to stop trying to sell her on everything; it's getting quite annoying. She liked the burning and dousing; she loved the images of the girl. A lot of the rest is boring and pretentious, but she doesn't need me to explain surrealism or postmodernism to her, thank you. I apologize, acting a little wounded. But it seems palpable, the way this place weighs her down with its grim corridors and stark stairways. It makes me want to play court jester to her sad majesty.

One thing that irritates me is that there is, apparently, some part of the show that you only get to see if you have a different, higher-priced ticket, and the museum guards are very particular about admittance. From some hints I get, I think the other part of the show has erotic content. *La Beaute* indeed. Perhaps this is a way of allowing families to shield children from this content, which, since this is France, means it must be pretty lewd. Every time a guard shoos me away from a room I have flashbacks to being a kid getting caught with a *Playboy*. Which never actually happened to me. In my case it was even more pathetic. I was very young, maybe six years old, and we were on our first family vacation, to Colorado. The same one where we crossed Trail Ridge Road and stayed in that cabin called *Pal-Ca-Ni-Ta*. Anyway, this night we were at a Ramada Inn in Colorado Springs. I was staring at a rack of greeting cards. They were completely unintelligible to me. A woman said to me, "Nice little boys don't look at those cards." I was mortified. To this day I am terrified of risqué greeting cards.

So now, in the damned Palace of Popes, I have that same nosey woman appearing in the guise of museum guards, and may be in danger of being ruined for erotic art.

We make the whole tour, floor by endless floor. When we are finally dumped out the back side of the palace, we find ourselves exiting at the same time as Dana. We invite Dana to lunch with us.

As one leaves the vast area in front of the Palace of the Popes, there is a broad avenue with some ornate administrative buildings, including the city hall, along it. A number of restaurants have covered dining areas in the park at the center of the boulevard, complete with barkers at each entrance. Dana leads us up and down the restaurant row, and we are no help either, hung up in that existential crisis where the outcome of the decision makes very little difference at all, and yet one is unable to decide. It has been little more than a week since we boldly braved the Door Men of Amsterdam, and even enjoyed their come-ons. But it seems like ages ago that we had that lightheartedness, that sense of fun. I sigh and trail along behind the women, who finally let the most pushy of the pushers push us into the most unpromising restaurant. The sun has come out, and the heavy plastic translucent screen that separates this restaurant from its neighbors makes it almost unbearably stuffy.

The name of the eatery is not on the receipt. Nor can I recall it, and it doesn't matter. All those places were alike. The receipt does remind me that my *Salade Niçoise* was a better choice than the *Plat du Jour* which both Janet and Dana, still in the throes of acute indecision, end up with. The featured meal of the day turns out to be a flat and gristly piece of meat—which the waiter straight-facedly referred to as "steak"—and a pile of underdone fried potatoes.

I don't remember what we talked about over lunch, except that it was certainly about boys, Dana's and ours, and that it fueled Janet's growing desperation to find some gift to bring them, not just some gimmick or some trash that they will just throw away, and certainly not some dumb t-shirt, but something they will actually *use*.

The sometime travel writer pays for lunch, and Dana the Victorianist takes off to find the hotel where one of the Brownings stayed, in partial fulfillment of her research bargain with the college.

Janet and I are at the edge of a fairly large shopping area—not just the tourist kind, but the kind where real people go, with clothing stores and sporting goods stores and who knows what else mixed in with the tourist stores. Janet wants to go there to look for gifts for the boys. I'm thinking that if we dive into that maze it's the last we're going to see of anything historical for the day, so I ask her can we please just go see the bridge first.

"What bridge?"

"The famous one. It doesn't go all the way across, but like, half way."

"You want to see a bridge that goes half way across the river?"

"Please."

So she follows me to the Pont St.-Benezet, which is a longer walk than I represented it to be, not made any shorter by my attempts to sing.

"*Sur le pont, d'Avignon, lonely dancer, lonely dancer,*"

"It's not 'lonely dancer.'"

"What is it then?" I ask.

"I don't know, but it's in French, not English."

"So it *could be* 'lonely dancer.'"

"Please. You know you're wrong but you act innocent and argumentative."

"Are you saying," I ask, "that I'm being ingenuous?"

"No." With forced patience, "You are being *dis*ingenuous."

"I think 'ingenuous' is more accurate. In the sense or a sort of affected or studied pretense of innocence."

"That's what 'disingenuous' means!" Janet throws up her hands. "Why are you doing this?"

"I like 'ingenuous' because I think it's one of those words that can mean itself and its opposite, like 'sanction' or 'cleave.'"

"I'd like to cleave you."

"Or cleave *to* me?"

"If I had a cleaver, you'd know which one I mean."

"Good! That was excellent. Hey, I'm just trying to lighten up the mood here, and you seem all oppressed by . . . "

"Please."

I am startled by her tone. "What? What did I do?"

"Please. Just stop."

"I was just trying to . . . "

"I know, lighten the mood. What it feels like is peck, peck, peck. Like a bird. I can't take it right now."

"Sorry."

"And don't go into the pouty boy routine."

"Sorry."

You have to pay an admission fee to walk out on the bridge, and while I'd like to buy a book, I make do with the pamphlet that outlines the storied history of the bridge. It is hot on the bridge, and hard to see in the bright sun and watery reflections. We sit down out near the farthest reach, where the bridge stops bridging and bridges nothing. Another silence stretches between us, and again I am uncomfortable. All day long I've felt Janet's melancholy, and my reactions have just made it worse, toggling between unctuous goofiness and unadmitted petulance. I tell myself to calm down.

Janet muses, mostly to herself, "When they were little it was so easy. The plastic toy inside the Happy Meal made them so happy."

"I'm sure it did."

"I never worried if they were going to like it. I gave it to them and they were just delighted. They'd play with it for hours. You should have seen them."

I hesitate to say what is on my mind. I want to help. I want her to feel better. "This anxiety," I say kindly, "this worry over finding the right gift for the boys, it's getting a little obsessive, don't you think? I'm starting to be afraid that you're letting it get you down, and you're getting upset about things like 'ingenuous,' and that you're not enjoying Provence because you're so concerned about finding a good gift."

"Is that what you think?" she asks in a flat voice.

It's not that I'm oblivious, but I've come this far. Now I want to finish making my point. "Well, I think it's obvious, don't you? That the gift is standing in for a range of broader anxieties?"

"Broader anxieties?"

"Yes, of course. You must know what I mean."

"No, I don't. Please go on."

"You worry about the boys all the time. You're scared for them, that they have to make their own way in this screwed up world, and they're not ready for it. So what you do is, you take the blame on yourself. You think it's your fault they're not ready. If you had been a better mother, you would have given

them something that would make school easier for them, or
given them something to make them more motivated to do
well in school. If they mouth off, you feel guilty because you
failed to give them something that would make them better
persons. They love shoot-up video games because you didn't
give them more sensitivity. And now, when you're over here,
you miss them, but you are even more afraid for them, more
acutely aware of what they lack. So these vague and overwhelming feelings of guilt get channeled into a compulsion to
get them something for them. It takes over your life."

Her arms are crossed. She looks me in the eye. "Are you
finished?"

"Listen, honey," I say with a little laugh, "I'm not trying to
add to your guilt, I'm trying to lessen it. We'll get something
for the boys. It will be fine. They'll like it or they'll toss it in
the closet or whatever. They'll love you just the same either
way. In the ultimate scheme of things, it doesn't matter all
that much. But in worrying about it so much, you are ruin-
ing your time here. We should cherish this time together, and
you're risking blowing it."

I am, I confess, rather proud of my little lesson.

There is a long pause before she answers.

NARRATUS INTERRUPTUS REDUX

We will return to the scene with its almost too perfectly symbolic setting at the edge of a useless bridge, non-bridge, bridge
to nowhere.

It may have occurred to some readers to question my current whereabouts, and Janet's. To be annoyed, perhaps, with
these occasional detours into my present setting of Chapet
and its environs, my kindly hosts George and Erica, my melancholy about the darkness overhanging our world, and about
the absence of Janet at this moment from my life. And what
about the three year abandonment of the story? Probably it is
best to start there, for the history of the narrative is the key to
the mystery of the present moment.

You may recall that Part I of *Eating Europe* ends with a Note From the Author which proclaims the invention of a new genre, *Interactive Meta-Nonfiction,* which promises that reader input will shape the second half of the book. More receipts, restaurants, and wine are promised, along with some spin-off Visible Products. And finally, there is that single word—a hope, a cry, a promise: Redemption.

Time has come for an accounting. We've eaten in several restaurants and sipped the pink wine of Provence. For those of you keeping score at home, the requisite Visible Product included a newspaper travel piece, "French, with a German Accent" (*Philadelphia Inquirer,* 19 August, 2001); a scholarly paper read at an academic conference, "Old Colonials vs. New Economies: Blurring Borders in the Postmodern Postnation State Euro-Transitional Era" (Popular Culture Association Annual Convention. Philadelphia, PA. 13 April, 2001); and a Baden Lecture delivered to the dean and faculty of Ursinus College, announcing the birth of interactive meta-nonfiction, along with a description of its chief characteristics.

The Underground Publishing Program went forward. Although I did have a dedicated email address for responses, I did *not* put *Eating Europe* on the Web. That would be too easy and undiscriminating. The word *blog* had not yet been coined, but I saw it coming over the horizon. This is a publishing venture. I manufactured one hundred intentionally low-tech editions and gave them away. They look like this:

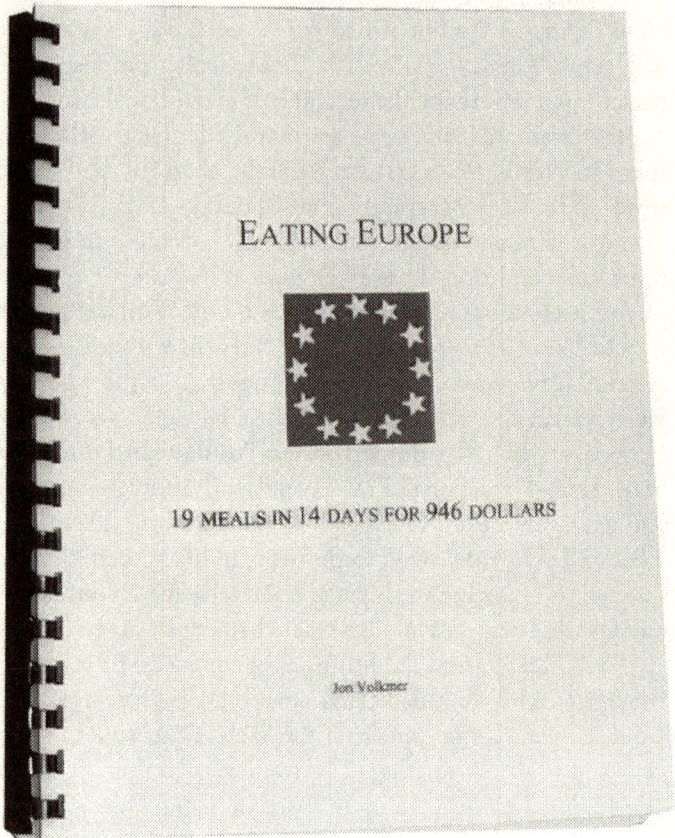

EATING EUROPE

19 MEALS IN 14 DAYS FOR 946 DOLLARS

Jon Volkmer

And in order to prove to the reader that I'm not making this up, the restaurant receipts are right there, embedded in the text.

1. GOLDEN TULIP BAR: $7.89

The oddity of Amsterdam is that we spent four days there and have only three receipts to show for it. The scarcity might be attributable to the overwhelming cultural and historical significance of this Great European Capital. The endless splendor of the Rijksmuseum, with all those Dutch Masters; the Van Gogh Museum; the terrible touching beauty of the Anne Frank house. These monuments are surely reason enough for awestruck tourists to lose their appetites. And for those times when one needs a shot of quick energy, there are coffee houses located on practically every street. These are not grab-and-go Starbucks-style stands, but cozy dens with upholstered chairs where service is languid and customers feel welcomed, even encouraged, to lounge back and speculate on the many euphonious words of the Dutch ... Hoogerbrugge, for instance. Odd that I never bothered to collect a receipt.

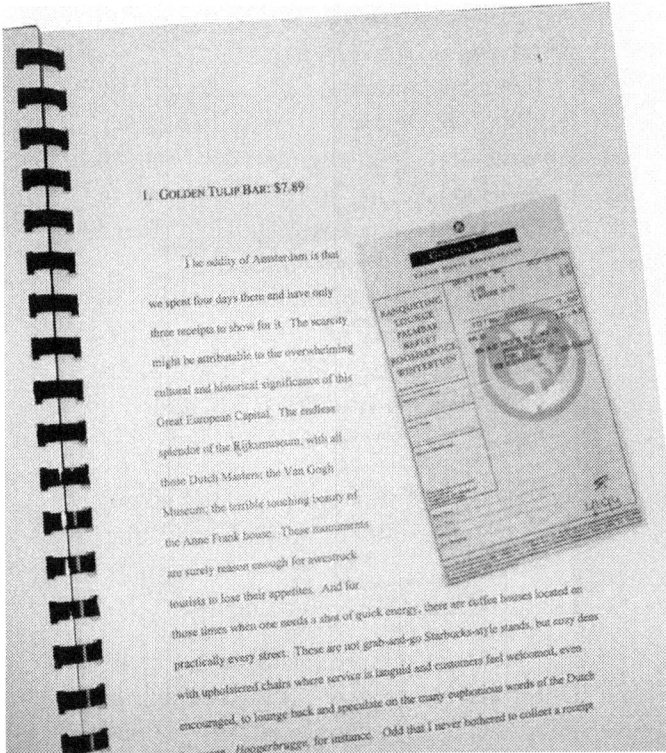

I sent about eighty of them to friends, colleagues, relatives, some writers I know. Most of the recipients were very good about following the instructions to send the thing on to someone else, and I hope that those people kept forwarding it. I have heard about copies sent to Hawaii, to Japan, to Russia. Plus—here's the guerilla publishing part—I took about a dozen copies and I smuggled them *into* large chain bookstores in the Philadelphia metro area. I put them in the travel narrative sections, right next to the *Best American Travel Writing 2000*, along with this note:

> Dear Reader:
>
> This book is Free! It is written by a real and authentic Travel Writer. (If you don't believe

me, go look at the also-ran section of *The Best American Travel Writing 2000*.)

If you love travel narrative, TAKE THIS BOOK. No alarms will sound when you leave the store. In taking this book, you will have an opportunity to become part of an Underground Interactive Meta-Nonfictional Alternative Publishing Experiment!

The second half of this book remains to be written: *You* may influence how that second half gets written. How? All will be explained when you READ THE BOOK!

Enjoy!

Jon Volkmer
Real and Authentic Travel Writer

Dear Underpaid Bookstore Employee:

Please do not toss this book in the trash. Only one hundred of them exist in the world. Someone will grab it soon and take it. It's free, so your Corporate Overseer is not losing any money on the deal. There's nothing slanderous or pornographic in the text that would cause anyone alarm. This *Underground Interactive Meta-Nonfictional Alternative Publishing Experiment* is a cool thing, and totally harmless. So, in the immortal words of John Lennon, "Let it be, Let it be, Let it be, Let it be."

Thank You,
JV

It has come to my attention Paul McCartney wrote "Let it Be." I resist the temptation to correct it here, in the interest of historical veracity. What happened to those bookstore infiltrators, you may wonder. And I may wonder too, because they all disappeared without a trace. Like spitting in the ocean. Pretty much the same thing that happens to most published books, or so I hear. Worse yet, something went wrong with the dedicated email address, EatEurope@flashmail.com, shortly after I placed these copies in the bookstores. So my public could not contact me. If you, present reader, happen to have one of these ninety-page prototypes, or have heard legend of one, may I humbly suggest you hold on to it as a rare and wonderful collector's item, or if you put it up for auction on eBay, not to accept a farthing less than $1,000 for the bidding to commence?

And now we come to the interactive portion of our postmodern travel narrative. The recipients of Part I were invited to contribute thoughts and suggestions, which I promised would influence the making of the second half of the book, using the flashmail address. The plan went awry when the damn thing became disabled somehow. But before it went kablooie, I received several insightful responses from readers. Here are some of them, rendered with one hundred percent accuracy:

> *Master: I am humble in your presence. I am the thought of mist, you are the ocean. I am the pant of a flea, you are the sky. I laughed and I learned. An enjoyable journey that left me wondering when the second installment would come. I thought it at least as entertaining as Peter Mayle with more bursts of laughter and a titillating bent (how I love that word!). Several of your experiences of course brought back similar events in my own travels. Obviously many fond recollections came back to me on considering the enormous marital aid.*

> —Dr. Richard Galeone
> Pediatric Dentist to Seth and Tristan

You know, now that I think about it, the only thing standing between Eating Europe *and, well, would "perfection" be too strong a word?? is more insight into the character of Janet. I mean, who is this person? How about if she had this friend—you know, a confidante—with whom she'd have after-the-trip conversations! These deeply perceptive, not to say frequently hilarious interchanges could be scattered throughout part II, further playing with the whole time continuum as we – uh, she and her friend – discussed the relative merits and drawbacks of, oh, being married to a writer who uses one as a foil.*

—Beth Johnson
Janet's Best Friend

The only suggestion I can make and it might even be defined as a reader complaint: finish the damn book.

—Shawn Witt,
Former Student

The anti-pomo lines were too throw-away, at least from my humble post-foundational and pro-Deleuzean perch. I wanted a better satire, that is, one that told me more about what postmodernism is and which aspects of it are truly ridiculous and why.

—Jane Bennett
Professor of Political Science

I disagree that Janet is "too perfect." She's acerbic, for one thing. And then there's that blood

*sugar thing, which isn't her fault, but why the hell doesn't the woman just carry some emergency pretzels or an orange in her canvas bag????
That's what I do.*

—Patricia Schroeder
Professor of English

Started reading your thing. Talk talk talk. These two ever have sex? Christ, Jon, you think people are interested in this shit? You need to get a clue what people want to read. Subscribe to Maxim.

—E. Scott Wingerter
College Roommate, 1975-6

Congratulations. You're accomplishing what every writer aspires to do in dialogue: you're doing Nick and Nora.

—Eric Kraft,
Novelist

So, I was wondering and searching for a unifying theme of "Eating Europe" and I wasn't sure I found one. There are a lot of genres being explored here. There's the travel narrative, the personal narrative, the wine advocation, the restaurant critique, the meta-non-fiction/fiction. The blending of genres can work, for me, as long as, for me again, that there's a direction I'm going with these people or at least where I'm being taken. What's at stake? That is the question that exists for all writing, and I wonder what's at stake here. This couple seems very well put together, very mature and they

*get along great, which is nice for them, but do
I just want to hear how wonderfully they get
along? Give me some red meat. Something I
can sink my teeth in. For my two cents, I felt
there was something else going on in the "Janet"
character. The stain on the white blouse and
the buying of another one, and especially the
angel running away. There was a deep and
mysterious sadness in the character that could
have been developed more.*

—D.G. Munro
Novelist

All these messages have been ingested, digested, are part of
the bone and red meat of me, their influence shot through
Part II like a jigger of single malt whisky loosed upon the
bloodstream.

Given the high rhetorical aspirations, startling original-
ity, and obvious literary merit of the work, one might wonder
whether any of these books made it into the hands of literary
agents. In the last dozen years, the writer known as Jon Volkmer has had preliminary dealings with seven literary agents
concerning various projects of his. It has not been pretty.
There are always those initial bright globes of promise—enthusiasm on their part, and wild hope on his—that burst like
soap bubbles, and have about the same life-span. Then there's
that period of unanswered emails and calls, and he begins to
feel like the person after the one night stand who didn't get
any *and* was given a fake number. He does not blame these
agents, who are all, he is sure, wonderful human beings and
very good at what they do. Something sad and mysterious
always happens. The Jon Volkmer that most folks encounter—the good professor, witty chum, loving husband, concerned citizen—all of them get locked in a closet somewhere,
and the guy in the sports jacket who shows up for the meeting
with the agent is his evil twin—a smarmy, oleaginous, self-

aggrandizing creep that exists in no other plane of earthly existence.

Through the good offices of a friend I delivered Part I of *Eating Europe* to a literary agent in New York. A sub-agent actually, but she has very good contacts with real agents, I am told.

> *Yes, I loved the characters, as you promised I would. You really are doing Nick and Nora, as Eric said—and what a compliment, coming from him! But the self-reflexive narration left me cold, and all that trickery and gamesmanship made me dislike just about everything about the book. Thanks for letting me see it!*
>
> —Helen
> A Sub-Agent

In the opening canto of the *Divine Comedy*, Dante seems close, very close, almost within hailing distance, of his destination and his goal. His life has gone off track, he tells us, and he is lost in a dark wood. He must relocate the path, and find his way up the Mount of Joy. It is just up the hill! Right there! He can see it! But then his way is blocked by the Lion, the Leopard and the She-Wolf. Virgil shows up and tells him they have to take the long way around. The way way long way, it turns out. The Mount of Joy is right there, but to get there he must pass through Inferno, Purgatorio, and many sub levels of Paradiso. It is the Divine Cartography, an objective correlative to the journey to salvation: Recognition of Sin, Expiation for Sin, Acceptance of Divine Grace.

Did you think I had overlooked the last item on my list: "Redemption"?

How little I understood, when I put down that word, how long and arduous the trail would be. I was like Dante, so close, it seemed, to concluding the book. The first half of the Trail of Nineteen Receipts had flown by, so easy to follow, so light and crunchy. At the end, true, there was a hint of trouble. A stain on a white blouse, a fleeing angel in Alsace. What of it? Into each life a little currant juice must fall.

I was not prepared for the journey I would have to undertake.

Taken in sum, I think my ten kindly interlocutors got it about right. It's not a bad piece of work, that Part I. Some funny moments, some nice insights. There is a wide variance in appreciation of the narrative gimmickry—all that stuff we've tossed into the meta-nonfiction basket. At points where the trickery seems to exist only for its own sake, becomes too cutesy or convoluted, readers turn away. At the heart of the work is the relationship between Jon and Janet—loving, witty, light and frothy. But ultimately unrealistic, sadly. I want Janet and Jon to *be* Nick and Nora Charles. I want all our adventures to be straight out of the *Thin Man* movies. I want to exchange witty barbs over martinis as we stroll down life's little lane, our life together providing courage and inspiration to all those who suffer and doubt. But it isn't that easy.

Just before the flashmail account stopped working, I found one other email there. Someone had sent me a partial transcript of an interview:

JL: With me today is someone who needs no introduction because we know her better than she knows herself— Janet, my creative nonfictional doppelganger, has eaten her way through Europe and straight into my heart. Like a cancer. She has sidekicked her way from Amdam to the Alsace—with me on her fictitious heels every step of the way. I've shared her sugar plunges, shoe obsessions, and shopping sprees. I've watched her pursue a fleeing angel down a cobbled street in a hard-to-pronounce town, which reminds me . . .

Janet: Did you say, "Like a cancer?"

JL: I get that the angel is a metaphor for whatever— happiness or self-esteem or a child-like sense of play or whatever, but is the point that like . . . the angel of whatever is leading you somewhere but you're so

unselfesteemy that you think it's running away from you?
Or is it more like the angel really is running away from
you because you're chasing it, which would be a kind of
Zen thing or maybe because . . .

Janet: I don't know.

JL: . . . Because you're a self-absorbed, culture-hating
shopping queen who wouldn't recognize an angel if it bit
you on the ass.

Janet: (muttering) You're the cancer.

JL: Oh get over it. I mean the good kind of cancer, okay?

Janet: What kind is that?

JL: More annoying than deadly.

Janet. Oh.

JL: Welcome Janet. Thank you for coming.

Janet: Thank you for making me.

JL: What does it feel like to be a creative nonfictional
character?

Janet: (Morphs into Nina Simone and sings a heart-breaking
rendition of "Don't Let Me Be Misunderstood.")

JL: And why do you think about shoes so much?

Janet: I don't.

JL: Right. And I suppose you're not obsessed with food
either.

Janet: I wouldn't say that I'm obsessed. I would say that I like
food.

JL: Are you kidding? You love food. And shopping.

Janet: I do not love shopping! That is a complete fabrication.
I hate shopping. I just like stuff.

JL: And you also hate castles and history and cartography
and anything remotely intellectual because . . . ?

Janet: (silence)

JL: Because . . . ?

Janet: (silence)

JL: Because those things are . . . what?

Janet: (sighs) Boring.

JL: Say again?

Janet: No.

JL: Now don't sulk. It's okay. Maybe you're one of those rare and
   fortunate people who don't need cultural cachet. Maybe you
   get to just be cute. Cute people are loveable no matter what
   they do. Look at Meg Ryan. I think Meg Ryan was adorable
   in that movie. The one where she co-starred with Kevin
   Kline's outrageous French accent, but if someone uncute
   played the role I might just find her character the kind of
   annoying that makes you want to . . .

Janet: Are you bitter?

JL: I'm asking the questions here.

Janet: Because you sound bitter.

I think we all know who sent that to me. The mysterious JL, who
at this moment is driving a car, or putting on a shoe, or opposing the war, in far suburban Philadelphia. When I try to bring
her alive on the page she becomes Janet, a signifier, displaced
and distorted from JL, the signified. In writing her, I create and
amplify the displacement and distortion that occurs in real life,
even as I strive for truth. The displacement has grown to be
ocean wide, literally, and the idea of writing my way back to her
via the receipts and restaurants of Provence, three years removed,
sometimes seems futile.

   For instance, at this moment, I picture Janet and Jon in the
bright sun on the *Pont St.-Benezet* in Avignon. I can clearly remember every point of my explanation for her shopping obsession, and how it seemed so tidy, so true and—I had hoped—so
helpful. The point seemed so obvious it was hardly worth saying.
And perfectly understandable; not a personal attack, certainly.

   And yet, from her point of view if was contrived, insulting,
and conveniently focused on her shortcomings.

   What's at stake here? asked D.G. Munro.

What's at stake, my fellow struggling writer, is the question of human understanding. In particular, can two humans create an ongoing, dynamic, and truthful understanding of one another sufficient for them to be happy, truly happy, together? Or is mutual understanding a myth that we agree to perpetrate together when we are in love, but that inevitably dries up and fossilizes into set patterns of accommodation?

I sit here at this table in this stone house of Chapet, obsessed with memory and melancholy. Melancholy as the natural state of human existence for Christians, reflecting the pain of our desire to be with God, and for Buddhists, reflecting the pain of our desire, period. Melancholy rides on the mistral and emanates from the stones of the Palace of the Popes. Melancholy seeps into our lives like sewage from fraudulent elections and belligerent foreign policy.

I look up from the table in Chapet, and see my host standing in the doorway.

"Can I interrupt the solitary writer?" Erica has a twinkle in her eye.

"Please interrupt," I say. "Please, please."

"The book not going well?"

"It's spiraled in on itself again. Another self-indulgent tangent that I'll end up throwing out. What's up?"

"George just called from the airport. He's waiting for his bags. Remember that stuff we were talking about the other day?"

"You mean the evil, banned substance?"

"I mean the Fountain of Inspiration for writers and artists." Erica grins. Her voice lowers to a whisper. "George got two bottles in Germany."

"No."

"Yes." She nods emphatically, her eyes large and owlish. "He has to stop by the office, so he won't be here 'til eight or nine tonight. I just wanted to let you know. The Green Fairy is coming to Chapet." Erica's head disappears from around the doorway where it appeared.

ENOUGH. I have interrupted myself long enough. I must swear off meta-narration and let the story unfold naturally, as it did in Provence. No more authorial intrusions. I must resist the urge to point out every damn conveniently symbolic half-bridge to nowhere that crops up in the story. We must go back to Avignon. We must be accurate and unflinching, and have faith that Janet will trust us to make it all right in the end.

Tonight, absinthe.

Avignon, part deux

I sit back on the stone curb of the bridge, leaning back on my hands, feeling the grains of loose stone beneath my palms. I am, I confess, rather proud of my little life lesson.

Janet says, "You took that trip to Japan, right?"

Uncertainly, "Yes."

"And you studied Buddhism and detachment and . . . "

"Well, it wasn't a formal course of study. I visited some temples and thought about . . . "

"That's great for you. Maybe one of these years I can go to Japan and learn to live each moment like the butterfly, soaring and free. Until then, I'm going to worry about whether I've messed up my kids. Get used to it, because I don't see a ticket to Tokyo coming my way soon."

"I only meant you've displaced your anxiety onto *shopping* for them. I'm just trying to help you get over it, so you can enjoy . . . "

"So I can enjoy driving people around and hearing about which king demolished which castle, and which this and which that . . . "

"That's unreasonable . . . "

"I try to tell you my feelings about something, and you tell me why I shouldn't have those feelings. I'm being unreasonable. Okay, forget it. Let's go." She gets up and begins to walk. "What's next?"

"What do you mean?"

"I mean, what else do you want to see? Is there some place where someone was beheaded or something?"

"What about shopping?"

Hands on her waist, she looks at me. "You expect me to go shopping now? After you, Dr. Freud, have diagnosed it as some kind of pitiful subconscious attempt to compensate for years of bad parenting? No thank you."

"I said you *think* you're a bad parent."

"No, I don't. I happen to think my boys are all right."

"Let's just go back to that shopping area and look around. Maybe we'll find something nice for them."

"Fine." Janet walks at a brisk pace back off the bridge, and I follow. We go back across the street, into the town, and climb the stone streets upward toward the castle. After a couple of hundred yards, Janet stops at an intersection.

"Maybe," I say, "some of those miniature knights, the ones made of metal and painted? I saw them in . . . "

"They're a little old for toys." Still, she doesn't move.

"What?"

Through gritted teeth: "Which way."

Trying to suppress a grin: "That way, I think."

"Thank you." And off she goes again.

"What about t-shirts?"

"Dumb."

"No, I didn't mean, like, Palace of the Popes t-shirts. I meant, like, those tight-fitting, cool kind."

"Like the ones they wear every day?"

I stop in front of a patisserie. Window full of brightly decorated cakes. But I'm not looking at them. "Can't we just go on and shop together and try to have a decent time?"

She looks at me for a long second, then starts walking again.

"What?" I say, catching up to her. "What? It's too much to ask just to get along?"

"Yes, let's just get along."

We walk several more blocks, if one can call them blocks in a town without a grid. I like grids. I grew up with them.

Nebraska City had one diagonal street in the whole town. We considered it exotic. But living in the East, and visiting France, I like being off the grid, having to feel one's way by cartography and intuition. I think I'm fairly good at it. I like to look out plane windows and try to name the city I'm flying over by clues I can spot and a general knowledge of location. Indianapolis, for example. Big town, no river. Columbus, Ohio. Lots of green (campus), big stadium. Fort Wayne had me stumped for awhile. Thought it was Akron, until one time the pilot came on and said it was Ft. Wayne.

Janet stops, turns to me. "You . . . "

"What?"

"I can't believe you."

"What?"

"This silence. This not saying anything."

"I've been saying things."

"A couple of lame suggestions, and then you just lapsed back into your own happy little silence. Drawing little maps in your head again."

"And, and, what are you, the Thought Police?"

She takes off walking again, in the wrong direction. But I don't think it's the right time to correct her. Anyway, it's down a side street where there are fewer people to witness the public bickering. "Okay maybe it's not about shopping," I say. "Maybe the real issue is that you feel neglected because we have to do stuff with people from school. And my response is, *Well, get over it.* I'm trying to balance time with you and time with the group, and I thought I was doing a pretty good job."

I've only been sailing a few times, but there's that moment when you're running with the wind, but going the wrong direction, so you need to change course, but it seems like the boat will shudder and break apart if you try to bring her about. This is the absolute wrong direction for me to be taking the conversation, but my tiller isn't strong enough, or my arms are too weak. So I just keep heading for the rocks in full sail. "I mean, sure, after going to Ansouis with a group, we should have gone to Venasque alone, but I *did* say to Natalie that we wanted to go alone, and then you were the one who insisted they go . . . "

"What? You *never said* anything of the sort to Natalie."

"I did too!"

"I know you. Here's how it happened: at some point the thought entered your head that maybe you should just tell Natalie that we're sorry, but this is our romantic getaway. You didn't have the courage to actually say it out loud. But later, you come back to it in your mind and because you *thought* of saying it, your mind backloads that into reality, and you tell yourself, *Yeah, now I remember,* and you *invent* the scene to make yourself look better."

"I do not." But uncertainty clouds my voice.

"Don't you read your own writing? What you call postmodern narrative blah blah everyone else has an old-fashioned name for—rationalization. No, wait, that's a clinical term. What is the common word? Hmmm. Oh yes. Lying."

"I create . . . "

"You *lie*, and not for the noble reasons people lie. You lie to make yourself look good."

We have been moving slowly down the sidewalk as we argue, and now we are under the marquee of a theatre. It is a grungy, back street film house, with dirty gray walls. The poster in the streaky window behind Janet is for the film *Eyes Wide Shut.* I'm not making this up. I can still see Kidman's wandering eye. As if this chapter wasn't already overloaded with too-convenient symbolism. Was it really there? Did we really begin our fight on the half bridge in the middle of the Rhone? Yes, and yes. And let me tell you something else. The time that we were in Paris before, the time we went on to Venasque, the first Venasque, Priam's Venasque, City of Gold—*that* time, the big movie in Paris was Altman's *Pret-a-Porter,* and everywhere giant billboards advertised it with rows of topless models, breasts blazing. It was a silly, sexy, wonderful touch to our Paris holiday, propelling us toward the ecstasies of Venasque.

Back on the dirty Avignon avenue, under Nicole Kidman's dubious stare, I try to take Janet's arm, and whine again, "Can't we just try to get along."

She backs out of my grasp, folds her arms across her breast. "Do you understand," she asks icily, "that there's a *reason* people made fun of Rodney King for saying that? It's not that easy. The issues don't just go away."

"What are the issues?"

"Are you kidding me?"

"We're in Provence, with my colleagues, trying to find balance between our time and communal time. Everybody else seems to be managing it. What maybe you need to do is just *grow up* a little."

Janet turns on her heel and walks the other direction. I follow her. By instinct she finds her way back to the shopping streets. When I start to talk, she stops me. "Listen," she says, "it's obvious we can't talk about this. We're on different wave-lengths, in different time zones, something. I'm going to look for something for the boys. You can do whatever you want to do."

"I want to be with you."

"Fine. Be with me. Only please don't try to talk with me. Not right now." And without another word she plunges into shopping. She goes from store to store to store, every aisle. But it's doomed. She's moving too fast, she can't see what's there, and there's nothing there, and every item that is either too dumb, too plain, too bulky, too expensive, whatever, is like a rebuke. Fiercely she continues. There is something almost masochistic about it. In each store Janet takes something up in her hands, looks at it, and feels the wrongness of it slap her in the face. Clothes, no. Sporting goods, what?—we've got six of everything in the basement. Ties, ridiculous. Candy. Seth and Michael don't touch the Halloween bags after they've collected them. Toys, games, wine, artwork, hardware, plumbing fixtures. Such futility is painful to witness. But she is too proud to give in. This is a shared kind of hell, more painful for being so separate together, like Francesca with Paolo in the swirling winds.

Finally, empty-handed and exhausted, we drag ourselves back toward the Palace of the Popes, where we are to meet Finn and Dana. Janet is staggering under the weight of desolation. I have to use a bathroom. An artsy-looking coffee shop has an open table in the shade outside. I ask Janet if she would like a cup. She sits down. I follow. We chat a little. The view is nice. The young leaves of the plane trees shimmer in the wind. Hopeful signs. Just after the waiter takes our order, a large and very loud truck rumbles up the pedestrian mall where no cars are allowed. It stops right in front of us, blocking our view, filling our space with noise and fumes. The back of the truck is a large blue tank. A hefty guy in blue coveralls grabs the end of fat black hose—it's a good four inches in diameter—and drags it into the coffee shop. If we do not move our feet it will unroll right over them. The guy returns, leaving the tube, which is damp and emitting a foul odor, running under our table and into the coffee shop. He turns on a loud additional motor. A pump, I would guess.

I say, "I really have to use the bathroom."

Janet says, "Good luck."

So I get up and follow the tube and sure enough it terminates in the only rest room, where the toilet fixture has been removed from its hole and is slumped uselessly against a wall. As I'm heading back out I see the photos on the wall. They are female nudes, done in glossy black and shadowy whites. Length of leg here, curve of breast there. I find them very nice, frankly erotic and understated at the same time. At any other time I would hurry to tell Janet: "Go check out the artwork!" and it would have become a titillation for us both. Now, they make my chest tighten with loneliness, and I recall Blake's quizzical couplets of similarity and separation:

> What is it men in women do require?
> The lineaments of gratified desire
> What is it women do in men require?
> The lineaments of gratified desire.

16 Le Clos de la Violette: $236.28

Le Clos de la Violette

Samedi 10 Juin 2006

Numéro de Table N° 6
Nombre de Couvert 2

Folio 1

2 Apéritifs   160,00
2 Ballade Gourmande   1200,00
1 Eau Minérale   35,00
1 Sainte Roseline Blanc 1998   210,00

                              NET A PAYER   1 605,00 F

Net à payer en euros   244,68

Dont TVA 19.6% 263,03 F

L'équipe du Clos de la Violette vous
remercie de votre visite

Brigitte et Jean Marc Banzo

10, avenue de la Violette · 13100 Aix-en-Provence · Tél. 04 42 23 30 71 · FAX. 04 42 21 93 03
S.A.R.L. / B.O.R. au capital de 50.000 F / R.C. AIX B 80 B 567
RESTAURANT FERMÉ LE LUNDI MIDI ET LE DIMANCHE

One book that does not make many people's top ten list when it comes to marriage counseling is the *Michelin Guide.* I had been planning this extravaganza since before Avignon, and it was a dumb idea then, too. Since I am a travel writer and can deduct my meals, I thought, why not have a real meal for once? I mean at the kind of restaurant the tire company gives stars to. Cecile, bless her, had called to make the reservation for me, and was excited for us, so Janet had to look excited at the prospect of sitting down for five hours with me in an intimidating atmosphere over food she can't pronounce.

Before setting out for Le Clos de la Violette, Janet and I spent the day apart from each other for the first time on this trip. Natalie was taking Peter to the airport at Marseilles, and asked Janet to go along to help navigate. I sat by the pool reading, drinking wine, chatting about history with Nelson. I didn't reflect much on Avignon. To the extent that I thought about it, I thought that my former assessment was about right, that Janet didn't deal well with the pressures of Life With Colleagues, and there wasn't much to be done about it. Anyway, there are just two days left. Today she'd have Rejuvenating Woman-Time, and tonight I would wow her and woo her with the Big Ticket Dinner. In the meantime, the Rodney King Impulse prevails, and I hope the tribulations of yesterday will recede and we can all Just Get Along. Sometimes my thinking comes in Three Word Phrases.

I take a wrong turn on the way to Aix, and we snap at each other a little over map-reading. I think it's going to be a long night. Then, out of nowhere, Janet says, "Listen. I'm sorry. We don't have much time left here. I want this to be fun, too. It makes me nervous to go to this place. Wrong Fork Anxiety or whatever. But I'll try not to take that out on you. I know I'm difficult. Let's just forget it and have a nice meal."

A giddy joy sweeps through me. "That was so generous. I know I'm difficult too. Yesterday was hard on both of us. I agree. A nice meal is the cure."

"No," she says, her voice dropping, "it's not the cure. Let's just try not to fight." Watching me droop, she makes her

188 ☙ Jon Volkmer

voice lively and adds, "Okay. Fancy restaurant. Let's do this thing."

La Clos de la Violette is a quiet street on in the north part of Aix-in-Provence. There's a wall near the street, and a gate. Inside, a lush yard, trees with low-hanging branches. There is a wide terrace for dining *al fresco*, but the evenings are still a bit chilly, and we are conducted indoors. When we ask for it, we are given an English version of the menu. It appears discreetly, sliding onto our plates, as if the host is aware of how embarrassing this must be for us.

I may as well admit that I can't remember the food. The receipt, like the meal, is large but unsatisfying. Soup. Something with shrimp. Something in puff pastry. Something else. The *ballade gourmande* turns out to be more of an epic than a ballad. Neither our brains nor our stomachs are prepared for many courses served at half-hour intervals. After the first three it starts to feel more like a forced march than a gourmet dinner. I am amazed that there exists a whole strata of society for whom this kind of experience approaches the sublime.

Among the phalanx of black-coated waiters are two skinny dark-haired guys who look like a young Jerry Lewis and a young Elvis Costello. The Elvis one develops a certain wry wordless dialogue with Janet. She reaches for a fork, stops, looks at him with eyebrows raised. He scolds her with his eyebrows. She touches the correct fork, and he gives the slightest of smiles. He manages it without making her feel censured, manages to make it seem as if he and she are in collusion against some large, evil, arbitrary, and unforgiving authority. Funny how even this—the bright spot of a dreary dinner— gives rise in me to stirrings of jealousy and loneliness. What happened to the joy I felt over the waiter's attentions to Janet in Ansouis?

Perhaps it was the Unnerving Oenological Event that soured me irredeemably on this restaurant. There is one place in the Inferno where the courage of Dante's guide seems to desert him. Virgil has been cruising through suburban hell, upbraiding surly ferrymen, chatting with dead poets, tossing slop to three-headed guard dogs. But when the buddies approach the walls of Dis, the City of Hell itself, the gate slams shut in his face, hydra-headed furies taunt him, and Virgil is left mumbling uncertainly to himself. It takes a visit from a Heavenly Messenger to spring the door and give him the confidence to lead Dante into the depths of hell. I had sailed the vineyards of Alsace, unfazed by the unpronounceable. I had swished the pink drink of Provence. But here, confronted with the massive leather-bound wine list, our Hero coughs and quails. The eyes of the Gorgon waiter taunt him, and the prices, he fears, will turn him to stone. When he speaks, the charade of sophistication is painful for all to endure, as he allows as how he favors a Provençal selection to match the cuisine, and hurries on to name his choice so as not to give the waiter an opening to make a suggestion. Rosé seems wrong for the formality here, so he orders the cheapest—*white?* That makes no sense at all. Maybe with the appetizer, a sprightly glass of *le blanc.* But for a dinner like this, one orders Red Red Red. Idiot.

Just at this precise moment when self-deprecating humor might have built a bridge from my isolation to Janet's, I commit the first sin, the worst sin, the sin that predates humanity, the sin of Lucifer: pride. I heave the wine list back to the waiter and turn to Janet with a bland smile. It would have been such a simple thing. I could have been clever in my self-effacement. I could have won from her a smile. Only now, years and oceans apart from her, am I able to relate my real feelings in that moment. Alone in Chapet, on this tiny stucco porch, with this three-euro bottle of Cahors on the glass top of the wrought-iron sun-dappled table before me. And yes, Janet, I selected it for the name—the town has a cameo in the Inferno. The sins of Soddom and Cahors. If only you were here to tease me, and let me tell you Dante's exquisite logic for linking sodomy and usury. You would tell me to shut up, and I would laugh and kiss you against the ivy on this wall.

For the record, this reviewer does not recommend the Sainte Roseline Blanc 1998. It was by far the most expensive wine that we drank on our entire trip, and the worst. A bouquet of strained dandelions, sour to the palate, with hints of rust and chlorine in the finish. The name is boring too, and fraudulent—at least in that I am unable to locate a Saint Roseline in *The Saints and Angels Directory*. We don't have fun making fun of it. We swish it around in our mouths and the most Janet will say is it's not her favorite wine, and the most I will concede it is that it isn't exactly what I expected. Nick and Nora do not make an appearance at the Clos de la Violette. We are just Stupid American Tourists. We are just another middle aged couple weighed down by our baggage of hurt and regret, our individual lives drifting in different directions the way married people's lives do.

Driving back to the villa in the dark, I take Janet's hand. I tell her that I'm sorry that the villa experience has put a strain on our relationship. I tell that if I had it to do over again I would schedule it the opposite way. I would arrange for the time at villa to be the first week, and then we would have a week together. I don't say what pops to mind next, which is the appropriateness of the cartographical analog; that is, an itinerary inscribing an upward arc from Provence, through Alsace, and on to Amsterdam, instead of the downward bend mirroring our descent into the slough of despond. This is, of course, presuming the top-equals-north bias, which is totally arbitrary. I once saw a world map with the southern hemisphere on top. It really makes you think.

Meanwhile, Janet has pulled her hand away from mine. Her voice is quiet and weary. "It doesn't matter which part came first. Your colleagues are not the problem. The boys are not the problem. The problem is that you don't see me. That you don't hear me. That you aren't really interested in me."

"What?"

"You don't see me. You don't hear me. You aren't interested in me."

"What? Never mind, I heard you. I just . . . I mean . . . that's ridiculous." My stomach tightens. "How can you even say that? I am focused on you. I spend every day with you. I could not *be* any more interested in you."

"I'm sorry." Her voice is not apologetic. "This probably sounds churlish to you. But try to listen. From my side of the car it seems that you are interested in an image of me that you create. You fashion this character of me, as if you are writing a book, and every time I try to break out of it, or peek around it, you get mad or hurt and shove me back into the shape that you've made, the one you're comfortable with."

I am driving on the narrow dark roads of France. I am tempted to say I got lost. That I took a wrong turn and couldn't find my way back to the villa. That I groped around in the dark trying to find my way. But that is not what happened. The heavy-handed symbolisms of Avignon, they were really there. And at times that week I did get lost on the back roads around Rognes and Purycard. But on *this* night I make the correct choices at the roundabouts and bring the Punto into the parking lot at the villa. I only mention this to demonstrate my commitment to the truth—at all levels. I am hurt and angry at the accusation that I would ever want anything but The Complete Janet. We do not get out of the car. We sit there and continue this conversation while we stare at the lights leaking out from under the stone arches of the villa.

I take a deep breath before I reply. "What can any of us do but create images of each other?" I ask. "We are all just characters to each other. Do you think there is some kind of 'Real Janet' lurking here that I haven't met? That I can just step outside of my perceptions, and there she will be? You act as if you could just toss aside my observations, just unzip and step out of them like they're coveralls, and say, 'Ta da! here's the real me!'"

"I could if you would let me," she says. "You were fine as long as I was the witty wife. Myrna Loy or Kate Hepburn. But there's more to life than snappy dialogue. When I'm unhappy, and when I tell you about it, that's the part of me you don't want to see . . . "

"Melancholy! Are you kidding me? I am *aware* of your sadness. It's not as if you try to hide . . . "

"Stop." Her voice is sharp. "Let me speak. You just did it again. You did what I'm describing. Every time I try to talk about how I feel, *every* time, you respond by telling me the reasons why what I'm feeling is not valid, why I shouldn't feel that way."

"But . . . "

"Or you lecture me about literature. Or you talk about maps. Anything to change the subject."

"Allusions, analogies." I thump the steering wheel for emphasis. "That's how we make sense of things, by comparing that which . . . "

"I tell you I feel sad, and you tell me I'm why I'm wrong to feel sad. I want to get something nice for the boys, and you say it's because I fear I'm a bad mom. I tell you I'm hurting, and you quote Philip Larkin. You don't *listen* to what I say. You analyze it for anything illogical or unreasonable, and then you hold that part up and say, *See, you shouldn't feel that way*—" she imitates my voice in a familiar way, foolishly pedantic Bullwinkle Moose, "—*I've got the proof right here*." She stares at me for a long moment. "While we were in the car all week, did you ever, even once, want to know what I was feeling because it was I, *Janet*, who was feeling it? Did you ever think to ask *me* instead of asking Yeats?"

"Yeats."

"I said 'Yeats.'"

"I thought you said 'Yeets.'"

She makes a strangled noise. "I would *never* say 'Yeets.'"

I put both hands on top of the wheel and lean my forehead there. "I've had it. You don't think I portray you accurately or honestly. Think you could do better? Fine, you go right ahead. Here, you drive."

"You don't mean that. You could never give up control."

"I mean it. Take the wheel."

"Fine, I will."

"Be my guest."

Janet seems to relax back in her seat. She says, "Thank you."

I glance away from the shadowed arches of the house and see a Cheshire cat grin on my wife's formerly sour-looking face. "For what?" I ask. This is *dis*ingenuous. I know what she's thanking me for. Why are my shoes so hellishly uncomfortable?

"Thank you," Janet repeats, "for inviting me to your little party." She cranks down the window and a sudden breeze whips her hair around her face. She closes her eyes. Sighs. Stretches. She turns to me and laughs. "Jon, This is wonderful! I haven't felt this good in a hundred pages."

"Party? What pages? What are you talking about?"

Janet pats my knee solicitously. "I'm sorry. I didn't realize. You're not in meta-mode. Hang on. Let me just make a few adjustments . . ."

The trees and shadows melt into a multi-hued stew and pour themselves over the Punto which begins to bubble or maybe it's my eyes that are bubbling and the colors howl and the wind bleeds and a thousand receipts from a thousand restaurants rise up like a flock of frightened doves swooping and diving over the ruins of a thousand castles and scattering into a boiling horizon and I am flying apart and I feel Janet's hand in mine. My heart stops . . . starts . . . establishes a new, unfamiliar rhythm and then the world belches and I am sitting at a corner table in a swank Manhattan restaurant, circa 1934. The wall is decorated with elegant black and white photography. Janet sits across from me, elbows on the table, chin cupped in one hand. In the other hand, she holds an impossibly long cigarette holder with an unlit cigarette. She is wearing crimson lipstick and a pearlescent gown with a gracefully plunging décolletage. Around her neck she wears a long strand of pearls, and on her face the same Cheshire cat grin she was wearing before the world melted and I went mad. A white-jacketed waiter glides past bearing a tray of martini glasses. Without bobbling the ridiculous cigarette holder, breaking eye-contact with me or spilling a drop, Janet snags one and takes a sip. In my right hand I am holding a glass of 12-year-old Laphraoig.

"Nicky, *darling*!" she exclaims in a voice not quite her own. "Rough ride? I'm so sorry. I tried to make it *fun*."

My wife shifts in her chair to present me with a three-quarter profile. She delicately places the cigarette holder between her crimson lips, and gazes languidly into the middle distance. She raises an eyebrow. She gracefully inclines her face in my direction. She lifts her chin, ever so slightly. She glances briefly at me, removes the cigarette holder, gives a discrete little cough from behind her hand, replaces the cigarette holder and resumes the cameo pose. She is motionless for a long moment. Finally, she rolls her eyes, shoots me an exasperated look and nods, rather sharply, toward my left hand which, as it happens, is grasping a surprisingly solid silver lighter with the initials "N.C." engraved decisively on it. I boggle at the lighter. I boggle at Janet. She smiles blandly into the middle distance. My hand, of its own accord, raises the silver lighter and lights her cigarette. "Thank *God*," my wife breathes. "I thought I'd have to do it myself." And she flops back in her chair in mock exhaustion.

"I hope the Laphraoig's okay," says Janet in her normal voice. "I know it lacks verisimilitude. Nick would be drinking a martini, but you're a scotch man through and through and I didn't want to belabor the *Thin Man* allusion—it's really just a little joke, between you, me and the Krafts—so I gave you scotch. I don't know scotch, but I checked the booze cupboard and we had Laphroaig and Cragganmore in there. I gave you the Laphraoig because it's more fun to say and I know that's important to you. Anyway, take a sip. You need it."

I take a sip. I need it. My feet are still killing me and without consciously deciding to, I kick off my shoes.

Janet smiles. "Sorry about the blisters," she says, looking not particularly sorry about anything. I bend to examine my sore feet, peel back my socks and discover impressive blisters on both heels. "I couldn't resist. Just a little payback for all that *shoe* business. Yes, I wore a new pair of shoes on a trip *once* and yes, they gave me a blister. *Once.*" She shrugs and blows a thin line of smoke in my general direction. "Hardly qualifies as a character trait."

"Janet?"

"Yes, darling?"

"Where's the Punto?"

She gives a silvery laugh. The cigarette and martini have disappeared. "The cigarette was just for effect, not that I wouldn't *love* to smoke it, and martinis go straight to my head. I need to keep my wits about me. Where's the *Punto*? Not where are *we*? Where is the *car*? Honey, the Punto is gone. Or, more accurately, the Punto was never here . . . "

The swank restaurant and the prints have dissolved, and we are sitting in the green wrought iron patio chairs on the deck at the back of our house. We're both wearing shorts and sandals. The heavy-leaved maple and ash enclose us (we badly need a tree trimmer) and goldfinches hover about the feeder. The TV blares from inside.

Janet takes my chin in her hand. " . . . Now pay attention," she says. "I can't stay long. Seth forgot his work clothes and I have to drop them off by 3:00. Tristan wants a sandwich. I have to take Nina to the vet – she's throwing up again. I have a client at 4:00 and I'm up to my ears in dirty dishes because the dishwasher is *still* broken, so I don't want to waste a lot of time on back story. Just enough to bring you up to meta-speed. Ready? Okay, we . . . "

"Stop!" My head is beginning to clear a bit. This is wrong. I don't know what's going on, but I know this isn't right. "I don't know what's going on," I say out loud, "but I know this isn't right. I swore off all this kind of . . . we're supposed to be sitting in the driveway of the villa in Provence, and you're supposed to be . . . you're *supposed* to be . . . ." Janet leans towards me, and my notion of what it is, exactly, that Janet is supposed to be vanishes down the scoop neckline of her t-shirt. She places a finger over my lips. "Shhh. I know, Jon. I'm *supposed* to be picking up the narrative thread where you left it and I'm *supposed* to be doing it in way that shows the true melancholy side of me in a sympathetic and accurate light. I know all that. But I also feel you've been neglecting the slyly fetching side of my character. Now please just sit quietly and listen." Janet takes her finger from my lips, leans back and gazes directly into my eyes and speaks in a brisk, businesslike tone. "Here's what happens. When we get home from France, you write half of an experimental book called *Eating Europe* in which you turn me into a snippy foil for the sake of narrative exposition and I *love* it. Three years later you begin the second half in a village called Chapet, outside Paris. This time, you turn me into a different kind of foil for the sake of something else, and this time I do *not* love it. Meanwhile, back in the Punto, *we*" (here my wife makes emphatic little quotation marks in the air with her fingers) "are arguing in the driveway of the villa and it will occur to me that if I'm forced to tolerate another paragraph of *my*" (air quotes) "pitiful company I'll have to beat us both senseless against the steering wheel. But then something happens, and 'Janet' seems to relax back in her seat and . . . 'Thank you.'"

"Thank you?"

"That's what Janet *says*, Jon. She says thank you. And she means it."

"Yeah, but I didn't mean you could just . . . "

Janet leans across the patio table. Her lips brush mine and I close my eyes. Then, instead of a kiss, she gives my lower lip a none-too-gentle bite.

"Ouch! What was that for?"

"For inviting me to drive and then trying to steer. And for turning me into her."

"I didn't turn you into anyone."

She leans across the table again, and this time she does kiss me, long and deep. We kiss the way she kissed me the second time we kissed. In a car. In the rain. When I feel her drawing away I slowly open my eyes. Janet is wearing a set of fake teeth. I jerk back reflexively and spill scotch all over my hand and the table. Janet removes the teeth and places them on the table where they chatter violently for a moment in a puddle of scotch.

I am not amused. "I suppose you think you're . . . " the teeth abruptly resume their chatter for a few seconds then lapse into silence. " . . . terribly . . . " the teeth chatter their way across the table in fits and starts and fall to the deck where they offer one last burst of chatter before settling down next to one of my shoes ". . . *clever.*" I finish with what strikes me as remarkable dignity under the circumstances. Janet giggles. Then she touches the puddle of scotch. Her eyes cloud and she shakes her head sadly.

"Oh Jon, Jon. Look what you've gone and done. You're making a mess of it."

This is outrageous. I'm making a mess of it? Please! I know a ham-fisted metaphor when I'm made to spill one all over me. Of course she made me spill it so she could make her little point. Criminal waste of single malt. Should have used a blend. She's probably scripting my thoughts right now. She really is quite brilliant. And attractive. I should buy her a present.

I scowl at my wife who is gazing at me, all radiant innocence. "Cheap trick," I mutter under my breath.

"Yeah," she says. "How does it feel?"

Back at the manhattan restaurant, in her Myrna Loy outfit, Janet inhales from the long cigarette holder and sighs rapturously.

"Having fun?" I inquire icily.

"Oh, I'm having a *grand* time. Finally. My question is, why aren't you? But go on. You were thinking?"

Yes. Okay. So I invited her to narrate. But I didn't invite her to hijack my narrative and turn us into a second-rate Nick and Nora, or worse (I give the teeth a vicious kick and send them skittering across the floor where they are discretely scooped up and pocketed by a passing waiter who bears a suspicious resemblance to Laurent), a third-rate Martin and Lewis. I invited her to contribute within the scope of that which I was creating. I mean, will create. Am creating. Whatever. The

point is, this is *my* show. She doesn't get to go around breaking frames, melting driveways and purloining Puntos willy-
nilly. That was *my* frame. That was *my* driveway and that
Punto was *rented*.

"Don't worry. I'll get it back to you without a scratch."

"Stop replying to my internal monologue."

"Make me."

I try.

"Nice try," she says. "Look. Just be grateful you're still
in the first-person. I didn't *have* to do that, you know. Now
play nice or I'll send you to shopping hell. Believe me. You
don't want to go there." She's still smiling but the smile has an
edge to it now. Her eyes are glittering and her jaw looks like
it's carved out of marble. I've seen this look before. It always
makes me want to . . .

"Correct my pronunciation?"

"Be careful, Janet. I think you're drunk on power."

"Oh, Jon . . . " Janet's eyes soften. She touches my arm. "I
didn't ask to drive so I could punish you. I did it because . . .
because I wanted us to play . . . have some fun. I need a laugh,
Jon. I need to hear you laugh. Look . . . I'm running out of
time here. I've only got a few more paragraphs in me. I'm not
like you. I'm lazy and undisciplined. I can't sustain this. I just
have to ask, though. Why are you so unhappy? Why am *I* so
unhappy?"

"We're not so unhappy," I tell her. "We love each other.
We're just going through a down phase. Why shouldn't we?
And the world's a mess. Real life isn't all fun and pomo games.
Godammit, I'm trying to be *real*."

"I know that." She stares at me, perplexed. "But do you
really think what you're doing is any more real than . . . " She
sweeps her arm around the restaurant and the lights come
up on the orchestra. They're playing a sweet, sultry rendition of "Bewitched, Bothered, and Bewildered." The hum of
conversation weaves its way through the music. Somewhere
across the room a girl laughs. Suspended above the middle of
the room, an enormous crystal chandelier sprinkles a sea of

reflected stars across the gleaming wood dance floor where couples sway and glide in perfect synchronicity. At the table next to ours, a smartly dressed silver-haired man stands and offers an arm to his lovely wife. She takes it and they step onto the dance floor where he dips her, and spins her off into the crowd.

Janet stands and tugs on my sleeve. "Come on, Jon. Let's dance. I don't have much time."

"I can't dance. You always make fun of me when I dance."

She winces. "I do? Well, it's very rude of me and I'm sorry. But that's there. Here you're a *great* dancer and here I am *never* rude to you." And she draws me to my feet, pulls me to the dance floor, and I find she is right. Here, I can dance.

Janet and I move in perfect synchronicity. Almost perfect. Janet turns when I'm trying to dip her, dips when I'm trying to turn her, and we nearly fall down. We step on each other's toes but we keep dancing. We laugh and we keep dancing. Finally, we get it right and no one's toes get stepped on. We're in each other's arms. Her head is on my shoulder and I close my eyes. When I open them we are dancing on the deck of our run-down little house in Pennsylvania. Janet is wearing shorts, sandals, and that white scoop-neck t-shirt. I can still hear "Bewitched, Bothered, and Bewildered," but it's coming from the boom box on the picnic table. From inside the house, the TV blares and a phone rings and footsteps thunder up the basement stairs.

"Mom!" Tristan's voice. "MOM! PHONE!" He opens the sliding screen door to the deck and hands Janet the phone. "It's Seth," he says flatly. "Oh yeah. I forgot to tell you. Nina puked again." He steps into the house, closes the door and opens it again to say, "Uh, Mom? How about that sandwich?" Janet takes the phone, turns to me, smiles and mouths silently, "That was *fun!*" I put my hands on her shoulders to anchor her because her body appears to be . . . wavering I suppose, but her shoulders shrug, shift and then dissolve under my hands

before resolving into the smooth steering wheel of the blue
rented Fiat Punto.

When I look across the car, the passenger side is empty. I am
not sure how long I have been sitting in the car by myself—it's
like I blanked out or something. I get out and walk toward
the house, feeling a little light-headed and nauseated. Seafood
reaction, maybe. And, strangely, my feet hurt. I enter the
house and spot Janet at the other end of the living room. She
is nestled deep in the leather of the living room couch, feet
tucked beneath her, glass of rosé in her hand, debating with
Nelson Barge.

"Okay, okay, I concede that point," Nelson is saying, "but
you also have to consider . . . "

I walk over and stand in front of the couch. "Well?"

"Hello," Janet says evenly, and turns back to Nelson.
"Sorry. I have to consider what?"

I have a tremendous curiosity to know what they are talking about, but hanging around seems intrusive. Cecile and
Paige are sitting at the long wooden dining table. Cecile wants
to hear all about Clos de la Violette, so I get some wine and
join them. I tell her about the bad wine and the celebrity look-
alike waiters, and she seems disappointed that we did not have
a sublime experience. I say it was more our problem than the
restaurant's, but I'm only half-there. My attention is on the
other end of the room. Janet arguing. Janet laughing. The
same person who was gripped by sadness in the afternoon can
sit there merrily outpointing the redoubtable Professor Barge
in the evening. Preposterous woman! A disinterested observer
might even choose the word *flirting.*

"Are you all right?" Cecile asks. "You look a little sick."

"Big night," I say. "Too much to digest. I'm going to
bed."

I am on the cusp of a dream when I feel the covers move,
and Janet gets into bed beside me. It's pitch dark; opening or
closing my eyes is no different. Janet, on her side, drapes an
arm across my chest. Her skin is soft and cool to the touch.

"Did Nelson give you a hard time?"

"It's just an act." Her voice comes softly out of the void. "He's really a sweet man."

"Sweet?"

"Yeah."

Silence, wordlessness, blackness. "You know," I say finally, "that was a wild ride you took us on, but I can't use any of that in the book."

"You said you were giving me the wheel."

"Not to drive off a cliff. Not for a total breakdown of narrative structure. How am I supposed to include that?"

"As if you haven't put it in that ditch about six times."

Her arm is all that's touching me. In the blackness, it seems as if I am having a talk with an arm. "Listen, Janet. You should just trust me. Everybody loves you from the first half of the book. You've got stored-up good will galore. If you just trust me, it will turn out all right for you in the end."

"Yeah? Like when? Look at me! Bitchy, miserable, antisocial. Even I can't stand to be around me. How many more meals was I going to have to drag my sorry ass through?"

"But look what you've done! Here we are lying in bed arguing about your characterization in a part of the book I haven't written yet."

"You started it."

"I may have started it, but you went ballistic. All that carnival pomo melting world bullshit. New York restaurants, Seth and Tristan, martinis and ballroom dancing, kissing on the deck."

"I had a lot of pent-up literary frustration."

"Wait a minute."

"Mmmm?"

"The bed's not squeaking."

"Mmmm?"

"Where did your arm go? Say something."

"......"

I pat around on both sides of me. "You're not here, are you? This is Chapet, isn't it?" I groan. My head is splitting.

I get weakly to my feet and grope for the door. The knob is always lower than I think it will be. Barefoot in my boxers, unsteady on my feet, I make my way through my outer room and into the hallway. Snores resound from the bedroom down the hall. I feel my way downstairs, pad through the kitchen to the bathroom, endure the glare of the light long enough to find the ibuprofen. Back in the kitchen, I get some water from the tap, knock back the pills, and stare out over the dull lights of Les Mureuax across the valley. It is quiet and beautiful.

"Don't do it."

I whirl around, but Janet isn't there. Just a cluttered kitchen table, some glasses, an open box of sugar cubes. The empty absinthe bottle.

"Do what?" I whisper.

"Try to pass off my writing as some kind of hallucination. It's not the absinthe talking. You may not like where I went, but you gave me the keys and I drove."

"But I didn't think you'd . . . " I grip the counter behind me to steady myself. "It's just that I was trying to stop using that kind of narrative gamesmanship . . . "

"I know. But I hated what you were doing to me."

"Do you feel better now?"

"Yes."

"Good. I feel like hell."

"You're going to have the shakes tomorrow, and even good French coffee is going to turn your stomach."

"You're enjoying this."

"A little. C'mon, you're off in France, being an absinthe drinker without me. How do you expect me to react?"

"Okay, okay. I'm going back to bed, and in the morning you're going to be gone, right?"

"Probably."

"And you're going to leave the narration alone."

"Maybe."

"Trust me, Janet. It's all going to turn out okay."

"You keep saying that."

17 Domaine de Janet

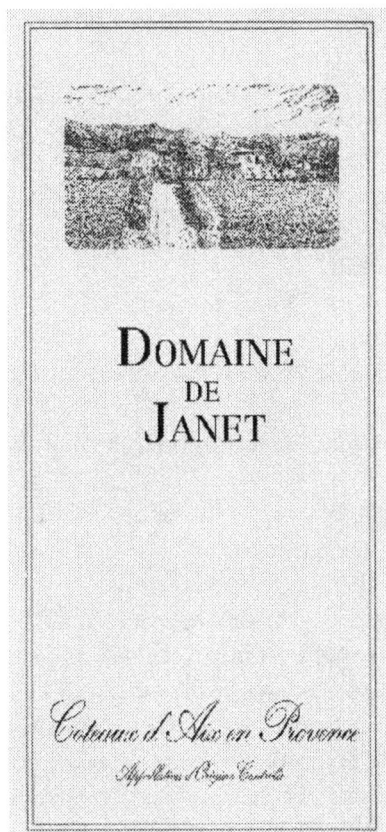

Sun and sand. We are headed for the blue blue Mediterranean. Janet is sitting there in the front seat of the Punto with the Michelin Map #245 *Provence & Cote d'Azur* spread out on her lap. She traveled this way with Natalie the day before, tak-

ing Peter to the Marseilles Airport. She is comfortable with
cartography.

"What's 'Janet'?"

"You're Janet."

"On the map. It says 'Janet.' It's right near here."

"Really? Close by?"

"Between Rognes and Lambesc."

"We've driven that road a dozen times. I've never seen
Janet."

"It looks like a back road."

I pull over to look at the map. Sure enough, a tiny black
rectangle 'Janet.' I just wasn't looking in the right place. "We
must go there!"

"I thought we were going to the shore."

"We will. It's only a few minutes out of our way. Maybe it's
a castle or chateau."

"And we're just going to walk up and knock on the
door?"

"If Janet doesn't want people to find her she shouldn't be
on the map."

She glances across the seat at me. "So how do I get on your
map?"

"You are the compass and the capital. You are the main
roads, you are the railroads . . . "

"All right, all right."

It is our last day in Provence. For tonight's dinner, Cecile has hired a chef to come to the villa to prepare a farewell
feast. Tomorrow morning, early, Janet and I will be heading
for Paris to turn in our Fiat Punto for an Airbus A300. Another set of wacky professors and their spouses will unpack
at the villa for another week of comedy. Sounds like a reality
TV series for PBS: *Tune in as addled and absent-minded professors from different disciplines attempt to make pasta primavera
together while explaining their diverse research projects that have
a more or less tenuous connection to Provence.*

Anyway, the sky was clear this morning when we got up.
Cecile mentioned it was supposed to be sunny and hot, and

that's when it hit me that we should head for the shore. For a week we'd been thirty miles from the Mediterranean, and neither of us had seen it yet. We put on swimming suits under our clothes, grabbed some towels and suntan lotion, and we were off. That's when Janet spotted Janet on the map, and that's what brings us to this long narrow driveway that crosses a vineyard flat on a valley floor and then rises to a group of white buildings half hidden by large plane trees. The foliage is dense, and the trunks must be four feet across. The place feels familiar to me, comforting. Ducks waddle about, dogs bark. A tractor sits beside a shed with hay bales inside it, and there's a red wheelbarrow, glazed with rainwater.

"Don't you *dare* mention chickens."

"You promised to stop doing that."

Janet looks up innocently. "What?"

"You know what."

"And you promised to lay off the cheesy allusions."

Janet is worried that we're invading someone's privacy. A truck rumbles by. I shout, "Wine?" The driver jerks a thumb over his shoulder behind him, and we keep going. We park beside a barn, and walk tentatively around to the front.

"I don't know if I could handle a wine tasting at this hour," I say, rubbing my forehead. "For some reason, I feel hung over as hell. I didn't drink that much. Maybe the seafood. Are you feeling okay?"

"I'm fine," Janet says, smiling pleasantly. "Look."

I turn where she's pointing and nearly jump out of my skin. A very large bird is very close by. Two of them. "White peacocks? I didn't know peacocks came in white."

"Shhh, you'll scare them."

"Then we'll be even."

The birds are magnificent. We stare at them, and then move on toward the large open barn door. No lights are on inside, but we can see wooden barrels on one side and packed cardboard boxes of wine on the other. In the middle, closer to the back wall, is a high wooden table for wine tasting.

"I think they're closed," Janet whispers.

"Look, it has 'Janet' right on the bottles. We have to get some."

The tiptoeing and whispering make us feel like children sneaking in somewhere not allowed, and suddenly we are giggling. When a woman comes bustling toward us from the farm house, we just get worse. *Yikes, a grown-up.* But it seems as if the woman has been laughing too, and the first thing we do is giggle insanely together there in the doorway of the barn. She is well-tanned, with long, very thick hair, reddish brown, cascading down her shoulders. She wears a white cotton top, jeans, and dirty sneakers. Although she speaks no English, it becomes apparent that what *she* thinks we are all laughing about is her unkempt appearance.

"*Très savage,*" she says, trying to smooth down her unruly hair.

How savage indeed, we think—for I am sure Janet is right with me on this. The woman before us radiates a farm-wife sensuality that nearly knocks us off out feet. I cannot reproduce the conversation. It occurred in some pigeon-patios of pointing, improvised sign-language, and laughter. Even three years later, alone in Chapet and missing Janet, the memory evokes a fluttery, giddy feeling that bubbles up from my sternum.

The woman turns on lights and ushers us to the tasting table. We convey that Janet is Janet, the same name as on the bottles. The woman points to another bottle, labeled 'Francine,' her name. She pours samples into small wine glasses with "Janet" inscribed in them. I take the first one with a trembling hand, afraid of unloosing the simmering headache. It's good. Better than good, it's great. It's the best wine I have ever tasted. Francine nods and laughs at our incredulity.

"Wow," I exclaim. "Janet."

"What?"

"I feel great. My headache is totally gone."

She laughs. "Hair of the Janet that bit you?"

We buy reds and rosés to carry across the ocean and drink on our deck to evoke this moment. And for years afterward, an empty bottle of Janet red will sit on the kitchen windowsill so that every day we will see it and smile to remember all the events of this day. Francine leads us to the farm house, takes us up to a second floor corridor to show us several large, plainly furnished rooms available to rent, and insists that when we return to Provence, we must stay at Domaine de Janet. From the front of the house we admire the remarkable view, green gorgeous hills of Provence unrolling before us all the way to Aix.

If the emblem of the Alsace is a fleeing angel in the form of a little girl, then that of Provence must be a welcoming angel, Francine in full womanhood. Driving away from Domaine de Janet, our booty stashed in the back, we confirm that we are on the same wave-length.

"I love her smile," I say, "the way she laughs."

"She's so funny," says Janet. "She kept apologizing for how she looked."

"And it wasn't fake . . . "

"I *know*. It was completely genuine. And she's so gorgeous."

"There was something about her. So wholesome and unpretentious."

"And so sexy."

I've never heard Janet refer to another woman that way with such conviction, and I admit, it stirs in me something *très savage*.

A little tipsy from the wine and Francine, we drive together toward sun and sand. It seems miraculous. The impossible distance of last night is gone. Finally, we are just happy to be with each other.

"You picked the beach today for me," Janet says. "There's probably some castle or ruin you wanted to go to."

"No, nothing else."

"This whole trip," she says, "has been a Jon vacation rather than a Janet vacation."

For once, some part of me clamps a hand over my mouth. Don't protest. Wait.

Janet goes on. "When you told me about the trips your family took when you were a kid, what hit me was how much it sounded like work. Starting off at 4 a.m., one day here, one day there, all those stops to make, sights to see. It sounded exhausting. In my family, we went to Ocean City every year, and rented the same house if we could get it. It had green siding and was three blocks from the beach. We put out chairs on the same stretch of sand every day, and we walked the boards at night. I can't think of it as vacation unless I lose track of what day it is."

Do not speak. *Listen.*

"This trip is a whole different thing, your kind of thing. It's the itinerary kind of a vacation. And that's fine. I can adjust to that. I'm having a good time. It's only," she pauses and looks at me. "You won't think I'm a slug if one of these days I'd like to have a vacation at the beach? Just you and me and the boys?"

"I would love it," I say.

"Really?"

"Sure."

We make a loop around Aix, and Janet navigates. A8 to A52 and south to sun and sand. For a while we have nice views out to the left of St. Victoire, the blunt mountain multi-colored by Cezanne. We ride in silence for awhile. We are headed for Cassis, just west of Marseilles. The closest nice beach town, according to Cecile. It doesn't take long. Pretty soon we are off the freeway and snaking through coastal mountains toward the sea.

"I can't believe we've been this close all week," says Janet, "and nobody has gone to the beach."

"Well," I say, "the prospect does pose certain problems of delicacy for a mixed batch of professors and spouses."

"What do you mean?"

"Breasts, my dear. This is the Cotes d'Azur. Sexy topless beach capital of the world."

Janet laughs nervously. "That means tops are *optional*, right? I mean, if I looked like a model . . . "

"I don't think it's just the young and the sexy. It's all shapes and sizes."

"But not everyone."

I shrug. After talking with Janet about Francine, I am feeling a bit feisty. "I think it's pretty much all the women. Let me put it this way, if every other woman on the beach is topless, wouldn't you feel conspicuous being covered up?"

"I probably would. But I don't think that's the case."

We park in a two-story garage in the city of Cassis. I grab the bag with towels and lotion, and soon we're hiking down hill through twisting streets until we come to the sea. A row of restaurants with outdoor seating under bright awnings faces a marina where pleasure boats bob in the maze of berths. A large concrete dock serves sightseeing boats that take people out to look at the Calanques, which are large cliffs that extend out into the sea like a set of fingers, leaving deep narrow fiords in between.

As I stand staring at the large map, Janet says, "I suppose you want to see them?"

"Not unless you do. But where's the beach?"

Janet laughs. "There doesn't seem to be any."

I lead Janet along the boat docks to the right, past the boat rental, to where private houses rise up directly out of the water. We joke about not being able to find the ocean. We go back to where we started and look to the left. The headland rises steeply out of the water just a hundred or so feet away. A high concrete wall runs along the dock. I cross the street to look and, sure enough, behind the wall, a small crescent of rough pebbles rings a tiny bay—the beach! People are sitting in chairs, walking around, splashing in the shallows. It seems as if they materialized out of air. A second ago we didn't even know there was room for a beach here.

We stride in among them, find an open place, and spread out the towel. "So," I say smugly, sitting down, "are you ready to concede?"

"What?"

"Look over there, ten o'clock. Not exactly a model." I am referring to a large woman, not young, lying on her back. Her heavy breasts tend outwards.

"I wish I could be like that," Janet whispers.

"Like *that?*"

"Her attitude, I mean."

There are few models in this crowd, which is mostly middle-aged—that is to say, though it is hard to admit—our age. My mind's eye always has me somewhere between twenty and twenty-five. I look at men ten years younger than I and think, *yikes, grown-up.*

Janet says, "You're the one who has to concede. Look around."

It turns out that a lot of women are wearing tops. Maybe half, maybe a third. Enough anyway that Janet does not have to feel conspicuous wearing hers.

"Okay, we were both right. Not all beautiful, not all topless. A draw." It surprises me that I feel vaguely let down. Why do I want my wife to bare her breasts on a tiny, rocky beach full of not-beautiful people? I do know enough not to badger her about it. *Aw, come on, honey, please . . . for me.* That would be unfair, and kind of pathetic. I do find my wife's breasts beautiful. Sometimes, after showering in the morning, she will put on jeans, and then, if I am lucky, get distracted and look for something in her purse, or pull out several shirts, trying to decide which one to wear. I made the mistake once of commenting—I forget what I said. Probably just some stupid male sound, a hubba-hubba or a va va voom. "Yeah, right," she said with pronounced sarcasm, turning her back to me. So now I lie in bed with my eyes almost shut, pretending sleep. The more businesslike, nonchalant and unselfconscious she is in just her jeans, the more beautiful I find her.

As long as a third of the other women are covered, the topless prospect is going to register off the top of her self-concionometer. And that's fine. Depends on what you grow up with, of course. Not the way it was done back in Ocean City. Too bad, I muse, watching a teenage girl saunter insolently by, cigarette in her hand, tattoo around her navel, sun-browned breasts as hard as young pears.

I feel Janet's hand grip my arm tightly, urgently. She doesn't say anything, but I can feel the direction of her gaze, and look there too. At first I see a fuzzy-headed boy sleeping in a sling chair. But it's not a boy, it's a very thin woman with one breast. She is to our left, twenty feet away. She is wearing sunglasses, but something about the tilt of her head—she has a small rolled-up towel behind her neck—confirms my first impression of sleep. It is impossible to guess her age, but I would say, maybe fifty. Her left breast rests flatly on her chest. Where her right one should be appears as smooth skin—we're too far away to see scars. Janet's fingers dig in tighter.

Janet is awestruck by the woman's courage. As am I. After our first gasp, we try not to stare. But her presence takes dominion everywhere. The psychic geography of youth and age, frivolity and gravity, sailboats and sunshine, tops and toplessness—all changed, utterly changed. The very word "beauty" suddenly needs quotation marks, for if she is not beautiful, then the concept itself must be questioned.

The humble chore of applying sun tan lotion becomes a slow, quiet ritual. This is our surface, our skin. Protect it. Anoint it. In all ways that can be measured and all that cannot, one thing is certain, our skin is not very thick. We lie on our towels, Janet on her back, blocking the sun with a forearm. I on my side, facing her, watching. I fall asleep then, perhaps. I've never slept on a beach before. Bright empty amphitheatre: eyelids from the back. Heat from her arm next to mine, heat from above. Waves, voices, motors, gulls. Pebble-bed soft. The childman weary. He rests. He has traveled.

When we sit up, some time later, the woman is gone, almost as if she had been a mutual hallucination. Where the sling chair used to be, a happy young couple sits on a towel. A tiny blonde girl child, naked, runs to them on unsure feet, squealing in delight, and making us smile. We stuff our towels back in the bag. Janet brushes her self off, wraps her long light skirt around her, and fastens it. We stroll past the waterfront cafes. We get little cups of gelato from a cart.

"Do you want to see the Calanques?"

Janet shrugs. "Sure, why not." And then: "Yes, I definitely want to see the Calanques. Whatever they are."

I lead her toward the boats, saying, "I'm not sure if they are the prominences sticking out into the sea, or if they are the fiords in between. We're going to check them out." I take her hand and walk toward the ticket booth for the tour boats. Only I don't stop there. A deliberate ruse. I keep walking, past the dock, around the marina with the boats at anchor, to a smaller dock with a half-dozen skiffs tied up. Half an hour later I am sitting at the back of a ten foot boat, my hand on the tiller of a tiny putt-putt engine that seems always on the brink of stalling. Janet sits in the bow. We leave the dock and I motor out into the harbor. We are somewhat under-prepared. The surly guy who rented us the boat was not interested in giving advice, and he didn't speak English. He took my money, my passport, growled, "*trois heures,*" and pushed us off with his foot. He did give me a map, though, if you can call this faded, one-page photocopy a map. On water I think you call it a chart. Anyway, thus cartographically equipped, I intrepidly point the boat out into the blue blue Mediterranean.

The swells, once we clear the harbor area, are larger than I would have thought. From the beach the sea had looked calm. Our little boat lurches over the waves, and sometimes Janet gets a spray of saltwater. I would have expected her to be anxious about such an expedition, full of questions, doubts and fears. *I'm* pretty damn nervous, especially when the wake of a tour boat nearly launches us into space. The little engine whines high and dangerous when the prop rides out of the water.

"Look back," Janet says.

When I do, I see the port of Cassis, the town rising behind it, and the high hills rising steep behind the town. Beautiful. "Which is port and which is starboard?"

"I think left is port," she says.

"Your left or my left?"

"I don't know." She laughs. "Do you know the words in French?"

"Dexter and sinister?"

"What?"

"Latin. Best I can do."

"Dope," she says genially.

"*Red right return*. That's all the yachtsmanship I know."

"What's that mean?"

"No clue."

"Oh well," she says, and laughs.

There are houses along the water, most with swimming pools set on patios above the rocky shoreline. As we get farther out, there are giant slabs of rock jutting out above the water. We are close enough to wave to the people sun bathing there.

"So *that's* where all the supermodels have been hiding," Janet says.

"I knew they had to be somewhere. This *is* the Riviera."

The water seems calmer here, not too close to the shore, not too far out in the open. After motoring awhile, we come to the first Calanque, which, according to the chart, seems to refer to the inlet rather than the land formation. The stony outcropping rises straight out of the water at least a hundred feet, forming a dramatic hump-backed ridge. As we pass the point, we can see the inlet, and I follow other boats in. Traffic is denser here. Sailboats lower canvas and use motors; speedboats and tour boats throttle down. I make educated guesses about which side I'm supposed to pass on. The fiord ends in a beautiful crescent of sand. There is no dock, and there are no buildings, and there appears to be no road in from the land side. Still, dozens of people frolic on the beach, with dinghies and skiffs and kayaks pulled up on one side. A joyful, pristine playground.

A joyful pristine playground protected by buoys and ropes and signs that I can't read, with many small craft maneuvering among them. "Do you mind if we just wave?"

"No, that's fine," says Janet. "I'm happy here."

As we leave the first Calanque and head out to less crowded water to round the second point, she unbuttons her light shirt, takes it off, and stashes it under the seat. That makes sense; it's damp from the spray. Then she reaches behind, unsnaps, and lets the top shimmy down her arms and into her hands. She puts it under the seat as well. She leans back in the bow of the boat, props one arm up along each side of the bow, and smiles at me. She has wide shoulders, like a swimmer, and nice arms. Indentation at her throat, hint of collar bones. Light blue skirt, long, riffles in wind, one leg bared between its folds.

The most beautiful thing I have ever seen in my life.

I use the word *thing* advisedly. For if I said *woman* or *person*, I would be restricting the fields of comparison to women or persons. That would be inaccurate and inadequate. She is more beautiful than other women I have seen or loved. More beautiful than starlets, models, college girls on the first warm day of spring. She is more beautiful than Auden's elegy for Yeats, more beautiful than Lincoln's second inaugural address, more beautiful than my father the last time I cut his hair before he died. She is more beautiful than Michelangelo's *Pieta,* than July corn on Otoe county bottomland. She is more beautiful than the view from the balcony the Palace Hotel in Lausanne, looking out across Lake Leman dotted with bright sails to the misty peaks of Savoy. All of those things she is more beautiful than. What I say is, "I can't tell you how beautiful you are."

"Please don't try."

"You look . . . "

"Zip it!" She holds up a warning finger. "One *hubba* out of you, and I'm back to sensible foundation garments, forever."

"I feel like I should be invoking high art, literature, music." (Forgot music. More beautiful than Chopin.)

"Don't do that either."

"I just thought of Francine."

"Oh great."

"No, listen. We talked about it in the car. The way she projected this aura of wholesome and sexy at the same time. That was just a preview, a glimpse, for the way you are right now."

"That's nice. Now will you shut up about it?"

"Okay, I will. I'll just drive the boat. In that skirt you look like a mermaid, waving to people in the other boats."

"They waved first. Anyway, they're far enough away that . . ."

"But they can see you. Listen, I can't just shrug off forty years of life in a culture that fetishizes breasts by hiding them. Naked breasts in the open air, on the open sea, in sunshine, in public. There's something transgressive about it. And yet, it's pure and spiritual and wholesome too. The sacred and the profane in perfect equilibrium. The lingerie shop and Strasbourg cathedral combined. You attitude is perfect too, it's like . . ."

"There you go again, telling me what my attitude is. Why don't you *ask* me about my attitude?"

"Tell me your attitude."

"Aren't you a little close to that white boat? Or is this part of your plan to give yourself a little thrill?"

"It's narrow here! I'm just trying not to run into them."

We're in the second inlet now, and the big white sailboat is coming up fast behind us, sails down, motoring. As it pulls alongside and then ahead, the people on board wave to us. Two men in polo shirts. Two women, one topless, one topped. We wave back. I say, "Well, that seemed pretty normal."

"It's surprising how fast you get used to it. It's so natural. Good old America."

"What do you mean?"

Janet frowns slightly, collecting her thoughts. Ahead are more boats, more congestion. I turn our ship around and head out toward open water.

She makes several false starts, blows air out of her cheeks, and starts again. "You ask me about my attitude, and the truth is I've got several different ones, contradictory, as usual. On the one hand it's fun and spontaneous, like you want it to be. On the other, I'm not really comfortable, and admiration from you makes it ten times worse, so shut up. Then I think about *why* I'm not comfortable, how every magazine and movie tells me that my body is the most valuable thing I've got, so long as it looks like it belongs to a twenty-year-old. And if it doesn't, then there's something wrong with me, and *that* pisses me off. But so do the politicians and the puritans—the ones that want to cover up Greek statues, and think breasts are 'dirty.' As usual, *they* manage to get you either way. Keep you in your place."

"We white males, you mean."

"Exactly." She braces her arms on either side of the boat so that she can scoot closer and kick me, hard, in the shin.

"Ow. Watch out, you're rocking the boat. What was that for?"

"Principle."

I rub my shin. "Was that your toe?"

"Sandal."

"Taking one for the patriarchy. Ow. Are you done?"

"For now."

"Good. Now get back on your pedestal and look beautiful."

"Watch it."

Leaving the inlet, I range far out into the open water. The Calanques drop away, and we get a perspective on all of them, rocky talons clawing the sea. The sun goes behind a cloud, the wind picks up. Janet sits up, gripping the sides of the boat. The hull bangs the trough, and a wave breaks across the bow. Cold water. Hard shiny arms. Wet skin. Warrior woman, goddess, amazon.

As abruptly as it came, the cloud is gone, the water smoothes out, and we are headed back to Cassis. Janet tilts her head and looks at me from underneath her eyebrows. "You did that on purpose."

"You shouldn't have kicked me. Poseidon was displeased."

As we approach the harbor, Janet takes out her shirt, squeezes water from one corner, and puts it on. The swim suit top goes in the bag.

"Is the skirt wet?"

"It's light. It'll dry fast."

Our rubbery legs surprise us. The harbor seems to be moving under our feet. We clutch each other, giggle, and walk like drunks along the quay. Janet stops. She pulls me close and hugs me hard, then steps back and looks at me with a very serious expression on her face.

I become tense. It seems that some threshold had been crossed, but I'm afraid of what she will say. She says, "Let me ask you something, Jon."

"Yes. What?"

"Are you hungry?"

"Starved."

An Ugly American in Paris

To the sprightly strains of Gershwin, the sometime travel writer bursts forth from the entrance of Gare Saint-Lazar, and throws his hands wide in joyful anticipation of the City of Lights. For several weeks I have been secluded in a stone house in Chapet, reconstructing my travels in Provence three years earlier. The going got rough, and I stopped writing for awhile. But lately something like a breakthrough has been achieved, a pent-up flow of words like lava rushing onto the page, so hot I have to let them cool before I can look at them again. I am rewarding myself with a day off—a day in Paris to walk, to take in the sights, and, of course, to eat.

The Boulevard Haussmann is dissected by the sharp shadows of morning, the sidewalks still damp from overnight rains. The city seems especially clean, as if fresh-scrubbed for my visit. I linger before the façade of the Jacquemart-André

Museum, trying to remember what George told me about it. My canvas bag contains only a spiral notebook and a battered copy of Elliot Paul's *The Last Time I Saw Paris*.

I feel clean and fresh-scrubbed myself, which is a miracle, considering how deeply I was mired in the slough of despond. Trying to write my way back to Janet, I found myself on a slippery slope that began with a stained shirt in Alsace, and slid inexorably (with the joyful exception of Ansouis), to the nadir of Avignon and the morass of Aix. No wonder Dante came so often to mind. Retracing that psychic descent, I was faced with the dilemma of how to be, in Larkin's heartbreaking phrase, "not untrue and not unkind." I wanted to share the chapters I'd written with Janet, and I hoped, despite some difficult parts, that their unflinching honesty would bring us closer together. And I would send them with a beautiful gift. I invited her to write the next chapter. It was the perfect idea, both structurally, as truly *interactive* meta-nonfiction, and psychologically, as a chance for Janet to be more than a portrait made from my memories. I sent Janet the chapters and an invitation. Here's your chance to speak, I said. Your chance to give background, to let the reader see *why* you are who you are. Maybe a story from one of those three-day tent revival meetings when you were a kid. Only, avoid the irony and meta-narrative gamesmanship. I'm trying to get away from that.

As I saunter down the Parisian boulevard, looking for a place to have breakfast, I remember Janet's reaction, and I shudder. While trying to hold myself to the highest standard of veracity, I wrote what seemed to Janet to be fiction—skewed and even at times malicious. On the phone she said, "How can you say that!" and "What have you done to me?" First I tried to reassure her. Then I argued with her. Then she hung up. As if three thousand, seven hundred and thirteen miles was not far enough, I pushed her incalculably farther from me.

A day later, by return email, I got her "chapter."

I called her again. We were terse. "That was a wild ride you took us on, but I can't use it in the book."

"You said you were giving me the wheel."

"Not to drive off a cliff."

"I don't expect you to use it. I wrote it to make a point."

"That any idiot can write self-conscious postmodern shit?"

"A couple of points, then."

"Well, thanks a lot."

"You're welcome."

We hung up, then. I stormed around for awhile, cursing and yelling. I'm glad Erica wasn't home. I spilled wine on her rug. And then I bottomed out. I quit. I gave up. No more phone calls or emails. I abandoned Janet to her melancholy—both in Avignon and in America—and settled down to dissolution in Chapet. Daniel and the regulars at *Le Relais des Saveurs* saw rather more of me than they might have wished. The evenings were given over to endless drunken iterations of Scrabble, much beloved by my hosts, and having a particularly satisfying self-flagellatory quality for me, as I nightly squandered whatever wordsmithy skills I owned, trying to stretch the *X* or the *J* to reach the triple-word score. I'm not even going to talk about the Absinthe.

The longsuffering reader will be relieved to learn that the sub-chapter Dissolution in Chapet has been removed from the text. Once considered crucial to the rising action and indispensable to the climactic breakthrough, this episode revealed itself, under cross examination, to be whiny, melodramatic and unnecessary. It was, therefore, retired to the Orphan Chapters Home. The sequence of events was telescoped a bit, and the tidy preceding paragraph was hired to fill in the summary business.

Still wandering down Boulevard Haussmann, I come to a large intersection where many streets come together. I spot a café with all its doors propped open. But the premises are dark inside, the chairs upended on the tables. A scowling man in a blue dress shirt is furiously mopping the floor. The look on his face drains me of all my optimism and joy as I am reminded that there is a world beyond the one I am crafting in my cave in Chapet. At this very moment, two-thousand four hundred and six miles to the south and east, American tanks are rolling through Baghdad. Statues of the dictator are falling, and the looting goes on and on. Every day the *Herald Tribune* brings me stories from an America that seems more foreign. Freedom Fries. Pouring Bordeaux in gutters. More talk of punishing France.

I notice the hard-faced commuters in raincoats hurrying down the sidewalks. They seem to be looking at me. I find myself whistling "Oh Canada." Inside the Café de Roma, that guy scrubbing the floor—does his scowl come from thinking about Americans? Is the place open or closed? Open, but not for me? A poster in the window advertises "Breakfast Française." If I try to order it, will he curse me, ridicule me, upbraid me for my country's sins?

So what if he does?

Perhaps he should.

An epiphany gurgles inside me like a fountain, climbing higher, making its way from my solar plexus to my brain. It is a bad war being waged for the wrong reasons by a bad president. My government has been arrogant, rude, and dismissive of friends who do not fall into lock-step behind it. I cannot change that. I cannot apologize to the people of France. But I can let them blow off steam. I can be the whipping boy for a day. In fact, I can make it easy for them. I will speak English in that loud slow way that indicates I think they are stupid, even adding a bit of Texas twang. My plan for the day is clear to me: I will walk from one end of Paris to the other, seeking French people to be rude to me. I will make myself an open target for their loathing, and I will face it with modesty and aplomb. Perhaps I will be able to achieve some small bit of expiation for my errant country. For this one day, I will be an Ugly American in Paris.

But what of that *other* epiphany, or breakthrough, or whatever it was? The one that got me back on track, out of the slough of dissolution and sent me soaring back to Provence, the happily named vineyard and the dizzying eroticism on the blue blue Mediterranean? The answer, like many great answers, is simple. It is Janet's story, too. Who am I to offer her the pen and then try to script her? If she wants to waltz me off to New York, torture me with tight shoes, and ambush me inside my own internal monologue, who am I to call it the wrong road? It was only when I suppressed my ego, and put her section into the book unedited that the road opened up for me again.

I was able to see that her memories of what happened in Provence were not self-protective shams any more than mine were. Truth is a negotiated thing, and I was duty bound to go back to the negotiating table. The emotional slide from Alsace to Aix was real, but it needed to be much more real; I needed to do it all again, every line of it, slowly, painstakingly, from the spot on the shirt to the overpriced feast. All of it, again, with the parallax vision of Janet's eyes and my own. And when I got to the end of it, suddenly, Janet's surrealism fit like the missing piece of a jigsaw puzzle—it clicked into place in the parking lot of the villa. And, suddenly, there was Francine. There was Cassis. The Calanques, the blue blue Mediterranean. It all came tumbling out in a rush. That truth had been there all along—we lived each moment I describe— I just had not been able to see it. Domaine de Janet indeed. In my fidelity to the highest standards of historical veracity, a small piece of narrative manipulation must be exposed. The woman on the beach, the one with her breast removed, the cancer survivor: she wasn't there. But that is not to say that she was made up. Janet and Jon did encounter her, in a different place and time and manner, and our reactions are authentic: we were in awe of the woman's courage; we were hushed to reverence at the fragility of life. The displacement of that one moment from elsewhere in our lives onto the beach at Cassis allowed my true vision of the events of that day to burst

forth, dazzling in its joy, its love, and its authenticity. The
Redemption I had wished for was at hand, made possible by
a kind of lie.

We will now proceed with the story of the Ugly American
in Paris, which features no manipulations or fabrications. At
8:45 on Thursday, April 24, 2003, I march inside Café de
Roma, yank down a chair, and park myself at a table facing
the street. The man in a blue dress shirt slowly puts aside his
mop and stalks in my direction, his scowl darkening.

"Breakfast Fran-case," I twang, pointing to the sign.

He nods. I cannot call it a rude nod. At worst, it is noncommittal, edging toward cordial. He disappears behind the
counter for a few minutes. The feast arrives without flourish
or insult. A split section of fresh baguette, buttered. Chocolate
croissant, coffee, juice. In case the man hasn't realized I am
American, I take out the paperback—that loving and condescending portrait of life on the left bank between the wars—
and settle in to occupy the table for a good while. No one
objects. In time, chairs come off other tables. More customers arrive and are served. Friendly conversation flows around
me. I crisply replace my bookmark and signal impatiently for
the check. The blue shirt is gone. His replacement looks like
something out of central casting from *cinema verité*: a portly
man with a graying whisk-broom mustache dressed in white
shirt, black vest, and jacket. I'm waiting for the surly attitude
that comes with the role as he takes the payment and the pit-
tance of a Eurotip. He smiles, thanks me, and wishes me good
day.

The newly-cleaned façade of the Opera gleams in the sun-
shine. The steps are packed with tourists, mostly Spanish and
Russian, from what I can tell. No point in antagonizing them.
So I circle wide, choose the wonderfully named Rue de la
Paix, and pirouette down to the Place de Vendome. I am ap-
proaching the epicenter of arrogance, the place that gave a
name to effete snobbery: the Hotel Ritz. A trio of fast-paced
French-jabbering businessmen in Armani suits are heading

for the hotel. They skid to a stop, their passage blocked by a heavy-set tourist bent over his camera. His hideously tight golf shirt doesn't quite cover his paunch, and he is calling out directions to his wife in loud Midwestern American English.

Mon frere!

His gaze is locked into his camera, deliciously oblivious to the pedestrians. He fiddles with buttons and stares in the viewfinder and periodically calls out to his increasingly uneasy partner to hold her position. I hold my position as well, savoring the ticking time bomb of French exasperation. The men in Armani, unaccountably relaxed, chat with each other through half a dozen camera snaps, and then toss amiable waves to the tourist who calls out his thanks in English.

C'est impossible!

The Tuileries Garden is lightly peopled on what is turning into a brilliant spring day. The tulips bloom in riots of pastel pinks, sunny yellows, and lipstick reds, contrasting the pale gravel of the wide walkways. I stroll up and down the length of it, savoring the morning. I walk around the outside of the Louvre for quite awhile, from the colonnades along the Rue de Rivoli over to the river side, growing increasingly displeased with its renaissance pomp and fussiness. So endless and so pretentious. Wait a minute, aren't these standard American complaints? Am I playing the Ugly American, or becoming him?

I look up and see the name of the street I'm standing beside, and I smile. Voie Georges Pompidou reminds me of my second favorite place in Paris, and I look around for the nearest Metro to zip over and see what's up at the Pompidou Center. I understand some people think the building over-explains itself, that it takes things that should stay hidden and hangs them out for all to see, as if infrastructure is art. Me, I love it. Fuck fancy facades. Give me the ducts and the pipes and the girders and the glass. Show me how the thing is put together, its tangle of visions and revisions. Give me the aesthetics of transparency.

But museums are not on the agenda of the Ugly American in Paris. I am not here to join the tourists; my mission is to offend the locals. So I saunter back along the tulip paths of Tuileries until I come to the great circular fountain. It is ringed by a couple dozen chairs, green, metal, low-slung. Most of them are taken by people who look like real Parisians. People reading newspapers, talking with friends. I could use a break. I take one of the chairs to rest and consider my options. I stare at the single stream of water shooting skyward, its noise creating an odd island of intimacy for those nearby. Across the river, another museum, Orsay, peeks at me coyly above the trees.

A vehicle resembling a golf cart rolls up to the fountain and squeaks to a halt. Two men in coveralls leap out, dispatched, no doubt, to inject some classic blue collar French surliness into this ridiculous tranquility. One of them inserts a T-shaped implement into a hidden hole near my chair, and the tall jet of water lowers suddenly to half-mast, then to a meter, and in another instant is gone. The other one clambers into a rubber suit that comes up to his armpits, and wades out toward the spout. The pool is surprisingly deep, and the worker has to clutch the rubber up around his chest while juggling a metal ladder and a handful of tools. Onlookers laugh and shout advice. He waves and hollers back good-naturedly. A woman in the chair nearby shouts something to me. "No comprende," I holler. "I'm *American.*" She does not seem at all afraid that I will punish her for opposing the war in Iraq. She laughs, mimes that I should turn the fountain back on, and laughs again, uproariously, with her friends.

My plan is not going well at all. Almost half the day is gone, and a French person has yet to be rude, arrogant, weak, or obnoxious. Maybe it's the weather: no one could be quarrelsome on a fine spring day like this one. Or else, perhaps everyone in Paris is just so goddamned glad their city is not swarming with Americans, for once, that they are willing to cut me a break. Apparently, I am going to have to make more of a nuisance of myself to complete my mission.

Noon. Rue de la Huchette. The street chronicled in *Last Time I Saw Paris* is well touristed these days. Just a few feet from the *Petit Pont*, it provides a narrow but well-worn funnel for masses of tourists leaving Notre Dame to launch into the Left Bank. Greek restaurants and kabob stands predominate. Scattered among them are souvenir shops, a pharmacy, and modest hotels whose only presence at street level is a doorway.

Looking back and forth from book to street, street to book, I finally enter the pharmacy. "Excuse me!" I say in loud, intrusive English. "Do you know if this used to be a police station?" I flash the book. "Back in the 1930s, I think this is where the police station would have been."

The pharmacist has salt-and-pepper hair, wire-rim glasses and blue lab coat. He stares at me a moment with great loathing. He is a bomb about to explode. He takes a step towards me. "I do not know," he says evenly. "Marie?" An assistant comes from another part of the store. He speaks to her in French, and then says, "She does not know either. Sorry."

She's on my side of the counter, so I push the book up to her face. "See, right here it is."

She glances at it for a second. "It says *Rue de Chat Qui Peche*. That is not here. That is just there, on the left." She points down the street.

Somewhere in the book Elliot Paul explains why the street is named after a cat that fishes, something to do with the proximity of the Seine. Anyway, the corner I'm looking for has a souvenir shop on one side and a Greek restaurant on the other. I pick a post card from the rack in front of the tourist shop, stroll inside, and hand over the Euro. The woman has Asian features, and doesn't seem to understand English very well.

"No, no police here," she says. "Down there . . . " She switches to French and rattles on.

"I mean *in 1933*," I interrupt, trying to show her the book. "I mean back when . . . "

"No, no police here," she repeats loudly. "No police. No police!"

She is quite alarmed, true, but that doesn't really count as *rude*.

Back on the street, feeling a bit peckish, I let myself be lured into *Le Moulin de Mykonos* by an aggressively friendly door man. *He's* not going to be rude. His restaurant is empty, and he wants me in that little table in the window to entice others. The waiter as well, decidedly unrude. They don't mind me pulling out my notebook and settling in for the long haul.

By two-thirty I am big-lunch-sleepy, despite the double espresso. I hit the street again, but the search for foul-tempered French is wearing me down. I pop into a hotel, one with a lobby and a black-coated concierge.

"Excuse me," I shout. "I'm looking for a place once called the Hotel du Caveau. I know your name is different now, but maybe years ago this could have been it? You see I've got this book, and . . . "

"Le Caveau is down the street."

He interrupted me! A thrill courses through my tired bones. I look at him closely and await further abuse. He says nothing. We stare at each other. His eyebrows go up. "Was there something else that the gentleman . . . " His palms turn upward, completing the disappointingly polite query.

I pause full seconds longer, trying to provoke him, but I break first. "Is it a hotel?"

"No. It is a jazz club."

And so it is. Not open, though, so I shake the dust of the preposterously courteous Rue de la Huchette from my heels and wander towards the Sorbonne, where notoriously impertinent French students will accommodate my masochistic whims. But the students appear to be even happier than the general populace. And more beautiful. I'm strolling through a fashion magazine layout. And more rapid. It seems that every one of them is on a skateboard or in-line skates or a bicycle. They whiz around me with easy grace. I would have to tackle someone to get out one of my Dumb Tourist Questions. The sidewalks and cafes teem with conversation. It feels as if I am walking in wet cement and surrounded by a bubble of invisibility. Damn these light-hearted beautiful Parisians!

Forlornly, I turn back toward the river, and stop in for a visit at what Elliot Paul calls "the most perfect small Gothic church in France," St. Séverin. Echoing Paul's actions seventy years later, I drop coins in the poor box. It is a cool and comforting space, unusually light, owing to the pale stone and a preponderance of high windows that make the roof seem to float above. From a habit I thought long dead, I hear myself muttering a prayer. Please God, let me find my arrogant Frenchie, take my medicine, and get it over with.

I leave the church, blinking a few times in the sunlight, and see someone approaching. As if in immediate answer to my entreaty, a scary French homeless guy confronts me, shaking a paper cup menacingly.

"Get a job," I sneer, looking him square in the eye.

Scary French Homeless Guy smiles, steps back, and gives a small salute as I pass. God is nothing if not funny. I glance back and realize the homeless guy is about as scary looking as Brad Pitt. That's who he looks like, in fact, scruffed up for the role of Homeless Guy With a Heart of Gold.

The church bells sound three p.m., and I am throwing in the towel. No more politics, straight up or ironic. No more Mr. Not Nice Guy. I am simply going to enjoy what remains of this day.

In her flashmail contribution to this book, Professor Jane Bennett asked for "more about what postmodernism is and which aspects of it are truly ridiculous." I wish that you could join me now, Jane, as I grab the Metro at Odeon, give coins to a gypsy fiddler, change at Gar de l'Est, and alight at my very favorite place in all of Paris, the Park de la Villette. The sun is shining on the green grass and the bright red structures called *folies*, a central design feature of Bernard Tschumi's park. There are dozens of them, laid out on a vast grid before me.

What you would find here, Jane, is not the ridiculous-
ness of postmodernism but the sublime. Perhaps the happiest
space on earth. Hundreds of children are playing on some of
the most imaginative playgrounds ever created. They giggle
on the floating bridge and scream on the Giant Dragon Slide.
The Garden of Mirrors casts reflections and Garden of Winds
whistles. The children present a picture of international har-
mony. Euro-white, Afric-black, pan-Asian, and Arabic—they
all play together, and their parents and guardians move easily among each other in civil respect. I am in the park for two
hours and never see a child cry. Veiled women picnic beneath
a giant Claes Oldenburg bicycle pedal. Teenagers kick soccer
balls on the vast greensward along the grand canal with the
delicious name of *Ourcq*.

A small carnival, complete with tinny organ music and
pink cotton candy, has set up temporary shop along the Grand
Promenade of the fabulous Park de la Villette. The carnival is
swarming with people, and the creaky, old-fashioned rides all
have lines of children waiting their turns. It warms my heart,
and makes me remember the excitement that would sweep
through me as a child, waiting for the Fourth of July, when
a carnival with rides and a midway would come to my small
Nebraska town for the weekend. Tilt-a-Whirl, Octopus, Ferris
Wheel. My reverie is interrupted by the curious sight of one
carousel ride spinning slowly in a circle with no one aboard,
and no one waiting to climb aboard. No one seems to be attending it either. Horses with empty saddles and fire trucks
with empty seats revolve forlornly. As it turns, one of the car-
riages comes around, and I see the reason that no one is riding
this carousel.

I wander away from the carnival and out onto the vast open spaces of the park, letting my melancholy slip away in the sunshine and green grass. I hang around by the Geode, the spectacular polished sphere outside the Museum of Science and Industry that houses the planetarium. Like a colossal diadem, its smooth surface gives back a carnival reflection of grass, people, trees, and *folies.*

It is a pity that the French don't understand the perfection of Free Market Capitalism. If they were not so arrogant we could have Mr. Cheney come over and explain to them: here they have hundreds of acres of prime real estate attracting many thousands of visitors, and no one is paying a single Euro to get in! The government is stuck with the bill for the all this pleasure, when stockholders could be benefiting. If the Park de la Villette were to be put up for privatization, a company like Universal Studios, say, eager to compete with Euro-Disney, would pay hundreds of millions of dollars for this place! Mr. Cheney could arrange it with a couple of phone calls. Then the French could afford to pay their fair share for Iraq, and the stockholders of a multinational corporation would get richer, and the world would be a much better place. Stupid socialists.

In the mellow late afternoon light I walk slowly toward the Swatch Tower at the Metro station to catch a subway back to Gare Saint-Lazar. I will take the train back to Les Mureaux, walk through the safe and clean public housing for immigrants, and cross the green fields to Chapet. The melodies of Gershwin re-emerge lightly in the background. I will tell Erica and George about my day in Paris, about how I tried and failed to find French people to be rude to me, and then I will get back to work on the denouement of my postmodern meta-narrative inquiry.

My walk toward the station puts me directly in line with a young couple sitting close together in the grass. She leans back in his arms as they stare into each other's eyes. They are whispering and smiling, alone together in this happy sea of humanity. If any people on earth would very much resent the intrusion by an Ugly American, they would be the ones. A bout of temporary insanity seizes me, and with renewed devotion to my mission, I stalk toward them shouting, "Excuse me! Excuse me!"

In a slow-motion moment their faces rotate in my direction, and I see their raised eyebrows, the beginnings of polite inquiry in their eyes, and I am ashamed of myself. Ashamed of everything I have done to try to provoke unkindness on this perfect Parisian day. At the last second I swerve, my gaze fixed above them, and stalk right by, still barking, "Excuse me!" into thin air, as if my ugliness were directed at someone else.

18 Cassis: $114.41

Among the many literary and intellectual flaws of this book, perhaps the most annoying is the propensity for auto-interruption. Just at the moment when one becomes engaged by the characters and scene, here we are in a different time-frame, or here comes the old gasbag again, putting his face in front of the camera, disrupting the flow. I imagine a reader standing on tiptoe, trying to see over, or around, this busybody narrator, gesturing to him to get the hell out of the way.

In a book organized around restaurants, Jon and Janet are about to enjoy the climactic feast. They have been restored to each other by the literal and figurative Domaine de Janet, and they will make it sacred by breaking bread in Cassis. The receipt hangs there on the page, unassuming, abashed, awaiting explanation.

But here comes the narrator again. First he had to grind his political axe, sending his Chapet self tripping down the boulevards of Paris. Now, worse yet, it appears that he is about to go off on one of his tedious *essays* about time or truth or something. Who does he think he is, the postmodern Montaigne?

ON RECEIPTAGE

This book began with the admission that since the English professor and self-declared travel writer had failed to keep an account of his journey, restaurant receipts would have to stand in. They would provide both narrative structure and mnemonic device for what dared not aspire to anything beyond that absolute lowest common denominator of academic effort, the Visible Product.

In retrospect, such an unassuming opening must seem coy and even a bit ingenuous (or *disingenuous*, if you believe, as some do, that the former term precludes self-awareness). It is time to take a more scholarly look at the Conceit of the Receipt. The most ancient written documents turn out to be account books. Before the earliest literary scribes began cuneiforming how Gilgamesh slew Humbaba, accountants were recording the price of grain, the number of bricks in the storehouse.

One lamb = ⟊ on a clay tablet.

As written analogs to reality go, you can't do better than that. It is no wonder that so many philosophers begin the quest to define reality with Mathematics, Queen of the Sciences. If mathematics is the purest simulacrum of reality, cartography cannot be far behind.

Here is the river, here is the mountain. You are here $\mathbf{X}$.

It might be argued that restaurant receipts signify the purest marriage of mathematics and cartography. As such, they are the surest foundation for a work whose goal is to achieve the highest possible level of equivalence between what you see on the page *here* and what exists *out there*. Like Descartes, I begin with what I can be most certain of, and build by logical inference. For him, that means starting with the self having an awareness of itself as a thinking entity. The present author goes to the surest reality *outside* of himself, the distillation of mathematics and cartography, and inserts the *actual receipt*—a digitized version of it—onto the page. From the receipts may be reliably inferred the existence of the restaurants themselves, settings in place, and the meals themselves, events in time. The iced tea at Bautezar in Les Baux was so fine we had to have it twice. Ergo, two receipts. When the reader eyes the handwriting from *Les Moissines* in Ansouis, is she not more persuaded of the existence of a handsome boy who was charmed by the narrator's wife? All of it can be faked, of course. No end to the ingenuity of novelists, Jonathan Swift to Eric Kraft, scheming to make you suspend as much of your disbelief as they can manage. But I am not faking the receipts, and I am a not a novelist. I am not a journalist; nor am I a memoirist. I desire more truth than any of those genres can frame, a truth that takes into account the passage of time and ongoing reactions—of the author himself, and of those around him—to the creation as it is made. Some time ago I gave a name to my new genre: Interactive Meta-Nonfiction. In its frank meddling with that which it creates while it creates it, my narrative resembles the current fad in television entertainment, the so-called Reality Show. However, I go them one better: it must be apparent that the convention of receipts—*receiptage*, if you will—far from the fumbling expedient presented at the outset, is, in fact, a groundbreaking *méthode de philosophie*, worthy to take its place alongside other epistemological processes.

Due credit having been given, let us now return, at long last, to the city Cassis on the blue blue Mediterranean, and to the meal correspondent to the particular *morceau de réalité* represented by the receipt that crowns this chapter.

Having returned the skiff and reclaimed our passports, Janet and I stand, rubber legged, holding each other, on the quayside of Cassis. We stroll by the dockside restaurants and wander the crooked streets. We peruse menus and we talk about food. We are hungry, but in no hurry. We are like lovers who dally playfully before undressing one another, full of wonder and anticipation at the exquisite upcoming event. We stop in a shop called *Le Herbier,* which is full of rich aromas of candles and herbs and lotions. A striking teen-age girl leans against the wall behind the counter smoking a cigarette, looking bored. A couple of teen-age guys are clowning around to one side, showing off, trying to get her attention.

"Remember her from the beach?"

"No," Janet says, "Do you?"

"I think so. Ask her to take off her shirt."

Janet pokes my ribs. But then she stops. She stands motionless, staring at the girl, then at the two clowning boys, then back at the girl.

"What?" I say. "Is something wrong?"

Janet marches purposefully toward the girl, and I have no idea why, until she stops at the counter and utters a single incantatory word: "Cologne."

Bingo.

Seth and Michael are just coming into the odoriferous age. A cloud of Polo proceeds them into a room; they leave behind an Axe essence. The girl speaks tentative English with a killer sexy accent. She knits her brow and seems annoyed, but when she figures out what Janet is asking, she becomes animated and friendly. Soon she and Janet are laughing. The Herbier proudly features the *L'Occitane de Provence* line of products. There are four men's fragrances, and Janet asks the girl to pick her two favorite. Then from her purse she gets out school pictures of Seth and Tristan. The girl makes mooning faces over both of them, forever binding her to Janet's heart. For older, adventuresome Seth, she picks *4 Voleurs.* Four robbers. For thoughtful Tristan, *Contadour.* Which means, according to the fine print, "one who counts sheep," but we'll tell him . . . guns. The gun-counter.

Our young friend turns out to be a master gift-wrapper as well, and we leave *Le Herbier* content that we have something the boys will like, will use, and is genuinely from Provence. We do not know, and better yet, it does not matter, that this particular line of cosmetics can be found in upscale malls throughout the United States. We are here at The Source, and we have discovered The Gift. Plus we have the story of the knock-out sales girl to tell them. Janet is practically giddy.

"The only thing better," I say, "would be to wrap up the girl and bring her too."

"Yeah. *You'd* love that."

"I've got mine," I say, pulling her to me. "Now let's eat. What about the seafood place with the striped awning?"

Darkness has long fallen on the Villa La Bastide by the time we return. The house is quiet, and the only signs of the Moroccan banquet are a lingering aroma of chicken couscous and a pile of wine bottles by the trash. A few people are still awake upstairs; the murmur of voices drifts down. We do not join them. We want no company tonight. We proceed to our room, take off our clothes, slide into the world's squeakiest bed, and meld together. Wordlessly we touch. Wordlessly hands slide along skin. We both know what we are doing. We are going to make love without a single squeak of bedsprings. For mortal lovers, this would be impossible. One cannot yawn in this bed without a corresponding sigh of springs. With infinitesimal slowness we come together, and I am inside her, and I move inside her, and inside her she moves. A tiny shift in the tectonic plates can cause harms and fears, but, as the poet says, the trepidation of the spheres is innocent. We say words that make no auditory vibrations; we make motions undetectable to the most sensitive instrument on the planet—that bed. We exist in a sphere of Zen physio-spiritual congress, transcending time, transcending space. I am on the boat, and she is leaning backward against the bow. The wind tugs at her hair and I am making love to her there, inside her and a part of her while at the same time detached and watching her, drinking her in. We are carrying on and completing what was begun on the boat, the perfect equipoise of the sacred and the profane. After the longest and almost imperceptible of careen-

ing crescendos we finish, together, and the tremendous tintin-
nabulations register not a whit with the bedsprings.

It is not a rival to Priam's Venasque. It is a sequel and its
complement. One more lucky turn across the zenith of For-
tuna's Wheel. All communication, all absolution, all redemption.

The perspicacious reader, although cheering the sensual-spiri-
tual congress of our heroes, may yet wonder what happened
in that restaurant in Cassis. If I hadn't made such a bloody
big deal about *receiptage* no one would care. But since I did,
well . . .

After finding the perfect gift for the boys, Janet and I wander back to the restaurants lining the dock and we eat at one
of them. Probably we eat seafood, and maybe the restaurant
has a striped awning. We drink wine. More than we should,
possibly, considering the drive back to the villa. But, to speak
truly, which is the only way I speak, I can't remember a damn
thing about that meal. Its details are swamped, swallowed up,
lost amid the momentous events of the day. A few weeks later,
when it comes time to submit the receipts for reimbursement
of expenses for my Pearlstine Grant, I will be, um, unable to
locate the receipt for the restaurant in Cassis. So I will select
another receipt from my stash of receipts, and I will, um, *re-
create* the computational evidence and analog for the meal.
That's why that receipt looks so crappy and is so devoid of
information, with the city named scrawled across it in my
handwriting. If the comptroller at Ursinus College wishes to
call me to account, I will say that I *know* that Janet and I had
dinner in a restaurant in Cassis, and that *somebody* wrote the
"778" on it—that number is not in my handwriting. And it *is*
a French receipt, no denying that. So perhaps it *is* the actual
correct receipt. It's just that I am unable to swear to its absolute authenticity, as I can for all the others in the book. Anyway, is there any doubt, given what came before and after, that

Janet and I had a great and wonderful meal in Cassis? Does anything else matter?

Well, yes. Because in admitting doubt to the correspondence of text and event, I am conceding a flaw in the epistemology of *Receiptage,* of restaurant receipts as the starting place for all knowledge. It was all so perfect: I paid, therefore I ate. I ate, therefore I existed in that time and place. All reality constructed upon the marriage of mathematics and cartography. Once again, and from another door, doubt has entered the matrix. As doubt will always enter the matrix. In spite of all innovation, the concept of "nonfiction narrative" either floats above as Platonic ideal, beyond the author's grasp, or is trampled under the mud of memory, time, and perspective.

Even after the final page has been turned, the interactive meta-narrative inquiry called *Eating Europe* will go on. For three more years, a post-exile Jon and a reinvigorated Janet will negotiate and renegotiate the truth of this interpretation of life—right up until the moment final page proofs are pulled from Jon's protesting fingers. Only then will the cacophony of flapping, buzzing, chirping, and squealing from these passages go silent, like insects arrested in amber. Upon publication, this book, like all books, becomes a fossil of its own creative process. And Jon will still be wondering if he got it right.

The hope for redemption, at this point, is transferred to the imaginations of readers.

19 Wancourt: $7.94

```
        COTE FRANCE WANCOURT
            AUTOROUTE A1
            62128  WANCOURT
     RCS: 391 378 239 00365 MARSEILLE
          TEL : 03 21 50 54 00

   24

        SUR PLACE
        SANDW.RUSTIQUE              27.50
        GRAND CREME                 12.90
        GRAND CREME                 12.90
          SOUS-TOTAL            53.30
   ------------------------------------
   TOTAL                       53.30
   ------------------------------------
        TVA 19.6%          8.73
        HORS TAXES        44.57
        ESPECES                   100.00
        RENDU              -46.70
   LUNDI
   29-05-2000 08:22:40 CAI 54 24X NOTE 540068/1

          MERCI DE VOTRE VISITE
        A BIENTOT - BONNE ROUTE
```

Janet looks at me from across the front seat of the Fiat Punto. Outside the car window, the gorgeous countryside of France flies by on the A-1. We are headed north to Paris on the *Autoroute du Soleil*. We are eager to go home after our travels to Amsterdam, Alsace, and Provence. We look forward to seeing the boys. We are happy. Janet smiles, and shakes her head at me.

"What?"

"Aren't you worried?"

"Worried?" I laugh. "I'm ecstatic. Yesterday was such a perfect day. First the winery named for you, then the beach and the boat at Cassis. Then we found presents for the boys, and then, last night was so . . . so incredible. What a last day in Provence! And today we turn in our trusty steed, Blue Punto."

"Yes," she says. "But aren't you worried about what you're going to write? For the grant, I mean. Your . . . ?"

"Visible Product?"

"You didn't take any notes when we visited any of those towns. You can't write about your colleagues. They'd kill you. And I don't even *remember* Amsterdam or—what was that town?"

"Goop-feeler," I say.

"Goob-vee-yay," she says.

"I'm going to write about you."

"Don't even *think* about it. Are we going to stop for lunch?"

"I'll write about how you're hungry all the time."

"And each chapter will be the name of a restaurant." She rolls her eyes. "Sorry, Eric Kraft already did that."

"Everything's been done," I reply. "I could write the most outrageous self-conscious postmodern hoopdy-doo, and I still wouldn't come up with anything that you couldn't find in *Tristram Shandy*. And that's eighteenth century."

Janet hits my arm. *"And that's eighteenth century,"* she mimics, sounding like Bullwinkle. "I hate when you patronize me, professor."

"In my head I'm writing dialogue for some traveling companion who is not so well read. I'm patronizing *her*."

"Is she pretty?"

"She loves to shop for shoes."

"I swear, Jon. I will kill you if you . . . "

"And sometimes she is very sad."

Janet looks out the window for awhile, and when she turns back to me, her eyes are serious. "My sadness belongs to me," she says quietly. "If you try to write it, you're going to get into trouble."

"Then you'll have to get me out of it."

"No, seriously."

"Very seriously," I say.

"Well, you'd better get it right." Janet turns slowly away from me, and stares out the window.

"Wancourt, ten klicks," I say, reading the road sign. "We'll get gas."

"And they will have great food," Janet says, "because this is Europe, where every gas station has better food than the entire state of Nebraska."

"That's a great line. And I will probably steal it," I say. "Except I'd change the name of the state."

"Really."

"Nobody expects Nebraska to have good food. Now, if you say all gas stations in Europe have better food than, say, Michigan. That would punch it up."

Janet laughs. "You just don't want to insult your beloved Nebraska. Admit it."

"Anyway, the details of the story don't matter so long as in the telling of it we do not depart one iota from the truth."

"Marquez?"

"Cervantes."

"You're insufferable." Janet takes my hand in her lap. She wraps her fingers around my thumb, gripping it tightly. When she speaks, her voice is quiet and serious. "We've had some rough moments this week," she says. "I just hope, when you do go to write about this trip, that you won't let yourself spiral down into some dark place. Focus on best stuff."

"But it all can't be light and fluffy, can it?" I say. "In order for transcendent moments to exist, they have to transcend something more ordinary. Don't I need some of the bad stuff to make the good stuff stand out? Wancourt, one kilometer."

Janet shrugs.

"Ice cream," I say slowly. "I'm having a vision of ice cream."

She glances down at her white blouse. "Does it show too much? Shouldn't I wear it?" She rubs at a faint spot.

"The blouse is fine. I was thinking of *eating* ice cream."

"I'm still mad I got a stain on this thing. Well, you go right ahead and have ice cream. I'm thinking panini."

"The spot on your blouse will become the lynch-pin for my grand opus. And I'll write about how you replaced it in Colmar with a new blouse, but the wrong blouse."

She wrinkles her nose, half in agreement, half in embarrassment. "I'm surprised you remember that. That other one was sexy."

"I have a good memory."

"You're going to need it."

I put on the blinker and ease my way into the rest stop. There are no lines at the pumps, a lucky break, and I pull right up to them, telling Janet she can go on in while I get gas.

Before getting out, Janet grips my hand and looks into my eyes. "Just whatever you do," she says. "Whatever you write, don't forget to *play*. Have fun with it."

"Play."

"Yes," says Janet, opening the car door. "*Play*. Play is the key. It's what you're good at."

"I'll play," I say. She starts to get out, but I grab her arm. "I'll play," I repeat, "but I will also tell the truth. Such as it is. Such as I make it."

Janet rolls her eyes. "Blurry *beurre blanc* in the post-nouvelle cuisine era?"

"Exactly."

She leans over, kisses my cheek, and goes into the station.

As I am taking off the gas cap, a scruffy attendant approaches. He's a big guy with long greasy black hair. His shirt is torn, showing parts of a large blue tattoo on his chest, and his earring is a silver skull. He points warningly to a sign. It says the attendant must operate the pump, and I hold it out gingerly to him, with an apologetic smile.

"*Touriste.*" He shakes his head, as if he can't believe how much crap he has to put up with.

"Yup, that's us, just dumb tourists," I say, stepping slowly away from the pump.

"Where are you from?"

"America," I say it apologetically. "Philadelphia."

"*Philadelphie,*" he says, nodding. "And how long do you stay een France?"

"Two weeks," I say quickly. "Just two weeks. We're flying home today."

"Two weeks," he repeats slowly, looking me up and down. "Ees not enough. You must come back." He holds a finger up to my chin, as if miming a gun. "You *must* come back and you must *stay* at least one month. Maybe then you will know something." He blesses me a warm, gold-toothed Gallic smile, and turns to fill up my car.

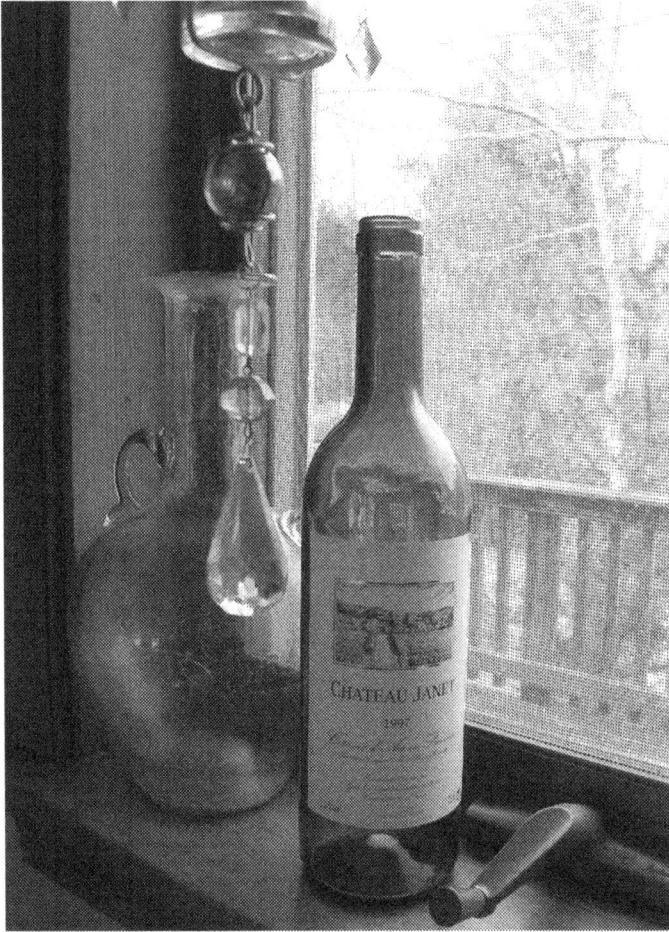

☙

About the Author

Jon Volkmer has written numerous travel features for newspapers and magazines. He is director of creative writing at Ursinus College, where he teaches travel writing and travel literature. He is an award-winning fiction writer, essayist and poet, with publications in such journals as *Parnassus, Prairie Schooner, Texas Review,* and *Painted Bride Quarterly.* He is the author of *The Art of Country Grain Elevators,* a poetry collection with photographs by Bruce Selyem (Bottom Dog Press.) He holds an MA in Creative Writing from Denver University, and a PhD in English from the University of Nebraska.